Narratives of Nation Building in Korea

The editors and publisher of this volume gratefully acknowledge the generous support of the Korea Foundation. The opinions, findings, and conclusions or recommendations expressed in this publication are those of the authors and do not necessarily reflect the views of the Korea Foundation.

Narratives of Nation Building in Korea

A Genealogy of Patriotism

Sheila Miyoshi Jager

An East Gate Book

M.E.Sharpe
Armonk, New York
London, England

An East Gate Book

Library of Congress Cataloging-in-Publication Data

Jager, Sheila Miyoshi.
 Narratives of nation building in Korea : a genealogy of patriotism / by Sheila Miyoshi Jager.
  p. cm.
 "An east gate book."
 Includes bibliographical references and index.
 ISBN 0-7656-1067-1 (alk. paper)
  1. Nationalism—Korea—History. 2. Patriotism—Korea—History. 3. Sex
 role—Korea—History. 4. Korea—History—20th century. 5. Korea (South)—History. I.
 Title.

 DS916.27 .J345 2003
 320.54′09519′09045—dc21   2002030853

Printed in the United States of America

The paper used in this publication meets the minimum requirements of
American National Standard for Information Sciences
Permanence of Paper for Printed Library Materials,
ANSI Z 39.48-1984.

BM (c)   10   9   8   7   6   5   4   3   2   1

Contents

Acknowledgments

Like all scholarly works, this book has been an outgrowth of a collaborative endeavor involving many people, including personal friends, colleagues, and anonymous reviewers who have generously given their time to comment on numerous chapters at the various stages of this project. The bulk of this work was researched and written in South Korea, and so I depended on many of my Korean colleagues, friends, and associates who, at various stages of the project, gave generously of their time and assistance. I'd like to especially thank Chang Chŏng-dok, Kim Yŏng-nam, Lee Sung-kwan and Choi Young-jeep, without whose help chapter seven could not have been written. For his insight into the netherworld of student dissident activism in South Korea, and for sharing this mysterious world with me, I wish to thank Song Ch'ŏng-yon. For aiding me to understand the subtle nuances of Sin Cha'e-ho's work, I'd like to acknowledge Ho "sŏngsaengnim." And for her help and companionship as we poured over hundreds of letters, photographs, and textbooks at the Saemaul Leadership Training Institute during those hot, hot summer days, as well as for tracking down many obscure journals and out-of-print books for me, my sincere gratitude goes to Kwan O-chŏng. Thanks also to Sea Ling Cheng and Elizabeth Lamoureux for all those long late-night discussions about Korean labor and gender politics. Janet Poole, a rare aficionado for Korean colonial literature, helped me rethink through many of my arguments in chapter two and three, and generously read through the entire manuscript. Thanks also to Nancy Abelmann for her incisive readings of several versions of the entire book. Throughout the project, I also benefited from the love and support of Bonnie J. Gordon and Katherine McIntyre Peters whose friendship has sustained me through the long years of research it took to write this book.

I am also grateful to the publishers of my previously published articles for allowing me to weave portions of them into this book. They include, "A Vision of the Future; Or, Making Family Histories in Contemporary South Korea," *positions: east asia cultures critique* 4, no. 1 (Spring 1996); "'Woman' and the Promise of Modernity: Signs of Love for the Nation in Korea," *New Literary History* 29, no. 1 (Winter 1998), and "Monumental Histories: Manliness, the Military and the War Memorial," *Public Culture* 14, no. 2 (2002). In addition, a revised version of my article, "Women, Resistance, and the Divided Nation: The Romantic Rhetoric of Korean Reunification," from *Journal of Asian Studies* 55, no. 1 (1996) was reprinted with the permission of the Association for Asian Studies, Inc.

The research for this project has been supported by the generous funds from the following institutions and agencies: a Daesan Foundation Fellowship (1999–2000); a Bernadotte Schmitt grant from the American Historical Association (1999); a NEAC travel grant from the Association of Asian Studies (1999); a grant from the Asia Research Fund (1999); an ACLS/SSRC International Postdoctoral Fellowship (1998–1999); a Postgraduate Fellowship from the Korean Studies Academy (1998); a Korea Foundation Postdoctoral Fellowship (1997); and another ACLS/SSRC International Postdoctoral Fellowship (1996). I am extremely thankful for the assistance from all these agencies.

Finally, I dedicate this book to my husband, best friend, and soulmate, Jiyul Kim, without whose patience and encouragement this project could never have come to fruition. Over the years of research and writing that it took to complete this book, our three children Isaac, Hannah, and Emma were born, and it is their love that continues to sustain and inspire me.

Note: The McCune-Reischauer system of romanization is used for the rendering of all but well-known names and for the names of individuals who have requested idiosyncratic spellings.

Introduction

This book is primarily concerned with the relationship between history, gender, and nationalism in Korea. More specifically, it reveals how the emergence of the nation, linked to the rise of the modern capitalist world system, transformed the ways in which Koreans perceived themselves as gendered beings. The idea of the nation that rose up toward the end of the nineteenth century was coeval with the creation of new forms of masculinity and femininity, and it is precisely this creative and transformative power of nationalism to produce new gendered subjectivities that is the subject of this book. The basic premise that informs my analysis is that the discourse of gender is not always or necessarily literally about gender itself. By conceptualizing gender in terms of the reciprocally constituted and historically variable categories of Man and Woman, my interest is to show how gender systems are reciprocally related, in multiple and shifting ways, to other modes of cultural, political, aesthetic organization and experience.

I begin my analysis by exploring the ways in which these new identity formations of manhood and womanhood in Korea were produced in the context of Japanese colonialism and Western imperialism. My interest is to discern the creative power of nations to produce new identities, such as those brought about by the particular combination of Western and Japanese constructions of Korea with Korean constructions of the West and Japan. In this sense, my book was written, in part, as a reaction to postcoloniality and the dominance that its discursive paradigm has had on the construction of identities, cultures, and politics of the non-Western world. In particular, I have taken issue with Bhabba's notion of "almost the same but not quite," whereby the colonized responded to colonial domination via a complex system of "mimicry," a mimicry that never succeeded in effacing the difference between the Western original and the colonized copy ("the subject of a difference that is almost the same, but not quite") (1994).[1] Robbed of any historical specificity, the concept of the postcolonial as "almost the same but not quite" is an abstraction for a vaguely defined ontological marginality that is equally applicable for *all* minority discourses and, hence, is specific to none. The categories of the "postcolonial," "women," and "race" assume the status of metaphors so that, as Suleri has pointed out, "each rhetoric of oppression can serve equally as a mirrored allegory of the other" (1995: 139). Moreover, by reifying the power of the dominator, non-Western cultures are reduced to a single possibility: resistance. The problem with postcolonial formulations of identity is that they are raised only in conformity to two basic binary modes: pure native "self-understanding" versus the "contaminated" identities brought about by the cultural appropriation of the Other ("almost the same but not quite"). Of course, the notion of "pure self-understanding" is a myth, since most cultures and societies around the world have long been "contaminated" way before Western ships ever reached their shores.[2]

If the "contamination" by the West has been viewed only in negative terms in recent years, we might want to consider the ways in which it has also provided the platform for new creative developments around the world. How did Korean "translations" of the myth of progress become reworked in the Korean context to create new forms of masculinity that drastically transformed the scholarly ideal of manhood associated with Korea's Confucian past? How did Western literary translations introduced to Korea via Japan become potent agents in Koreans' nation-building efforts and their imaginary/imaginative construction of "modern" men and women? How were these translations later re-appropriated in the nationalist rhetoric of Park Chung-hee and student dissident rhetoric about the reunification of the peninsula? Indeed, to view gender historically in terms of multivalent "translations" that generate and perpetuate cultural meanings and values, is to reveal the myriad of local and individual sites of social reproduction, variation, and change of collective social structures.

One of the central aims of this book is to chart the complex inheritance of all these creative "translations" and to demonstrate their narrative coherence (and inconsistencies) throughout Korea's modern history. As a collection of readings of some key texts/moments, the book's purpose is to offer insight into how particular events and works throughout Korea's modern history have been discursively linked to one another and to discern the underlying logic of these narrative connections. This requires a form of critical inquiry that, borrowing from Hayden White and Harold Bloom, has been designated as "tropical." A tropological approach to the nation provides us with a way of examining certain key historical events or texts that have played an important role in the national imaginary and linking them together by discerning the ways in which they have been emplotted by key narrative tropes. As White explains, "the tropic derives from *tropikos, tropos* which in Classical Greek meant 'turn' and in Koiné 'way' or 'manner.' It comes into modern Indo-European languages by way of *tropus,* which in Classical Latin meant 'metaphor' or 'figure of speech'" (1978: 2). In this sense, the trope is as much a *trans*lation as it is a *re*lation between one reference point and another ("reference" from the word *refero,* to bring back), functioning, as it were, as a kind of map or topography, that connects key moments/texts to one another in an endless chain of reference.

In this way, my project also connects to Benjamin's notion of montage, what his friend Theodor Adorno referred to as "picture puzzles which shock by way of their enigmatic form and thereby set thinking in motion" (Taussig 1984: 89). Whereas my analysis of particular texts/moments have little shock value, they do provide a way of thinking about otherwise concealed or forgotten connections with the past which can only be revealed by their juxtapositions with other texts/moments. Moreover, by drawing upon Benjamin's notion that "to discover in the analysis of the small individual moment the crystal of the total event" (Benjamin 1999: 461), my book provides alternative ways to think about historical categories and methods used to study nationalism. Far from merely replicating the myth of progressive history as sanctioned by the nation-state and the modernist conception of historical time, this book is organized as a *fragmentary* history of modern Korea, a kind of literary "montage" that attempts to decode the narrative patterns of Korean nationalism while staying clear of their progressive claims. Throughout the book, past and present meet in a continual process of narrative "reconstructions" so that each text/moment under consideration contains within it a past, present, and a future.

Thus, the organization of the book, while chronological, is eclectic in the sense that I travel from one narrative "site" to another, skipping over some key historical moments while focusing very intently upon others.

The thread that weaves these chapters together as a whole is the premise that particular narrative tropes that extend back to the colonial period (1910–1945) have remained important, albeit transformed, over the modern period and into the contemporary moment. Throughout the book, I explore a variety of discursive texts/moments in which these key narrative tropes are employed, transformed, and redeployed to make sense of particular national events. Tracing these narratives to contemporary Korean society, I show how these "master-tropes" were successfully redeployed in the context of the Korean national division.

Part One, entitled "Modern Identities," sets the stage for the six chapters that follow. Chapter 1 sets out to explore the relationship between martial manhood and the nation-state that was made during the early decades of the twentieth century. Through an analysis of certain styles of nationalist self-critique and colonial discourse, I show how key concepts and representations, like the image of weak and ineffective manhood embodied in the figure of the Confucian *yangban* (Confucian literati) was appropriated by nationalist historians like Sin Ch'ae-ho as an example of how the "true" record of Korea's past had been distorted. I show how Sin's unexpected usage of the *yangban* as a vehicle for nationalist self-critique served not only to promote "civilization and enlightenment" but also to justify the complete erasure of the Chosŏn dynasty—and the forms of "effete" masculinity associated with it—as an *aberration* of Korea's authentic national history.

While Chapter 1 is devoted to the analysis of manhood and nation in the new historical writings that were being produced during the colonial period, Chapter 2 examines the connection between "translated" literary practice and the role that women played in the politics of nation-building in Korea. Focusing my research on the works of Yi Kwang-su, widely considered to be Korea's first modern novelist, my interest is to discern how the "particularized" concept of modern Korean literature that developed during the first decades of the twentieth century became an important medium for national self-definition and how women emerged as the primary subjects in the nation's quest for authenticity. Chapters 3 and 4 explore these themes further, to show how the trope of the loyal wife/enlightened woman was repeatedly used to give expression not only to Korea's colonial predicament but also to the tragedy of the national division. In particular, I pay special attention to the way in which various "translations" of the *Tale of Ch'unhyang* were rewritten onto a variety of modern texts/moments and how, through these revised interpretations, newer "versions" were used to create a plausible story about the Korean nation.

The last chapters of the book once again take up the theme of heroic/virile manhood discussed in Chapter 1 to explore how this trope was variously resurrected throughout Korea's modern history, both by Park Chung-hee (Chapter 5), student dissidents (Chapter 6), and the military regimes of Chun Doo-hwan and Roh Tae-woo (Chapter 7). In my analysis of the Saemaul Undong (New Community Movement) (Chapter 5), for example, which was launched under the Park Chung-hee regime in 1970, I show how stories of heroic manhood were variously played out in the practices of the movement, which sought to bring about not only significant economic improvements to Korea's rural communities but also attempted to inspire a "spiritual" revolution in the minds and hearts of Korea's farmers. This "revolution" aimed to transform Korea's "backward" and "lazy" Confucian farmers into "self-reliant" and "progressive" modern citizens. By employing these familiar heroic tales as a basis for revolution, Park inspired change to create his idea of a model, rational, and disciplined modern (militaristic) society. Moreover, by presenting himself as the descendent of Silla and the spirit of the Silla Youth Corps (*hwarang*), Park sought to present his regime, particularly after the declaration of the draconian Yushin Constitution in 1972, as the sole legitimate heir of Korea's nationalist "traditions," which he contrasted to the iconoclastic and "wayward" Marxist regime of North Korea.

Likewise, Chapter 7 takes on the theme of struggling and redeemed (heroic) manhood in the context of my discussion of Korea's (official) view of national reunification, which I explore in detail through my examination of the War Memorial. In this reinterpretation of the heroic narrative motif, I show how the story of national reunification by the Roh Tae-woo regime was written as a narrative of brotherly reunion: South Korea as the elder brother whose magnanimous "forgiveness" of his weaker and wayward northern brethren becomes the condition upon which reunification is achieved.

How these themes relate to recent developments in South Korea's political discourse following the 1997 presidential elections is the subject of the last chapter and epilogue. Kim's triumphant "rise" to presidential power can be read as another variation of the pervasive plot of "manly" redemption found in the nationalist rhetoric of Kim's military oppressors. However, I show that, in stark contrast to the forms of manhood promulgated by Korea's past military regime, Kim's version of manhood idealized not martial prowess but the spiritual strength that comes from Christian forgiveness.

These ideas have bearing on the multiplicity of nation-views and the idea that political identities are not fixed but shift between different loci. Indeed, in order to understand just how historical actors mobilize certain representations of the nation against others, it is important to realize just how *similar* these contested representations sometimes are. The mobilization of opposing claims, in other words, is not incommensurate with the fact that these claims are often made by privileging the very same narrative strategies. While it is important to keep in mind that the nation, even where manifestly a recent invention, is designed to include certain groups and exclude or marginalize others, the very terms of inclusion and exclusion are very often couched in the *same* language.

This has been particularly true of South Korea. Unlike most modern nations where the contests between various groups have been drawn along ethnic, religious, or linguistic lines, in Korea these contests have been drawn, broadly speaking, between the generations. This may explain why there is so much focus in Korean nationalist discourse on the generational link between father and son, "patriotic" genealogy and ancestral piety. Underlying these fundamental concerns that are characteristic of both student dissident *and* State national discourse is a primordial anxiety about paternity. Ideas about the loss of fatherhood/manhood and its idealized "recovery" in the paternalistic image of Kim Il Sung—seen in student dissident nationalist discourse of the late 1980s (Chapter 6)— is matched only by that *same* concern for ancestors and paternal legitimacy evinced by the State's preoccupation with its ancestral national legitimacy (Chapter 7). In each case, North Korea is central to the representational strategies of both versions of national history. While the young have (historically speaking) idolized North Korea as the repository of authentic national values, the old see their northern brethren as an illegitimate offspring, the wayward younger brother in need of an elder brother's guidance and salvation.

The striking discursive similarities of these opposing claims derive, I argue, from the way in which certain narrative configurations have been interpreted (and reinterpreted) against other claims of "faithful" representation. The search for heroic manhood is a good example of this dominant (shared) narrative strategy of ambiguous cultural signification. As I show in Chapter 1, the colonial historian Sin Ch'ae-ho was one of the first Korean nationalists to adopt a heroic narrative strategy in his project of defining the national "essence" (which he variously linked to the great military exploits of such renowned Kogurŏ warriors like King Kwanggaet'o and General Ŭlchi Mundŏk). Both dissident and State usages of Sin's hero-centered view of history show just how unpredictable the mobilization of particular interpretations against others can be in the reconfiguration of the nation. This is because the multiplicity of nation-views derives not from some inherent, intrinsic, or prediscursive "identity" that is in turn mobilized by particular groups. Rather, the multiplicity of nation-views, I argue, finds its commonality in a *shared* and recognizable narrative strategy that is selectively interpreted by historical actors against similar claims to faithful interpretation. Likewise, Chapters 3 and 4 reveal that the canonical Confucian romance narrative of separating and reuniting couples also takes on a completely new significance from its "original" or "intended" reading, so that what once was a story about Korean romance gets transformed into the story of national self-enlightenment (Chapter 3) and later, national reunification (Chapter 4).

What I hope to make clear in my study of nationalism in Korea is that ideas or ideological concepts, whether they stem from politically "dominant" or "subordinate" cultures or groups, are never *intrinsically* oppressive or liberating in themselves. The significance of the loyal wife as a symbol of either traditional oppression or potential liberation/reunification, for example, depends upon the *unexpected* usages to which these images are put. The privileging of the "intrinsic core" of an original idea and the culture of which it is effectively a part negates the potential power of the idea to be employed for *other* (and unforeseen) ideological or political ends. Nation and nationalism have always drawn upon narratives about progress and civilization, but people with *very* different political agendas often deploy these *same* narratives in a variety of ways and for very different ideological ends. Student dissident and State nationalist rhetoric used very similar representational strategies (strategies that evolved from a series of unexpected "translations" of particular dominant narrative tropes related to a family-centered universe) in their particular claims to legitimacy. While dissidents relied on the narrative of benevolent fatherhood and lineage in their vision of the reunified nation, progovernment groups relied on the cult of virile manhood and ancestral piety in their search for national recognition. It is by charting the contested nature of this interpretive enterprise that I show just how the dispersed meanings of the past are (re)appropriated in the dynamic (re)formations of the national imaginary.

Part One

Modern Identities

ety through the attainment of "civilization and enlightenment" (*munmyŏng kaehwa*) in the hope that Korea's failed traditions and institutions could be remedied. Many Korean nationalists had come to the conclusion that the so-called backwardness of the Korean national character (*kukminsŏng*) had lead to the nation's collapse. Concerns about strengthening the national character through a program of reform raised questions about the continued validity of Korean Confucianism and its institutions. It was in this context that some nationalist writers began to reevaluate their previously held views of the military, including the role that the military establishment had played in Korean history. Through the embrace of a new and alternate history of the Korean people in which the military played a dominant and central role, these nationalists hoped to resurrect new ideals of martial manhood from the nation's past in order to resuscitate Korea's failed national traditions and institutions.

One of the first modern Korean historians to link issues of martial manhood with nationhood in Korea was Sin Ch'ae-ho (1880–1936). In his attempts to come to terms with the colonial reality, Sin linked the crisis of nationhood with the crisis of (Confucian) manhood. By looking back to the Three Kingdoms period (57 B.C.–A.D. 668) of Korea's ancient history, and in particular, to the great military exploits of Koguryŏ (37 B.C.–A.D. 668) and Silla (57 B.C.–A.D. 668), Sin tried to resurrect ancient warrior male ideals as he forged to build the nation's future. The effete and ineffective Confucian scholar-bureaucrat (*yangban*) of the Chosŏn dynasty (1392–1910) was largely blamed for Korea's colonial predicament and thus became an effective ploy justifying the attack on Confucianism in the name of a more "authentically" ancient, and hence more manly, Korean tradition: the Koguryŏ *sodo* and the Silla *hwarang* warriors. The liberation of the nation was thus conceived in terms that reflected Korean nationalists' concern with both Japanese colonial overrule and with the rebuilding of a powerful "manly" ethic that starkly contrasted with the traditional "effete" and "effeminate" masculine characteristics associated with Korea's Confucian past.

In his groundbreaking book, *Korea Between Empires,* Andre Schmid reveals the vital role that representations of the *yangban,* the metaphorical personification of the Chosŏn dynasty, came to play in Korean nationalist and Japanese colonial discourse. For Schmid, both Korean nationalists and Japanese colonialists shared the same conceptual vocabulary, cultural representations, and narrative strategies, and he shows in detail how the stock figure of the *yangban*—"with his black horsehair hat, flowing white robes, and traditional shoes" was used as a major symbol of Korean backwardness in vital need of reform.[3] Implicit in both these reformist agendas was the connection that was also repeatedly made between failed nationhood and failed manhood. The pervasive image of the weak and emasculated *yangban* that became a centerpiece of the rhetoric of nationalist self-critique had led Korean nationalists like Sin Ch'ae-ho to embrace new and idealized images of the military man.[4] While many nationalist intellectuals continued to extol military heroes of Korea's past, some of these same intellectuals also became engaged in restoring and recuperating the legacies of Sirhak (practical learning) of the seventeenth and eighteenth centuries. These reformers carried over Neo-Confucianism's faith in the civilizing function of moral self-improvement and thus attempted to limit Korea's problems to those "corrupt Confucians" while salvaging what they saw as the core of Confucianism (Schmid 2002). By contrast, Sin's representation of the emasculated male was different from these and other instances of nationalist self-critique because Sin declared the *yangban* to be an *aberration,* not a veritable representation, of the "authentic" Korean national tradition. The question became not one of reforming the "corrupt Confucians" to revitalize the nation (or to attain civilization), but of declaring Confucianism an alien culture altogether, and then searching for an alternative (military) tradition that could replace it.

The purpose of this chapter is twofold: first, I trace how Sin's usage of the *yangban* as a vehicle for nationalist self-critique promoted an *alternative* image of the national past. Second, I show how the "rediscovery" of Korea's martial roots in the military kingdoms of Koguryŏ and Silla brought forth alternative perceptions of Korean manhood as distinctly different from the weak and effeminized male figure that came to be associated with the Chosŏn dynasty. To this end, we shall see how the "re-making" of the national past had important implications for the re-making of Korean manhood.

Militarism and Nationalism

Like the majority of Japanese neologisms brought into Korea, either directly or via China at the turn of the century, the concepts of national character (*kukminsŏng*), national essence (*kuksu*), and national soul (*kukhon*) were frequently used by Korean intellectuals to develop their theory of the modern nation-state. While the teleology of history was relentlessly progressing toward the modern, the viability of a culture was measured by its contribution toward this advancement. In the wake of Korea's colonization by Japan in 1910, Korean intellectuals thus sought to identify the flaws and weaknesses in the Korean national character responsible for the deplorable state of the Korean nation. What were the primary causes that had prevented Korea's evolution toward civilization, and how might these flaws be remedied? For most, the answer lay squarely in Korea's traditional relationship to China. Throughout the five hundred years of the Chosŏn dynasty (1392–1910), China functioned as the "Middle Kingdom" of a transnational cultural realm within which Korea's Chosŏn elites had participated (Schmid 1997). By the late nineteenth century, however, Korea's participation in the old world culture began to be questioned as new intellectual elites, themselves trained in the old school of Chinese learning, became increasingly convinced that the deplorable condition of the nation was rooted in its historical "subordination" to China. Whereas Chosŏn elites had participated in what they perceived as a universal transnational cultural realm of civilization, by the first decades of the twentieth century, Chinese civilization was no longer viewed as universal. Now deemed particular to China, Chinese civilization was rejected on the grounds that it was alien to Korea (Schmid 1997). As Sin related in his essay "Imperialism and Nationalism," Koreans' survival in the universal struggle for existence could only be achieved through the complete recovery of their "national essence" as separate from China:

> Any nation that wants to protect itself has no other recourse than to stick to nationalism. If, consequently, nationalism displays its physical strength [ch'aeryŏk], it can protect the nation from aggression attempted by an expansionist form of nationalism, that is, imperialism, no matter how atrocious and sinister it may be. In short, imperialism can find its way into a country whose nationalism is enfeebled [pagyak]. Why has the Korean peninsula, as beautiful as silk and flowers, been degraded to a dark den? It was because the Korean people failed to develop their nationalism strongly enough. It is sincerely hoped that my dear countrymen will promote their nationalism. As masters of our nation, we decide our own fate and work to ensure our national survival. (Sin 1962: 108)[5]

The task that immediately became apparent to Sin and to others who were striving to cultivate their nationalism through the rediscovery of their nation's spiritual essence was to define what exactly this "essence" was. Among the myriad Korean ideas and customs that had been "suppressed" by Chosŏn Korea's assimilation of Chinese culture, it was the loss of the nation's ancient military culture and traditions that Sin Ch'ae-ho most lamented. Discarding the enfeebled scholarly traditions of an "alien" Confucian past, the modern period would be one of national "renewal," one in which a new kind of "fighting" people would be reborn. As an editorial of the *Taehan maeil sinbo* (June 4, 1909) put it:

> It is repeatedly urged that we must create a new people. What kind of people can be called a new people? Are they docile people? No. Docility leads to cowardice, cowardice to regression, regression to defeat, and defeat to extinction. Trying to create a docile people at this time when the East and the West are soaked with bloody rains can be likened to setting sheep free among a herd of ravenous tigers. Are they serene people? No. Serenity leads to conservatism, conservatism to effeteness, effeteness to defeat and defeat to extinction. Trying to create a serene people can be likened to leaving a sleeping person in a pool of gushing water. What should our people be like? They should be determined and forward-moving people. Why? Because without determination, no people can fight gallantly for their survival in this age of rampaging swords and devils.

The modern period ("the age of rampaging swords and devils") was thus viewed as a period of renewal—the creation of a new fighting people—toward progress. As Sin Ch'ae-ho related, the present age required people of conviction and determination who must "call forth the [original] martial spirit of the people and cultivate the military ethos" (Sin 1962: 201). "The people," he said,

> must climb the Samch'ŏdae dais of Im Kyŏngŏp and grab the Paekgunju iron pole of the Knight of Ch'anghae (kingdom) [Ch'anghae Yeoksa] and embark on whatever risky venture that is necessary to fight and win. (Sin 1962: 201)[6]

As Sin Yong-ha (1984) has noted, Sin Ch'ae-ho emphasized physical conditioning and military training as the basis for developing a newly enlightened "fighting" citizenry. Despite his strong anti-Japanese bias, Sin nevertheless turned to Japan as a model of the ideal modern militarized nation-state:

> Physical education exercises the body, strengthens the will, and, by practicing certain skills, develops soldiers. In Japan primary school students

are taught physical education and machinery familiarization [*kigye undong*] and middle school students conduct military training with weapons such as marksmanship. These students display an orderly and disciplined appearance in formation. They are the future supporting and reserve soldiers. There is no one in the entire country who does not go through this military training. Students are future soldiers and merchants former soldiers; machinists too are future soldiers while farmers are former soldiers. Only when a country can count on all of its people to become soldiers in time of mobilization can it be a strong nation. (Sin Ch'ae-ho 1962: 139)

In response to the perceived need among Korea's national elites to promote and educate a new "fighting" citizenry, numerous Self-strengthening societies began to emerge during the first decade of the twentieth century. Examples of these include the Kukminhoe (People's Association, 1904), Taehan cha'ganghoe (Great Korea Self-Strengthening Society, 1906), Taehan hyŏphoe (Great Korea Society, 1907), and the Sinminhoe (New People's Association, 1907), all of which supported military operations and training (Kim Dong-pae, 1986). The New People's Association, in particular, lent its support to the activities of the *uibyŏng* (righteous armies), in addition to overseeing plans for the establishment of a military officer school in Manchuria to support the Independence Army, which was later based there (Sin Yong-ha 1984, 1985, 1986; Wŏn Ui-tang 1964). Following Korea's annexation by Japan in 1910, leading members of the Society, including Sin Ch'ae-ho and An Chang-ho, exiled themselves either to Manchuria or the Russian Maritime Territory, where they founded military schools and organizations to further their armed struggle against Japan. Like many of these self-exiled former Sinminhoe members, Sin Ch'ae-ho ended up for a time in Vladivostok where he helped to establish the Kwangbokhoe (Restoration Association) in 1913 and became the organization's vice-chairman (Sin Yong-ha 1996: 43).

As most scholars of Sin have noted, the majority of his historical works written before 1910 were heroic biographies of military leaders. After completing his translation of Liang's *Biographies of Three Great Men in the Founding of Italy* in 1907, Sin embarked upon writing a biography of General Ŭlchi Mundŏk (1908), Admiral Yi Sun-sin (1908), and General Ch'oe To-t'ong (1909). Like Liang's own heroic narratives, these works about Korea's ancient military heroes linked collective action to purposeful individual existence as integral and inseparable (Tang

1996). Unlike Liang, however, Sin focused his efforts on writing entirely about military leaders, those personages who had been sorely neglected in the traditional Confucian canon. Pak Ŭn-sik, who was himself the prolific author of several dozen heroic biographies and an active member of the New People's Association, shared this hero-centered world-view. As he put it, "history embodies the spirit of a nation and heroes are its vigor. All civilized nations of the world respect their history and worship their heroes" (Pak Ŭn-sik 1906).

If the new history of Korea was the record of a people's struggle to achieve nationhood, then the people's warrior-heroes were the nation's principle protagonists. In Korea, where human agency had always played a significant role in Koreans' view of their past, the question became not so much how to define the role of the hero in the new history of the nation, as it was about how to *redefine* the very ideal of heroism.

This ideal underwent a radical transformation during the first decades of the twentieth century. Together with nationalist scholars like Pak Ŭn-sik and Chang Chi-yŏng, Sin set out to "rediscover" the role that the martial hero had played in Korean history. Through this reassessment of the military hero as the new principle agent of Korean history came new ideas about the traditional relationship that had existed between the scholarly (*mun*) and military (*mu*) elite in Chosŏn Korea. While tensions between the literary and military elite had always been present in Chosŏn society, it was Sin, more than any other nationalist writer working during this period, who exploited these tensions further to launch a scathing attack on the Chosŏn dynasty's scholarly elite (*yangban*) who were, according to him, "devoid of national spirit." The project of heroic rediscovery, in other words, became intimately connected to the project of forging a new history of the militarized nation rescued from the clutches of Korea's "slave literary culture" (*noyejŏk munhwa sasang*) (Sin 1976: 195). And it was in the name of the new military hero—strong, combative, loyal, courageous—that Sin sought to strengthen the weakened nation to ensure its survival in the battle for existence.

Mun (文) and Mu (武)

Before turning our attention to the specific content of Sin's "militarized" view of history, it is important to grasp how traditional tensions within Chosŏn Korea had become exploited to give rise to new definitions of the nation. Running throughout Sin's early historical writings, and in particular, his biographies of military heroes, is the loathsome portrait Sin painted of the *yangban*. This view was shared by many of Sin's contemporaries. As one of the most vilified and satirized groups, the *yangban* played a prominent role in both nationalist and colonial writings to critique the Korean past and Korean national culture. For his part, Sin berates the *yangban* for engaging in "disgraceful" and "laughable" scholarship that had "nothing useful to say about our four-thousand-year history" and even accuses them of "concealing the great accomplishments of our heroes" (Sin 1990: 183). Expressing his grief over the state of the weak and emasculated nation, Sin urges his readers to "abandon their brushes" and to take up the armed struggle (*mujang t'ujaeng*) (Sin 1962: 367–68). The Korean people, he laments, have been stripped of their honor due to the "slave-culture of Korea's China-loving elite" who, like an "old *kisaeng* who has made the habit of prostituting herself," no longer recognizes her disgrace (Sin 1995: 183).

> They [the Confucian scholars] weakened the military, killed the gallant and righteous soldier and spoke sternly at the people, saying: this is *Ŏnmu Sumun* (偃武修文 "end war bring peace"). Oh, what a cunning scheme it was! The civil and the military [*munmu*] are two parts of a whole. Only after achieving integrity and courage [derived from the military] can civilian interests be pursued. Only after impartiality is guaranteed [by the military] can civilian affairs flourish. Therefore, how is it possible to have a civil society without the military?
>
> They [the Confucian scholars] seem only to know the "*mun*" of *munyak* [effeminization, emasculation due to literary indulgence] and not the "*mun*" that represents the whole of civil society. Because of this, they have corrupted the people's dignity and by deceiving them in this way, have caused chaos, bewilderment and a sense of inferiority among the people. (Sin 1995: 396)

Sin's disdain for Korea's Chosŏn's scholarly elite was not limited to the Chosŏn period, however. Like other former members of the Self-strengthening societies who left Korea in 1910 to establish military schools, join the Tongnipkun (Independence Army), or advocate the "discourse of armed struggle" (*mut'ujaengron*) abroad, Sin also became severely disillusioned with the aims of the cultural nationalist movement (Sin Yong-ha 1986).[7] His later essays reflect this increasingly critical stance, particularly after the failed March 1919 uprising. In both his "Declaration of Chosŏn's Revolution" (1923) and his "New Year's

Ramblings of a Vagabond" (1925), Sin not only offers a virulent critique of the principles of the cultural nationalist movement, he also questions the appropriateness of culture (*munhwa*)—and cultural institutions—to achieve Korea's nationalist aims. Linking the writings of Korea's new cultural elite with the "escapist attitude" of their Confucian predecessors, Sin laments the deplorable state of the nation fatally weakened by Korea's new "corrupt poets and writers." These new literary men were no more use to society than the depraved Chosŏn poet Chŏng Su-dong, who abandoned his wife in the midst of childbirth to seek poetic inspiration in the Diamond Mountains:

> Chŏng Su-dong was a poet of sixty to seventy years old. One day he went to the herb doctor to get the Buddha's-Hand Powder for his wife who was suffering from a hard childbirth. On his way home from the doctor's, he met a friend who was riding a donkey. When he asked the friend where he was going, the friend answered that he was going to the Diamond Mountains to enjoy the scenery. Upon hearing this, the poetic mood of Chŏng Su-dong was aroused. He put his Buddha's-Hand Powder into his sleeve pocket and went off to the Diamond Mountains.
>
> Can we not find a similarity between his attitude and those of our literary men of the present time who are specialists in love affairs? Someone might say how could it be possible? Isn't Chŏng a corrupt old poet who only wrote slavish Chinese poetry and are not these literary men of our time whom you accuse of resembling the advocates of new poetry and new writing? How can you say that there exists a similarity between them? But I still insist that the similarity exists. The similarities lie in the escapist attitude they share. I mean that these new poets and new writers are avoiding the reality and suffering of the Korean people. . . . For instance, what do they care about the iron bridge over the Han River or the rice market in Inch'ŏn or the depression? Would they be able to declare that the depression that is descending over all spheres of commerce and industry and the mass immigration of Korean farmers to the West and North Kando districts are not a reality? In my opinion, the crisis of our nation exceeds the degree of urgency that the house of Chŏng experienced sixty or seventy years ago. And yet, these new poets and new novelists only seek pretty scenery of the Diamond Mountains in the vulgar literature. How can one not help lamenting this? (Sin 1976: 169–73).

The image of the abandoned wife is a motif that resonates throughout Korea's Confucian and early modern Korean literature (Chapter 3). But whereas this motif was widely used as a metaphor of the colonized nation in the literary works of Korea's new poets and writers, it was the image of absent husband, not the abandoned wife/lover, that became the focus of Sin's historiography. While poets like Han Yong-un (1879–1944) and Kim So-wŏl (1902–1934) portrayed Korea as the victim of Japanese imperialism ("My lover is gone/O my lover gone away/as you loved me so I loved you!/ A robber has taken all the color away from the green mountains . . ." [Han1970: 17]), Sin sought to find the causes of Korea's colonial predicament in the "absence" of loyal men. Like other nationalists of his time, the figure of the absent/weak *yangban* was read as an allegory of failed national character. Yet, far from employing the *yangban* as an example of weakened manhood/nationhood in need of reform, Sin advocated instead the eradication of the *yangban* from the annals of Korea's "true" national history, in order to resurrect a new ideal of masculinity that would replace the old. Strong, brave, industrious, war-like, and enlightened, the most striking feature of these new protagonists of Sin's history was how different they were from their *yangban* counterparts.

After 1910, Sin's hero-centered history shifted from the examination of the ancient military hero as the primary subject of nationalist inquiry to the historical investigation of the military exploits of the Koguryŏ, Silla, and Paekche kingdoms (Sin 1979: 190). The period after 1925, however, marks Sin's wholehearted embrace of the tenets of anarchism (Sin Il-ch'ŏl 1981). Just as the gallant military hero/military nation had been the subject of nationalist inquiry in Sin's earlier writings, the heroism of the fighting *minjung* (oppressed masses) became the object of his nationalist interest after 1920. Already by 1923, Sin introduced the notion of class struggle—the liberation of the *minjung*—and advocated armed revolution to achieve this end (Sin Ch'ae-ho 1979: 194–95).[8] If war was legitimized as the "natural" expression of nationalism ("the survival of the fittest") through the adoption of Social Darwinian principles in the first decade of twentieth-century Korea, by 1925 this same struggle was *expanded* beyond the limits of nation-state to encompass the transnational struggle of a now universally oppressed people in search of global "liberation."

> We must destroy the entire old social system, including law, politics, ethics, the royal family, the government, banks, business and the rest of our existing social framework. By so doing away with all these institutions, we hereby cry out for a global revolution which we hope can be heard by all the [oppressed] men and women of this earth. (Sin Ch'ae-ho 1979: 198)

Although Sin's anarchism toward the end of his career has been characterized by some scholars as an anomalous conclusion to his nationalist career, his later advocacy of "total violence" as the solution to humanities' problems was actually rooted in the *same* discursive conditions that produced nationalism: transnational imperialism (Duara 1997: 1039–40). Among those narratives that extended beyond the territorial nation, transnational ideologies like imperialism, pan-Asianism, and other utopian radical ideologies like anarchism and communism were justified in the name of a higher calling (or civilization) celebrated as a transnational idea. Far from being an aberration of his nationalist thinking, then, Sin's anarchism actually represented the logical unfolding of the evolutionary paradigm that had produced Korean nationalism. The notion of a self-contained nationalism whereby the territorial nation was to be perfectly coextensive with a homogenous community (in Sin's case, the Puyŏ race) had always coexisted with the transnational desire of the national subject (here linked to the soldier-hero/warrior-nation/ revolutionary *minjung*) to *transcend* the limits of the territorial nation. These transnational imaginings linked an aggressive militarism with a redemptive nationalism aimed to revive the former greatness of a lost "imperial" Korea in Manchuria: Ŭlchi Mundŏk's Koguryŏ (Schmid 1997). Both Sin's nationalism and his anarchism gave rise to similar hypermasculine ideals about the "subjects" of universal progress and their struggles to attain it.

National and Transnational Ideologies

If Sin's early career is characterized by a hero-centered view of national history, the masculine ideals that became associated with such powerful military figures as Ŭlchi Mundŏk and Yi Sun-sin were soon incorporated into Sin's ideal of the authentic "warrior" nation. Sin made his first attempt to articulate his radical interpretation of the national past in *Toksa sillon* (A New Reading of History), published in 1908. After his self-imposed exile in 1910, he began researching and writing about Korea's ancient history, producing his well-known *Chosŏn sangsa* (History of Ancient Korea). Although these later historical works were not published until the 1930s, most Korean scholars agree that they were researched and written well before then, probably between 1915 and 1925 (Sin Il-ch'ŏl 1981).

The evolution of Sin's thought can thus be characterized into three main stages: (1) a hero-centered view of national history; (2) the examination of the territorial nation/race (*minjok*); and finally (3) his embrace of anarchism and the transnational investigation of the "nation-less" *minjung* (oppressed masses) as his principle subject of inquiry.

Although these stages represent distinct phases in the evolution of Sin's thought, their continuum lies in the connection made throughout Sin's work between war and progress, militarism and nationalism, and violence and liberation. According to this framework, the decline of the nation must be traced not only to Chosŏn's disavowal of Korea's "authentic" militaristic spirit, but also to the nation's loss of its imperialistic ethos which Sin associated with the great military exploits of Koguryŏ. Presumably, then, we can understand Sin's anarchism at the end of his career as an attempt to retrieve this original transnational and imperialistic ideal, located no longer in the lost conquered lands of Manchuria, but in the revolutionary potential of the *minjung* and the transnational utopian society he had hope to eventually create.

Thus, Sin begins his history of Korea as a retrospective narrative of decline which he links to the nation's loss of its ancient territorial holdings. At the end of this history, however, Sin offers a way to "resurrect" Korea's original imperialistic ethos in the revolutionary potential of the *minjung*, the harbingers of a new global and revolutionary (yet still very Korea-centered) society. The circulatory of this narrative thus begins and ends with the resplendent image of Korea as both (ancient) imperialist conqueror and (future) revolutionary agent.

Focusing just on the first two stages of Sin's career, the beginning of this history records the military exploits of the Puyŏ race through Koguryŏ (37 B.C.–668) and Parhae (698–926). According to Sin, however, this militaristic "spirit" had been progressively weakened ever since the loss of Korea's ancient territories in Manchuria, an event that was eventually sealed by the unification of the peninsula by Silla in A.D. 668. While the official Confucian view of history had praised Silla for its role in unifying the Korean peninsula, Sin saw Silla's feat as a "betrayal" of the *minjok* because it had relied upon the support of T'ang China to defeat Koguryŏ and Paekche (Sin 1995: 50).

> The reason that the nation became weaker and its territory reduced in size lies in the fact that the people of the same *minjok (tongkok)* considered their brethren enemies. . . . It was Kim Ch'un-ch'u who caused the demise of his own people by relying upon a foreign enemy power (the T'ang).
> (Sin 1995: 50)

Because the unification of the peninsula had not included Manchuria, the original birthplace of the Korean people, Sin argued that "unification had only been achieved by half" (1995: 55). This semi or "half unification" (*panp'yŏnjok t'ongil*), more than a source of national pride, was in actuality cause for collective shame.

After the fall of Parhae, the territories west of the Yalu River were occupied by the Kitan and Mongol peoples. For the past 900 years, we have lost half of the land of old Tan'gun Chosŏn. . . . People say that the unification of our country was achieved only after Kim Ch'un-ch'u. However, if one is to discern the real meaning of unification, it did not happen after Tan'gun Chosŏn. How, then, can we say that Kim Ch'un-ch'u was a unifier? (Sin 1995: 55)

To Sin, the "semi-unification" achieve by Silla signaled the beginning of the country's decline, as it had gone from an aggressive, militaristic and imperialistic nation, to an inward-turning, passive, and peninsular nation. But more than the physical loss of Manchuria after the fall of Parhae in 926, it was the erasure of any memory of Manchuria in Korea's official history that Sin most lamented. In bursts of emotional outrage, Sin lashes out at the Confucian scholar Kim Pu-sik (1075–1151), a man he considered to be a "China-loving lackey" who "possessed no esteem for his own country and its heroes" (Sin 1995: 59). It was this tragic obliteration of Korea's great Manchurian past from Kim's *Samguk sagi* (History of the Three Kingdoms, 1146) that had led to the erasure of any recollection of Korea's great imperialist past and martial "spirit." As a result, Korea had become progressively weakened over time, a process that eventually led to the loss of Korea's national sovereignty altogether.

If the nation's former glory was tied to its territorial holdings, the more land Korea's leaders had ruled over, the greater the nation had once been. Thus, Sin's nationalism had always extended beyond the notion of the self-contained territorial nation. In his biography of Ŭlchi Mundŏk, for example, Sin praised the Koguryŏ general not only for his martial prowess; he extolled the Koguyrŏ general for his imperialist vision. What will it take to recover Korea's glorious past for future generations? "Ŭlchi Mundŏkism," Sin answers. And what is "Ŭlchi Mundŏkism?" he asks. "It is imperialism" (Sin 1995: 87).

The issue of national decline that became intimately tied to the loss of national territory was also linked to the problem of race. The extensive use of the term *minjok* (race-nation) first appeared in Sin's *Toksa sillon,* but it is clear that Sin's view of the original *minjok*—which he traces back to the original Puyŏ race—shared many of the same masculine features that were attributed to the heroes of Sin's biographies. If the ups and downs of Korean history were described in stark Darwinian terms ("history is the record of struggle between the I [a] and the non-I [pi-a]" [Sin1995: 61]), the new subject of national struggle was no longer the individual warrior-hero, but the original war-like *minjok.* Recounting the course of the Puyŏ *minjok*'s struggle with the Xianbi, Chinese, Malgal, Jurchen, and other local tribes, Sin records the triumphs (as well as setbacks) of the *minjok* in its battle for existence (Sin 1995).

The picture that emerges from *Toksa sillon* is one of an aggressive, war-like race becoming progressively weaker over time. Whereas once the Puyŏ *minjok* had been renowned for its fierce and combative spirit, this spirit had become progressively "corrupted" by a literary and dilettantish elite that began to look to China for military support. This corruption, as we have seen, first emerged when Silla relied upon the T'ang to defeat Koguryŏ, leading to the "semi-unification" of the peninsula and the loss of Korea's ancient territorial lands. It was imperative, therefore, that the new historian not only recover the memory of Korea's lost Manchuria, but rediscover this lost martial spirit (which Sin later connected to the revolutionary *minjung* that signaled his embrace of anarchism). In order to rid the *minjok* of its "slave mentality," this authentic national spirit had to be revived. As we shall see in Chapter 5, the re-evaluation of the military (and later, the militarized *minjung*) as the principle agents of Korean history deeply influenced the nationalist ideology of postwar leader Park Chung-hee, who structured his own views about the "strong" and "self-reliant" nation from Sin's version of Korea's "emasculated" past.

Manly Redemption

In 1916, Sin published *Kkŭm hanŭl* (Dream of Heaven), one of only two novels he wrote over the course of his career. Like the rest of Sin's historical work, the project of creating a racial/national subject was intimately tied to the circular themes of struggle, history, and nation. Unlike his other works, however, Sin introduced the concept of patriotic redemption, that is, the means by which Korea's "failed" men/husbands could be turned into "successful" patriots.

The story begins when Hannom (which literally means "one man" or "any man"), "who dreams even while he is awake," finds himself seated under a *mugunghwa* tree. Out of nowhere, three voices begin speaking to him. The first is the voice of the Heavenly Official who has come to visit Hannom from the Heavens of the *nimnara* (roughly translated, "beloved Country," which is, according to the author, the place where all good patriots dwell); the second is the voice of the *mugunghwa*, the Korean national flower; and the third is the voice of Ŭlchi Mundŏk, the Koguryŏ general. Each in turn urges Hannon to take up the sword and fight:

> (*Heavenly Official*) There is only war for men. If you triumph in it, you will live, and if you lose, you will die. And all of this will happen according to the will of Heaven. . . .
> (*Mugunghwa*) Hannom! Open your eyes!! Why are you so weak? This is the true face of the universe. It might have been different had you not come in the first place. But you came, and there is no other way but to enter the fight. If you avoid going to the fight, it will be the same as avoiding your responsibilities. Open your eyes, Hannom, at once. . . .
> (*Ŭlchi Mundŏk*) The spiritual world is the shadow of the physical world. If war does not cease in the physical world, it will not cease in the spiritual. . . . The master in the physical world remains master in the spiritual world and the slave in the physical world remains slave in the spiritual. (Sin 1990: 11–15)

As soon as Ŭlchi Mundŏk has finished speaking, "the reddish clouds in the sky formed these words":

> Yes. Yes. Ŭlchi Mundŏk's words are correct. Physical world or spiritual world, they are both on the side of the victorious. The place called Heaven is only occupied by those with the strongest fists. Those with weak fists shall all be chased into Hell. (Sin 1990: 16)

Stirred from his dream-like stupor, the "re-awakened" Hannom is aroused to action. Determined now to join the war on the side of the *nim* (which can be translated here as the "Lord," but also refers to Tan'gun, the founding father of the Korean nation), Hannom is accompanied by six men who the *mugunghwa* has given him for his perilous journey. Full of "fighting spirit," all seven men then set off for the battlefield.

This fighting spirit is short-lived, however, as Hannom's companions decide one by one to abandon him. One man surrenders to the enemy while another is lured by the temptations of riches and gold. Likewise, the fifth companion declares, "I will go among the blue mountain and the white clouds and become the deer's friend" and flees the world of reality. Thus losing all six friends, Hannom arrives at the battlefield alone. Just as Hannom is about to slay the enemy, however, he becomes briefly distracted by a beautiful woman. Suddenly, he is transported to Hell, the land of traitors.

Unable to understand why he has ended up in Hell, Hannom meets up with a Visiting Official from Heaven who helps him realize his wrongs, thereby setting him on the path toward patriotic redemption. "Hannom," the Official says to him,

> No matter how deep your devotion for the nation may be, you cannot achieve a patriotic deed through devotion alone. Take a look at the *toryŏng gun* [literally translated as a "band of unmarried men" which means "brotherhood of warriors"] that Tan'gun established. (Sin 1996: 44)

The Visiting Official then proceeds to offer Hannom a lengthy explanation of the origins of this "core" martial spirit as exemplified in the idea of the "brotherhood of warriors" (*toryŏng gun*). Established during the Three Kingdoms period, these warriors were called different names by Silla, Paekche, and Koguryŏ, although they all shared the same essential beliefs and ethics. It was during periods of victorious martial exploits carried out by this band of chivalrous warriors that the spirit of the nation had most clearly manifested itself. Pressing Hannom to remember his duty to these heroic martial ancestors, the Visiting Official urges him to take up the sword and revive the original martial spirit of the nation tragically suppressed during the Chosŏn dynasty. Thus Hannom, now fully repented of his ways and having finally realized the true meaning of the Korean warrior "spirit," ascends to Heaven. There he encounters the nation's greatest patriotic heroes. Garbed in the fashions of the Three Kingdoms period, the inhabitants of Heaven dwell in the perpetual fullness of a glorious Korean past.

> At every house were spread animal skins from Koguryŏ; people wore clothing with patterns from Puyŏ and silk woven from Chin-han, and wrapped around them were shawls made of silk from Pallhae, with dragon designs from Silla. Everywhere, one hears the music of Pyŏnhan's zither [*kayagŭm*], the gentle sounds of Silla's flute [*p'iri*], Paekchae's *konghu*

[string instrument], and the music of Koryŏ. Seeing all this Hannon exclaimed in ecstasy: "So this is the Kingdom of Heaven!!" (Sin 1996: 38)

But it is a past marred by the "corrupt" deeds of the nation's traitors. For the sky is not blue but a milky white, and the Sun and the Moon have turned black and square. Inquiring why all the inhabitants of Heaven are sweeping the white dust from the blue sky, Hannom is told that the "traitor" Kim Pun-sik is responsible: it was shortly after his successful repression of the Myongch'ŏng Rebellion in 1136, which marks for Sin the beginning of Chinese overlordship in Korea, that the true fighting spirit of the *minjok* was at last suppressed. Thus Hannom—one man and every man—takes up a broom and, in the company of the nation's greatest warrior heroes, begins to sweep.

Of course, the act of sweeping is also a reference to historical memory and commemoration. In order for the nation to rediscover its true past, the false history—the "white dust" of Confucian historiography—had to be cleared away. For Sin, then, the warrior and the historian each played complementary roles: if the warrior went to battle to defend the *minjok* against its external enemies abroad, the historian fought to preserve the memory of his martial achievements against the nation's internal "enemies" at home.

2

The Quest for Feeling: Yi Kwang-su

Like the new field of national history that emerged during the first decades of the twentieth century, the rise of modern Korean literature
(*munhak*) also played an important role in the "recovery" of the Korean
national character. While the emergence of popular forms of vernacular
literature began to appear as early as the late nineteenth century, it was
not until the first decade of the twentieth century that Korean writers
began to become preoccupied with issues of national identity, the modern vernacular language, and the status of literature (Cho Tong-il 1978;
Yi Son-yŏng 1981). Yi Kwang-su (1892–1950) was among the first generation of these elite intellectuals concerned with the relationship between modern literary practice and nation-building and his pioneering
position in the production of modern knowledge about literature has
been widely recognized. In particular, his essay entitled "Munhagiran
hao" (What Is Literature?) (1916) is considered to be "the first establishment of modern literary theory in Korea" (Kim Yun-sik 1978: 65),
an appraisal that is still valid among Korean literary theorists today
(Hwang 1999; Kim T'ae-jun 1994; Kim Yun-sik 1999; Cho Tong-il 1978).

Simultaneous with the cultural othering of China that was taking place
during this period, Yi Kwang-su advocated a new and "particularized"
concept of Korean literature that would become the new medium for
national self-definition. At the same time, however, the very possession
of cultural or national uniqueness required Yi Kwang-su to subscribe to
a new universalized lexicon of modernity (nation, progress, enlightenment, civilization, and so on) borrowed from Japanese "translations" of
the same terms from the West. The multiple "translations" and global

flows of transnational ideas and resources reveal how the possession of national uniqueness was conditioned by the acceptance of a new universal "civilization" now centered around the West.

These observations are significant to the extent that they shed light on two central themes that will be explored in detail in this chapter. The first concerns the relationship between the act of translation and the recovery of national identity. Yi Kwang-su's work was the product of multiple translations (a point I also explore in detail in Chapter 3), and most of his early works describe the process of national self-discovery—the awakening of *chŏng* (情 feeling)—as a transformative experience linked to a voyage of self-discovery (Hwang 1999; Kim Yun-sik 1999). His early fictional writings are replete with scenes of "translations"—traveling between cities, voyages abroad, train rides, illness, and recovery—many of which coincide with moments of individual emotional (and national) awakening. I am interested in analyzing the interrelationship between these two levels of "translation": both as global discourse (the transnational flow of ideas between Korea, Japan, and the West that gave rise to a new lexicon of modernity that Koreans used to construct their national subjectivity) and as particularized experience ("translation" as a process of self-discovery and patriotic "awakening").

The second theme concerns an examination of the differential structure of relationships that allow the translation (and the voyage) to be recognized as such: the movement between home and world. Implied within the metaphor of the voyage is a set of gender determinations that define the boundaries between home and world, women and men. I show how these points of departure and return functioned in Yi's early "travel" narratives, particularly with regard to the recurrent theme of (male) displacement and homecoming (to the wife and the family). The trope of homecoming that was linked to issues of emotional self-awareness, conjugal love, and national "recovery" was a recurrent theme in Yi's writings and had important implications for the development of Korean nationalism in years to come.[1]

Literature as Translation

Modern Korean literature originated as translated literature (Hwang 1999; Kim Ta'e-jun 1994; Ku In-hwan 1983). This point is underscored by the fact that many early modern Korean intellectuals and writers began their careers either by translating Japanese works or writing their first literary endeavors in Japanese, not in Korean.[2] Yi Kwang-su, for example, spent his formative years in Japan from 1905–1910, when he attended the Meiji Gakuin school (1907–1910) before returning to Korea in 1910. One of his earliest published works of fiction, "Sarangin'ga" (Is It Love?) was written in Japanese when he was just seventeen years old (Kim Yun-sik 1999: 251) As Hwang has observed, a striking aspect of scholarship during this period was the attempt "to reorganize human life in all spheres—from the political system to hygiene—into translated discourse" (1999: 8).

This observation is underscored by the fact that the modern Korean word *munhak* (literature; Jap., *bunkagu*; Chin., *wenxue*) was a term created during the process of introducing Western culture to Japan. Although the Chinese characters for *munhak* (文學) were familiar to Japanese, Korean, and Chinese scholars at the time, these characters now designated something entirely different from the traditional meaning of *munhak* which had originally referred to scholarship or erudition (Hwang 1999: 6). In the Chinese tradition, *mun* (Chin., *wen*) was a much broader concept than the modern reevaluation of the term, encompassing both literary activities as well as various political, cultural, and social practices, such as government, education, and social relationships (Hwang 1999; Chong Tong-il 1969, 1978). The delineation of literature as an autonomous field, however, was the product of a new lexicon of modernity whereby thousands of specialized words and phrases of Classical Chinese origins were given very different meanings in the modern discourses constructed in Japan. The modern Japanese term *bungaku,* which was later translated by Korean and Chinese intellectuals during this period, reveals how this new transnational vocabulary became the very cultural resources through which these writers were able to construct their new national subjectivities.[3] In the case of modern Korean writers and novelists, this reevaluation of *munhak* from a broadly defined scholastic endeavor to a particularized discourse changed their view of the spoken word and its relationship to *mun* (Chinese writing).[4] As Kim T'ae-jun (1994) and Kim Yun-sik (1986) have observed, the modern term *munhak* was linked to the idea of a spoken word, not written (Chinese) language.[5] In this way, the definition of *mun* (文) was broadened to include the spoken vernacular (*mal*) (Kim T'ae-jun 1994: 143–44). The concept of literature, now freed from the traditional understanding of *munhak* as scholarship (which required the mastery of Chinese characters) was perceived as an autonomous field able to articulate the "particularized" experiences of the Korean people outside of the cultural sphere of China (and Chinese *ecriture*).[6]

Yi's pioneering position in this translingual endeavor has been widely recognized, and his essays "Munhakŭi kach'i" (The Value of Literature)[7] (1910) and "Munhagiran hao" (What Is Literature?) (1916)[8] are considered to be foundational works in the history of modern Korean literary theory (Hwang 1999; Kim Yun-sik 1979; Cho Tong-il 1978; Ku In-hwan 1983). By insisting that "literature" was a translation of *bungaku*, Yi not only changed the traditional understanding of *munhak* as it had been understood in the canonical works of traditional Confucian scholarship and learning; he also opened up the possibility for introducing other new concepts and terms that became attached to it. One such new concept was his modern usage of the term *chŏng* (literally translated as "feeling" or "emotion"). For Yi, *munhak* was that which gave expression to a people's unique feelings, or *chŏng*, as "books that satisfy human feeling" (1979a, 547). It was the privileging of *chŏng* over any other human activity that became the basis for his modern theory of literature.

Both Cho Tong-il (1978) and Kim T'ae-jun (1994) note that Yi's usage of the term *chŏng* was a modern invention rooted in new psychological definitions of the term rendered from translated Western sources. These new definitions had very little to do with the traditional understanding of *chŏng* as it was used in the Chinese Confucian canon.[9] Indeed, most scholars agree that Yi Kwang-su was very likely unfamiliar with the Confucian Classics and thus had no historical knowledge of the term's prior meaning (Kim T'ae-jun 1994; Chong Tong-il 1978). Through this lexical effect, *chŏng* was given a very different meaning in the modern literary practices advocated by Yi where it now came to be conceived of in *direct opposition* to Confucian morality and institutions. Throughout "Munhagiran hao" for example, Yi criticizes the detrimental effect of Confucian morality which, in his view, had caused irreparable damage to the sensual and spiritual lives of the Korean people:

> Korean thoughts and emotions were suppressed by the narrowminded morality during the 500 years of the Chosŏn dynasty, not to mention the pre-Chosŏn periods, and thus did not have the opportunity to develop freely. Only if this sort of suppression and obstruction had not existed, then the flower of [Korean] literature [*munhak*] could have bloomed brilliantly during Chosŏn's past 500 years and provided nourishment for the minds of its people and become the source for their pleasure. (1979b: 549)

Confucian morality had stifled the expression of the people's feelings and as a result, Korea's literature had been unable to flourish like the "great literatures of other modern civilized empires" (547–48). If the primary aim of literature was to satisfy human feeling, then the primary task of the author was to liberate "feeling" from the oppressive structures of Confucian morality and institutions.

Yi Kwang-su's insistence upon literature's independence and autonomy from Confucian morality had its own theoretical basis. Based upon the thinking of Christian Wolff, who had forged the rationalist turn in psychology in the late eighteenth century, this theory divided the human spirit into three categories: intellect (*chi*), feeling (*chŏng*), and will (*ŭi*) (1979b: 550). Hwang (1999) notes that Wolff's theory was later revised by Kant, among others, and then ended up circulating among Japanese enlightenment thinkers during the late nineteenth century (1999: 19). For early modern intellectuals in Japan and Korea, the theory provided a basis for understanding human activity as a rational system and was subsequently applied by Yi Kwang-su in his doctrine of *chichŏngŭi ron* (知 情 意 論) (Doctrine of Intellect, Feeling, and Will).[10] In particular, the application of this theory had important implications for Yi's aesthetic ideology, for by categorizing human activity into three main functions, Yi devised a method to distinguish between the variety of human pursuits (for example, the arts, science, and ethics) on the basis of a psychological division within the human mind (feelings, intellect, and will). If science was concerned with the intellect (*chi*), then literature concerned itself with feeling (*chŏng*). In either case, this popular threefold psychological division justified literature as an independent and autonomous endeavor, equal but distinct from all others.

According to Yi Kwang-su, the special status that had been accorded to *chŏng* in the West as something worthy of investigation was missing in the Chinese Confucian intellectual tradition: "An examination of the ancient arts [literature, music, and fine arts] reveals that while *chŏng* was not ignored, it was also not the central focus. *Chŏng* was employed as a supporting or accessory device to examine intellectual, moral and religious issues" (1979b: 548). Whereas Chinese civilization had given credence to only intellectual and moral pursuits, Europeans had recognized the importance of feeling: "As the result of the European Renaissance that occurred nearly five hundred years ago, *chŏng* achieved independence from *chi* (knowledge) and *ŭi* (righteousness) and was treated as equally significant" (1979b: 548). By granting *chŏng* equal status with *chi* and *ŭi*, Europeans had allowed their aesthetic, emotional, and cultural life to flourish, and with it, the means by which they could express their *particular* national spirit and identity.

Yi Kwang-su's insistence upon creating an autonomous sphere for literature as a separate field—"not a slave to politics, morality or science, but *equal to them*" (1979b: 509; my emphasis)—was thus motivated in large part by what he perceived to be the degenerate effects of Confucian morality upon Korea's cultural identity. The privileging of feeling that became the basis for his new definition of literature was made in response to what he perceived as the moral despotism of Korea's traditional Confucian moral culture. Overwhelmed by the power of Chinese writings and ideology, Korean literature had been unable to flourish.[11] As a result, the Korean people had lost their creative power to define the particularity of their national culture, becoming instead "slaves to Chinese civilization."

> Literature is the spiritual culture of a people and the foundation of its national character. The most powerful agent for transmitting one's precious spiritual culture is literature. Nations without literature pass on their spiritual culture through customs or oral traditions. However, the content of these customs and traditions do not become enriched over time and they cannot help but remain primitive and uncivilized. It is said that it has been 4,000 years since the Korean nation was founded. Within this span of time, the kingdoms of Silla, Koguryŏ and Paekche possessed brilliant cultures and as a result, there must be a spiritual culture of the Korean people that contained unique characteristics of Koreans which cannot be found among other peoples. However, the literature of these periods has vanished completely and thus we have been denied the contentment of receiving this precious inheritance. While lamenting the fact that our idle Chosŏn dynasty ancestors have not left us anything of tangible value, I am also deeply vexed that they have not left behind anything of spiritual worth due to their incompetence. However, this situation cannot be blamed only on our ancestors. *As a result of the intrusion of Chinese culture, Chosŏn culture became extinct. Underneath the overarching dominance of China, Korean culture withered and died. Our careless and idle Korean Confucian literati [sŏnin] foolishly allowed themselves to become slaves to Chinese culture and as a result, our own nation's culture was eradicated.* (Yi 1979b: 551; my emphasis)

What is striking about the various passages in both "What Is Literature?" and "The Value of Literature" is Yi Kwang-su's critical rethinking of China as completely Other. This cultural "othering" of China was the result of Yi's insistence upon a new and particularized understanding of literature as the vehicle for Korean national self-definition. Through this new conception of literature, now isolated from the traditional ideology of *mun*, Yi attempted to "resurrect" Korea's national self from the oppressive strictures of Confucian morality. Whereas traditional Chosŏn elites had functioned within the transnational cultural realm of Chinese civilization, by the late nineteenth century new definitions of "civilization" had shifted Koreans' geographical locus from China toward the West and Japan. The reconstruction of Korean identity in this new world system, in other words, "was accompanied by a reinvention of China," a process that entailed the "decentering of the Middle Kingdom" and the embrace of a new universal order focused toward the West (Schmid 2000: 84–85). This new sense of separateness from China was achieved in large part through Yi Kwang-su's appropriation of the modern concept of *munhak* as translation.

However, to characterize "What Is Literature?" as representing a complete rupture from the past would not be entirely correct. As Hwang has aptly observed, Yi's new theory of literature "is not a rupture in the sense that it negates traditional literary practices, but in the sense that it changes the rules in the production of the concepts, principles and knowledge of literature" (1999: 22). This observation is especially relevant when considering Yi Kwang-su's view of morality (*todŏk*). Although Yi attacked the moral despotism of Chinese Confucian culture, which he believed had repressed Koreans' sensual desires and stunted their aesthetic development, his theory of literature did not promote feeling to the exclusion of morality and moral principles (Kim Yun-sik 1999: 258). The cultivation of feeling was not defined as the negation of morality, in other words, *but its very source*. Yi believed that *chŏng* was the spontaneous expression of moral principles and that which caused people to voluntarily realize society's ethical and moral ideals: "Work hard on cultivating feeling [*chŏng*]. Feeling is the driving force of all our duties and the foundation of all our activities. It makes people spontaneously filial, polite, and loyal as well as gives us faith and love" (quoted from Kim Yun-sik 1999: 259). Morality and moral principle, instead of being imposed from above, would arise spontaneously from within, through the cultivation of *chŏng*. Moreover, with the particularization of the concept of literature as the imaginative and fictive expression of feeling, literature came to be seen not only as a means for national self-definition, but the necessary vehicle for moral self-cultivation:

> If I was to add a word to eliminate a possible misunderstanding it would be this: when I say that a writer should liberate himself from the oppressive restrains of [Confucian] morality, I do not mean that he should create literature based on lurid and indecent thoughts that could cause harm. What I mean is that a writer should not be explicitly concerned about morality but should vividly describe the realities of human life that are in front of his eyes. In short, he should not write literature to inculcate a moral principle or to examine the consequences of virtue or vice, but, without writing directly about morality, he should recreate the thoughts, emotions and life of the real world [and so create a moral society]. (1979b: 549)

The psychological development of the people which Yi demanded in the name of the satisfaction of feeling, was of course one of the major tenets of cultural nationalism, which began to take root during the second decade of the twentieth century (Wells 1990; Robinson 1988).[12] Like other cultural nationalists of this period, including An Chang-ho and Yun Ch'i-ho, Yi Kwang-su argued that individual self-cultivation was the basis upon which national Self-strengthening could be achieved. "It is strength alone that will save Korea, and strength derives from the youth cultivating themselves morally and mentally; and again after that, from perseverance in education and industry" (Wells 1990: 95). The cultivation of feeling was thus proffered as a moral duty that had social and political implications beyond the sensual and emotional life of the individual. This is because the new moral freedom achieved through literature provided the possibility for the production of new national subjects—the "awakened Korean"—who would, in turn, reconstruct the nation's identity. If literature was the means by which this new national subject was aroused to the sensual and emotional particularity of his/her own individual experiences, it also provided the source for his/her political identification with the unique community of people who were now identified as "Korean."

Thus far we have examined Yi's theory of literature as translated practice, that is, *munhak* as the particular instantiation of a more central, national, or imperial East Asian discourse of the modern. By pursuing the universal criteria of "civilization and enlightenment" from the modern discourses constructed in Japan, Yi Kwang-su was able to argue for the *particularity* of Korean identity. The question that remains to be explored is how Yi Kwang-su's theory of literature was worked out at the level of literary practice. That is, I want to show how scenes of aesthetic, emotional, and national awakening described in Yi's work were also construed as a process of "translation." The subsequent sections thus take up the problem of translation as inseparable from the project of creating the national subject evolving into modernity.

Travel and Translation

One of the striking characteristics of Korea's early modern literature, and Yi Kwang-su's writing in particular, is its preoccupation with travel.[13] Train and boat rides, scenes of homecomings as well as voyages abroad (usually for educational purposes) all figured prominently in the new literature that emerged during the first decade of the twentieth century—a literature commonly referred to as the *sinsosŏl* (new novel). Train rides, in particular, figure prominently in Yi's early work, and often coincide with scenes of sensual and emotional "awakening." Michael Shin (1999) has observed that these scenes of travel typically function in Yi's writings as a kind of "translation" in the sense that they most frequently represent moments of physical or psychological displacement between places and people that must be resolved. This observation is reinforced by the recurrent theme of the loner-hero-in-search-of-*chŏng* motif, which appears throughout Yi Kwang-su's early writings (Kim Yun-sik 1999; Shin 1999). Indeed, out of this principal theme Yi creates a fluid, transitional landscape of continuous movement and dislocation that demands resolution (translation). Yi's narrative can thus be characterized as one in which the transgression of losing or leaving home is mediated by a movement that attempts to fill the gaps of that loss, which usually constitutes the moment of the protagonist's "return": the "rediscovery" of home, subjectivity, interiority, selfhood, or nationhood as *translated* practice.

Of course, the metaphor of travel is one of the most commonplace tropes in the Western tradition, and Yi's appropriation of it was undoubtedly a "re-translation" of Japanese translations of the modern voyage.[14] As Van Den Abbeele has pointed out, "the dearest notions of the West nearly all appeal to the motif of the voyage: progress, the quest for knowledge, freedom as freedom to move, self-awareness as an Odyssean enterprise, salvation as a destination to be attained by following a prescribed path, and so on" (1992: xv). But the voyage also posits another kind of possibility, namely, the educational value of travel. In this case, the fundamental dislocation of the voyage provides the "critical distance" for the traveler to formulate new opinions about everything he has left behind. The voyage, in other words, enables the traveler not only to discover new landscapes, but to "rediscover" old ones. All of these evaluations of travel figure prominently in Yi's early writings. My own reading of his work will explore this motif in relation to how the "discovery" of selfhood and nationhood described in these texts was achieved during moments of both dislocation and return.

The Quest for Chŏng

One of Yi Kwang-su's earliest literary endeavors, entitled "Sarangin'ga?" (Is It Love?)[15] (1909), raises important questions about the relationship between travel and translation, and will serve as a preamble to my discussion of the voyage motif. Written in Japanese in 1909 when the author was only seventeen years old and a student at the Meiji Gakuin in Japan, the story opens up the possibility of travel and "translation." Like most of Yi's early work, the main character of the story is a loner who briefly finds love and companionship that is prematurely cut short when the object of love suddenly becomes unavailable. The search-for-chŏng motif, which runs throughout Yi's early works, thus functions as a sort of subtext upon which descriptions of displacement and travel are mutually reinforced within the text.

The story begins with a scene of walking. Mun-gil, a Korean student in Japan, is on his way to visit his friend Masao, a Japanese student and classmate. Scheduled to return to Korea the following day, Mun-gil has decided to visit his friend in order to bid him farewell. However, when he arrives at Masao's house, Mun-gil is overcome with apprehension and begins to have second thoughts: Will Masao be happy to see him? Should he knock at the gate or not? Berating himself for his lack of courage and indecisiveness ("Oh, why am I so weak!" [Yi Kwang-su 1972: 443]), Mun-gil begins to pace up and down in front of the gate when the proprietor of the house, hearing the commotion outside, takes notice of Mun-gil and invites him inside ("Ah, don't stay out there in the darkness, come in! [443]). The description of this transitional movement from outside to inside, from darkness to light, signals a moment of hope for Mun-gil, who expresses warm feelings for the proprietor as he eagerly anticipates his meeting with Masao. However, this hope is quickly dashed when Masao fails to appear. Unable to state why he has come ("Mun-gil was too shy to tell the proprietor that he had come to see Masao" [444]), he begins to speak loudly in the hope that his friend will hear him and show himself. However, as time passes, Mun-gil grows increasingly despondent as it becomes clear that Masao will not come out of his room ("Mun-gil heard whispers coming from Masao's room so it was clear that he was there" [444]). Confused and now completely in despair ("that he would treat another human being like this is so cruel. Really cruel!" [444]), Mun-gil leaves the house, feeling both rejected and humiliated. Returning to the darkness outside and realizing that he can no longer live with his anguish and suffering ("Mun-gil now understood that Masao didn't love him and even more than that, even felt antipathy toward him" [445]), he decides to kill himself. Walking swiftly toward a railway crossing (as it happens, in the direction of Korea), Mun-gil lays his head upon the rail "as if on a pillow." Looking up at the stars, Mun-gil begins to cry ("His hot tears would not stop flowing" [446]) as he contemplates his own death.

The failure to find *chŏng* is thus represented as both a physical and emotional displacement that fails to be "resolved" (translated). Mun-gil, after all, is a Korean student in Japan who is due to return home, but his homecoming is cut short by his suicide. Moreover, instead of riding a train—an object that became associated with a whole host of related issues about self-discovery, patriotic "awakening," the quest for modernity[16]—Mun-gil waits to be killed by one. Likewise, Mun-gil's journey to Masao's house is not resolved, as the object of his quest—saying good-bye to Masao—is cruelly cut short and Mun-gil "returns" empty-handed, back into the darkness from where he came. In this sense, "Is It Love?" is a narrative about a quest unfilled, a voyage cut short, a "translation" that is incomplete (meeting his friend, the voyage home, the search for *chŏng*, the suicide, the train that kills instead of transports).

These same travel themes are reiterated in "Yun Kwanho" (1918), which also culminates in the suicide of the protagonist who fails to find *chŏng*, as well as in "Panghwang" (Wandering) (1918) and "Tonggyŏng-esŏ kyŏngsŏngkkaji" (From Tokyo to Seoul) (1917), both of which employ similar motifs of dislocation (illness and travel) to describe the protagonist's quest for *chŏng*. However, the travel motif takes on a new twist in Yi Kwang-su's "Sonyŏnŭi pi" (The Sorrows of Youth)[17] (1917), which deals explicitly with the motif of *return*. The work is different from Yi's other short stories written around the same period in that the protagonist's displacement sets the stage for the reader's own displacement with regard to his/her view of "home" (traditional Korean society), to which the protagonist returns at the end of the story. The voyage thus posits another kind of increment, namely the educational value of travel (travel as a way to call into question the existing order, whether by placing oneself "outside" that order or by taking a "critical distance" to it). As such, the spatial and temporal displacement encoded within the story is constituted as a kind of social critique that is established between the returning (educated) traveler and the sedentary (uneducated) savage.

The Fork in the Road

Sorrows of Youth is also a story of failed love except that it is structured in such a way that the failure to find love is posited as a critique of traditional Korean society. The principle characters are Mun-ho and Nan-su, male and female cousins, respectively. Although they love each other dearly, the fact that they are cousins has made it impossible for them to consummate their passion. Hence, their relationship is purely an intellectual and spiritual one; while they share an occasional moment of physical intimacy by holding hands, their love, for the most part, transcends earthly passions.

When Mun-ho receives word that he will soon be able to leave for Seoul to begin his studies, he secretly harbors a plan to take Nan-su and his younger sister with him so that they can study as well. But his plan is foiled when he learns that his beloved Nan-su has been engaged to another man. Nan-su's parents have entered into a contract to marry their daughter to the son of a local *yangban* family. However, when it turns out that the husband-to-be is severely mentally retarded and an obviously unsuitable mate for Nan-su, Mun-ho begs his cousin to disobey her parents' wishes and come to study with him in Seoul instead. With Nan-su unwilling to stand up to her family, Mun-ho confronts Nan-su's father directly and pleads with him to cancel the marriage:

> "But a *yangban*'s honor is just a momentary thing. Isn't Nan-su's marriage a life-long issue? It is unthinkable to consider sacrificing a person's life for the sake of momentary honor," said Mun-ho.
> However, in an angry tone, Nan-su's father replied, "It is now beyond the power of man to change," and no longer listened to what Mun-ho had to say.

Mun-ho hated this thing called "*yangban*'s honor." He cried alone. And when he met Nan-su later that day, they cried together. After consoling Nan-su for a while, Mun-ho blurted out, "It's all because you are so weak! Why didn't you do as I had told you! [and run away to Seoul with me]," and ran out. (1993a: 89)

The marriage between the beautiful Nan-su and the village idiot therefore takes place with the blessings of both parents. Thus separated forever, Mun-ho leaves to study abroad and Nan-su stays behind to endure her tragic fate.

The basic themes of the novel are almost identical with Yi Kwangsu's later work *Mujŏng* (1917): unrequited love, the idealization of companionate marriage, the critique of traditional marriage practices, and the call for female enlightenment and emancipation (see Chapter 3). Unlike, *Mujŏng* (Heartless), however, the story of Mun-ho does not resolve itself in any meaningful manner, so that the reader is simply left to ponder, at the end of the novel, "Mun-ho's bygone youth." Mun-ho's return home thus provides the critical space within which the reader "arrives" at a fundamentally new reading of "home" (traditional society). Mun-ho's homecoming is not a triumphant or even a happy one, but instead is marked by a profound sense of sadness and loss. His return, in other words, serves to put into question traditional Korean society and, in particular, the "barbaric" practice of arranged marriage. In this sense, the tragedy of the plot can only be resolved by its didactic value: resolution (translation/return) comes in the form of a "lesson" whereby the reader is asked to consider the evils of the traditional system that allowed Nan-su's marriage to take place.

Such a critique was possible only by inventing a new gender discourse that could support Yi's modern claims about love and marriage. Here, man's union with woman was supposed to be based not upon the idea of male sexual appropriation, but rather on the male/female spiritual union. Mun-ho's love for Nan-su is idealized as the perfect meeting between pure souls: their love transcends all physical desire. Thus it is interesting to note that whereas Mun-ho is described only in terms of his emotions and his "heart"—"passionate," "romantic," and "warm-hearted" —Nan-su's future husband is portrayed in terms that are purely corporeal: wide-eyed, with huge lips and spittle drooling down his chin. The vividness of his mental deficiencies is made plain by the detailed description of his physical grotesqueness. Unconstrained by the mind,

Nan-su's future husband is pure body: he drools, his nose runs, his mouth remains forever agape.

And it is precisely the grotesqueness of this image that alerts the reader to the travesty of this doomed marriage, for what can the union between Nan-su and the idiot mean except the fulfillment of (male) sexual desire? The debasement of marriage as a union between sexual partners (whereby the idiot now represents the savage/primitive part of the equation) is contrasted only by the spiritual love shared between Mun-ho (the evolutionarily more advanced man) and Nan-su. The sham that is Nan-su's marriage thus becomes tragically clear when Mun-ho realizes his beloved will marry not a man governed by feeling but a beast ruled by physical urges. Pure body, the nameless fiancé is all instinct, all impulse, with no mind to control either:

> The groom drooled as he laughed with his mouth open. Mun-ho smiled as he thought, "so he remembers the woman he met yesterday." Someone next to him introduced Mun-ho to the groom.
> "This gentleman is your wife's older cousin."
> But the groom continued to drool and just looked at Mun-ho's face while saying "older cousin??"
> The groom's eyes suddenly looked like those of a dead cow. Mun-ho felt nauseous and turned away.
> And he thought, "Ohh!!, how can that thing be my Nan-su's husband!" (1993a: 93–94)

Strikingly, it is Nan-su who emerges as the focus of male rivalry between "civilized" and "primitive" man. Her spiritual purity unquestioned, she becomes the "marker" and thus implicit critic of a "primitive" Korean past. The travesty committed against her by that tradition thus also becomes symbolic of savage man's travesty against all women.

Yet, despite this obvious linear paradigm of Woman as a measure of progress, the evolution upward from sexual depravity to sexual restraint, primitive corporeality to civilized spirituality, is presented by Yi Kwang-su as a *choice:* by asking his readers to consider the evils of a "backward" marriage custom, he also produces an alternative to those evils. In this respect, companionate marriage is offered as a *remedy* to "savagery," just as Woman's self-enlightenment is presented as a "cure" for tradition. Woman and nation thus merge at the point of intersection between *two divergent paths:* one leads upward toward the realm of love and civilization while the other leads downward toward the baser world of primitive urges and loveless desire.

This voyage is thus posited as much as a *translation* as a *relation*—the differential relationships between one place and another, between barbarism and civilization. But the story also posits another relation: that between *chi* (intellect) and *chŏng* (feeling). Applying his theory of literature to this fictional narrative, Yi Kwang-su creates two opposing characters who, as Michael Shin has observed, "embody two very different conceptions of literature" (Shin 1999: 273). Mun-ho's foil is his male cousin Mun-hae, Nan-su's older brother, who is "distant and logical," as opposed to being "warm and emotional." Thus, whereas Mun-ho "admired literature with emotional and aesthetic qualities," Mun-hae preferred literature that "was intellectual and morally good" (Yi 1993a: 85).

But as Yi Kwang-su reveals, Nan-su's marriage to the idiot awakens no compassion in Mun-hae, and his moral virtue is revealed to be meaningless since he feels no empathy for his sister. Like the indifference of Nan-su's other male relatives toward her tragic fate, Mun-hae shows himself to be equally "barbaric." In this sense, Mun-hae's morality, like the idiot's grotesque physicality, both serve as *reference points* that allow the reader to gauge not only the "backwardness" of Korean marriage customs, but also to plot the new "course" toward civilization: marriage as the fulfillment of *chŏng*. In each case, the problem that Yi poses for the reader becomes a question of choosing the "enlightened *path*." Both Mun-hae and the idiot thus function as reference points against which Korea's future "civilization" must be measured. This topographical structure enables the reader to be cognizant of the "voyage" he/she must travel toward the attainment of *chŏng*, civilization, and enlightenment.

The explicit attempt to define this new civilization in terms of the fulfillment of *chŏng*—the "liberation" of feeling as a national imperative—is most clearly developed in Yi Kwang-su's novella "Ŏrinbŏt ege" (To My Young Friend) (1917).[18] Employing once again the search-for-*chŏng* motif, the story is written in an epistolary style consisting of four letters. The first letter begins with a scene of illness: as the hero lies sick in bed, he begins to contemplate the "coldness of the world" and the loveless relationships between Korean couples:

> Is there any other place in the world which matches our nation's monotonous and colorless society? Is there any other place which boasts peoples of such foul character and base feelings? The cause of our nation's meanness lies in its inferior education and in the shortcomings of our social system. Although many factors can be blamed for this situation, such as

an inferior education and imperfect society, it is the lack of an intimate bond between man and woman that is the cause of this situation. Think about it. In a household, intimacy between couples is discouraged and for many couples, except for sexual intercourse, they cannot approach one another outside of the bedroom. As a result, it was thought that coupling was only done for procreation and anything beyond that was considered unacceptable. (Yi 1993b: 290)

The distinction between physical and spiritual love that was posited in terms of a narrative of development (barbarism to civilization) in the "Sorrows of Youth" is posited once again in this text as a problem of "liberation": "On our peninsula, love has been imprisoned. And along with it, many other things linked to love have also been shut away. We cry out in desperation to liberate love. Like the newly sprouting spring grass, we want our oppressed spirits to flourish and like the spring flowers, we want them to bloom" (290). The quest for *chŏng,* in other words, is likened to the search for national authenticity which has to be "liberated" from Confucian morality now deemed foreign and Chinese. In this way, Yi posits the search for *chŏng* (or lack thereof) in this story as a national, not individual, problem:[19]

I am a Korean. Although I am familiar with the word "love," *I, like most of my countrymen, have never actually experienced it.* Most married couples in Korea do not come together in love. Why is it that within the Korean man's heart, love has no place and any affection that might blossom into love is crushed before it is allowed to bloom, killed off by our society's customs and morals? (286, my emphasis)

In the second letter, the hero is roused from his philosophical musings by the presence of a woman whom he later refers to as his "savior." He later learns that she is Kim Il-yŏn, the younger sister of a close friend from Waseda whom he met six years earlier. The scene that follows is a flashback to their first encounter. Though married, he confesses his love to her but she rejects him. Later, however, she sends him a note begging his forgiveness and requests that they meet in a park, but the whole episode turns out to be a dream. The third letter begins as another experience of dislocation. The hero, traveling on a Russian ship to America, meets up with Kim Il-yŏn again just as the ship encounters an accident and begins to sink. The two are saved from death by a boat called *Korea,* and the story ends with a scene of the reunited lovers on a train. Like similar travel motifs that appear throughout Yi's early writings, the transgression of losing or leaving home is mediated by a movement that attempts to fill the gap of that loss through the fulfillment of *chŏng*. The discovery of the emotional, authentic, and spiritual (national) self is thus constituted as a process of (national) self-recovery: the moment of "return" closes the spiral of loss.

The epistolary style of the narrative serves to reinforce the spatial and temporal dislocation of the novel as a voyage that is *re-lated* back to the reader (as the recipient of the letters). In this sense, "To My Young Friend" can be read as a kind of travelogue that recounts the process through which the hero must travel to find his love and attain *chŏng*. The constitutive movements within the text (from despair to happiness, loneliness to reunion, *mujŏng* to *chŏng*) are reinforced by descriptive scenes of similar transitory movements (from illness to recovery, dreaming to awakening, death to life, and so on), all of which serve to reinforce the basic structure of the novel as a series of dislocated experiences that are, in the end, resolved (translated).

Yet, in spite of these scenes of transitory movement toward resolution, it would be wrong to characterize Yi's "travel" narratives as being simply voyages that posit incremental gain (whether this gain be in the form of self-awareness, the attainment of *chŏng*, enlightenment, or whatever). Rather, despite the progressive linearity of the travel motif, Yi's modern voyages are as much about gain as about the recovery of *what has been lost*. This recovery is posited as a movement to reconnect to a lost and authentic Korean past through the disavowal of a Confucian "middle age" associated with China. The search for *chŏng*, in other words, is as much about returning home as it is about leaving it.

Take, for example, Yi's reading of the *Tale of Ch'unhyang,* Korea's most renowned love story.[20] The love shared between Ch'unhyang and Yi Myong-nyong was, for Yi, the most authentic expression of the original Korean *chŏng* (or spirit) tragically suppressed by the stringent codes of an "imposed" Confucian morality. In this case, the search for *chŏng* entailed the recovery of this authentic and idealized past/feeling as the prerequisite for "charting" the modern nation's future. Yi writes:

> Even though Koreans may not admit it, they are, deep inside, looking for this kind of love [shared between Ch'unhyang and Yi Myong-nyong]. But such a love is as precious as gold or jade and perhaps one person in a thousand, one time in ten or a hundred years, can ever really experience

this type of love. Thus, women envy Ch'unhyang while men envy Yi To-ryong. Since such a love is so rare, people have turned to novels, plays and poetry to experience it and to laugh and cry.

Early on in Korea's history, the only kind of love that existed between man and woman was the one which blossomed between Ch'unhyang and Yi To-ryong. Every woman aspired to be like Ch'unhyang while every man sought to be like Yi To-ryong. . . . *It was the Chosŏn dynasty's brutal marriage customs, however, that killed this flower of love that had for centuries blossomed in the bosoms of the Korean people.* (1996: 313; my emphasis)

Of course, the connection Yi poses between the *Tale of Ch'unhyang* and the nation's "authenticity" ignores the didactic aspects of the story, which served as a means to "uplift" feminine virtue as well as to enforce proper Confucian moral behavior. Nevertheless, the interesting point here is that Yi connects the *Tale of Ch'unhyang* as being authentically "Korean" and as such, appropriates the story as the veritable expression of the nation's *chŏng*. Whether the search for *chŏng* is about leaving the "home" (and) or returning to it, the absence of *chŏng* serves as both the point from which the voyage begins and the point to which it circles back in the end. In this sense, self-discovery is posited as a movement of rediscovery: *chŏng* functions as both the absolute origin (the authentic expression of Korean identity) and the absolute end (the "recovery" of Korea's [lost] authenticity) of the voyage.

Both these evaluations of the voyage (that which offers incremental gain or recovery of what has been lost) remain circumscribed within the limitations of two conceptual points: departure and destination, and the spatial relations between them. For Yi Kwang-su, the departure point, or "home," functions as the transcendental point of reference that organizes his narrative insofar as scenes of "recovery" (the fulfillment of *chŏng* and patriotic awakening) are almost unanimously portrayed as a *circular* voyage (the "home" as the absolute origin and absolute end point of any movement at all). This also explains why the home—including related issues such as domestic happiness and conjugal love—is so intimately tied to issues concerning spiritual bonding and national "awakening." Indeed, one very important aspect about Yi's definition of *chŏng* was that it represented the *spiritual* coming together between husband and wife that was ultimately devoid of physical or sexual content.[21] The foundation of civilization that was forged in the home by these "spiritual" bonds thus constituted both the starting and ending point of the hero's quest for enlightenment (and *chŏng*). This is because the quest for *chŏng* was posited as much as a discovery as a "recovery": the spiritual fulfillment of a love *that had always* been present (albeit long suppressed by Confucian morality and social codes). The home—here associated with a host of related issues about emotional awakening, spiritual love, enlightenment, progress, civilization, and so on—thus constitutes both the beginning and ending point of Yi's "traveling" narrative.

More than simply an abstract principle, however, Yi's theory of literature had deeply personal implications. When Yi Kwang-su met Ho Yŏng-suk at the age of twenty-seven in Tokyo, he was already a married man and the father of a son. She was a twenty-two-year-old medical student at Tokyo Medical College for Women. Having completed her primary education in Korea at Ehwa school for girls, she had come to Tokyo to finish her medical education in Japan. Their love was to provide the inspiration for Yi's earliest literary endeavors.[22]

The circumstances of his failed marriage to his first wife left him bitter and, recalling his abandonment of her, he wrote simply that "he never loved her":

> I don't believe she was a mean person who looked down on others. She is a gentle person. Even though I recognized her merits, I just could not love her, and I resented myself for it. Perhaps I wished for a more beautiful and better wife. But, it wasn't that either. I am not trying to vindicate myself. I simply didn't love her. (From Kim Yun-shik 1986: 315.)

Like the sick and dying hero of "To My Young Friend," Yi Kwang-su experienced his own miraculous recovery from tuberculosis under the care of his new wife. Functioning as a kind of surrogate mother (Yi's real mother died when he was a child), Ho thus became the mother Yi never had. Attending to his "rebirth," Ho thus assumed the role of both mother (civilizer) and wife (companion). Her moral beauty had uplifted him from his original/primitive "depravity." Whereas (primitive) marriage had once meant to him the socially sanctified union for unleashing (male) carnal lust, he now recognized (civilized) marriage as the idealized bonding between like-minded souls.

> Traditional (arranged) marriages have only two meanings. The first is that the couple becomes an ornament, to be viewed by the groom's parents. The other is to obtain a child just like a pig farmer eagerly awaiting

piglets for future income. Thus our Chosŏn couples simply end up as their parents' plaything and as a reproductive machine. Under these circumstances, when a man looks at his wife, *all he is capable of seeing is a "body" that satisfies his animalistic sexual desires and produces his children. Men could see women only as a way to satisfy their lowly carnal lust. The purpose of the relationship between man and wife thus resides simply in sexual intercourse* and reproduction. . . .

Only the uncivilized believes that happiness in a relation between man and wife is based on physical contact (sexual intercourse). *It takes a civilized gentleman with a solid moral foundation to appreciate the supreme satisfaction of disregarding the physical appearance, to praise the grace of the heart and thus, to love a woman solely with the mind. A relationship between man and woman is not solely based on the physical, but it is also based on affection and the fusion of the heart. This is true of the more civilized people.* (1993b: 287–88; my emphasis)

If the path toward civilization and enlightenment begins in the home (an idea that is linked to Yi's description of his own spiritual "rebirth"), then women, as the traditional guardians of the home, function as the spiritual base from which all "voyages" both begin and end: civilization, progress, self-knowledge, and nationhood. A poignant moment in *Mujŏng* is the scene in which Hyŏng-sik asks his bride-to-be to confirm her love for him with a verbal declaration (1996: 279–82). Although Sŏn-hyŏng is thoroughly confused and embarrassed by the question, what Hyŏng-sik actually demands of her was a verbally articulated confirmation of love, more than her real and still inarticulate feelings for him. The verbal declaration of love demanded by Hyŏng-sik thus has more to do with the emancipatory possibilities of conjugal love, linked to his image of himself as a modern and civilized person, than the actual sensual experience of it. In this way, the ideal of "conjugal love" was viewed as the departure point from which the hero launches his quest for progress and nationhood (his studies in America as well as his imagined "triumphant" return). Although Hyŏng-sik is unaware of the true meaning of love, he nevertheless understands the necessity of its existence *in order* to embark upon his journey abroad.

Homecoming: Nation, *Chŏng*, Women

The metaphor of the voyage as a critical trope had important implications for the development of Korean nationalism. The notion of domestic bliss that was idealized by Yi Kwang-su was appropriated into a variety of national contexts, from colonial representations of the raped and violated woman as the symbol of Japanese colonialism (the "loss" of home and homeland), to the narrative of separating and reuniting couples as the expression of the division and national reunification (see Chapter 4).[23] As will become clear in the two chapters that follow, the intrinsic tensions between home and world, loss and recovery, reveal a distinctive characteristic of Korean nationalism in which the "resolution" (or translation) of loss (colonialism, division) was discursively connected to a kind of "homecoming" (*chŏng*, liberation, and unification) symbolized by women. Whether this resolution took the form of female empowerment (see Chapter 3) or romantic reunions (see Chapter 4), these images acquired their symbolic significance through the discursive possibilities first opened up by the translated term *munhak*.

Part Two

Women

3

Signs of Love for the Nation

*It is the model narratives that give "meaning" to our readings of
ourselves and others. We are used to working with variations on,
critiques of, and substitutes for, the narratives of Oedipus and
Adam. What narratives produce the signifiers of the subject of
other traditions?*

—Gayatri Chakravorty Spivak[1]

*Especially in Korea a woman was no better than a domestic
animal. She was denied the privilege of an education. To assert
her personality or to engage in an independent livelihood was
never dreamt of. But it is the blessing of Christianity that has
induced her to attend church services and to engage in acts of
worship along with men, giving her the conception that men and
women are sons and daughters of God on equal terms.*

—Yi Kwang-su, 1918[2]

So wrote the novelist Yi Kwang-su on the status of Korean womanhood
and the "civilizing" benefits of Christianity in early colonial Korea. That
women came to occupy a singularly important position in the new fiction writing of this period raises some interesting questions about the
way in which colonial literatures recode traditional notions of gender
and femininity in the context of colonial modernity. This chapter will
critically examine the way in which "woman" became the sign and sub-

ject of early-twentieth-century Korean nationalist discourse. I will highlight how early modern Korean literature, by appropriating Western religious and scientific notions about Woman as a "natural" and ontological
category distinct from Man, transformed traditional Confucian images
of womanhood in family life into a political "sign" of colonial oppression. I explore how the new gender coding of sexual "difference" became linked to other sites of political opposition (state/society; past/
present; modernity/tradition, and so forth). One of the consequences of
the appropriation of this new gender coding, I argue, was the merging of
private and public spheres whereby political discourse translated itself
through women into the private context of love, marriage, and loyalty.
Just as women's personal happiness (most significantly in family life)
was suddenly made the consequence of national concern, so her private
life was turned into a stage for politicizing national desire.

This "appropriation" of woman as a sign was not, however, a one-
way hegemonizing process. The way Korea's early modern writers used
the new category of woman in their political discourse was, to a very
large extent, patterned after traditional narrative configurations about
women found in Korea's canonical literature. Whereas traditional hero-
ines had been revered for their virtuous loyalty to their husbands, that
loyalty now shifted to the nation and the colonized state. The nation in
Korea rose up not by excluding (or oppressing) local forms of communal imaginings, including women's traditional roles in patrilocal Korean kin fields. Rather, it merely transformed those imaginings, in a
process of accommodation and struggle, in such a way that traditional
loyalties were never entirely abandoned, but merely transferred to a newer
object of affection (the nation).

To examine this problematic of gender, nation, and fiction writing, I
will focus my analysis on Yi Kwang-su's *Mujŏng* (Heartless), a work widely
perceived to be Korea's first modern novel.[3] Published in 1917 and considered a classic in Korea's modern literary canon, *Mujŏng* engages the
"woman's question" as a way of coming to terms with the traumatic experiences of Koreans after their colonization by Japan in 1910. In the book,
Yi Kwang-su opened a new battlefront in his struggle to claim "modernity" and to reject "tradition," for traditional Confucian culture was widely
perceived to be the root cause of Korea's downfall into colonial dependence. In his efforts to create a new, improved, and modern social order,
particularly in a world beset by internal political crisis and Japanese en-
croachment, Yi Kwang-su put supreme faith in the power of literature to

transfigure the tradition by way of modern narrative modes.[4] To this end, *Mujŏng* represents a discursive intervention of the past. By virtue of the novel's self-conscious difference from the Confucian canonical texts which it sought to self-consciously revise—and the ideal gender models associated with them—the novel serves as a prescriptive example of how tradition could (or should) be rewritten. This rewriting of Korea's literary canon destabilizes previous traditional notions of femininity and masculinity and reassigns them new (political) value. It opens up an important avenue toward our understanding of the problematic of nationalism itself.

The "Woman's Question"

One of the most curious features of early-twentieth-century colonial (and semi-colonial) nationalist movements around the world has been their seeming reliance on domestic issues involving women. Lydia Liu, for example, notes that the story of women's liberation in China was inextricably tied up with concerns of nation-building (Liu 1994). Likewise, in Korea, women's happiness in marriage and family life was made an essential feature of early Korean nationalist and resistance movements against Japanese colonialism.

These concerns for women entailed a radical rethinking that involved their historical reconstruction into a universal "generic" political category. In the context of the Chosŏn dynasty, women were framed according to kin-specific situations as instances of "things women do," not what they inherently "are." The discursive positioning of a woman marked her gender in terms of some very specific roles she was expected to fulfill within the domestic kin structure. What appear in the ancient Confucian texts "are not the 'sexes' per se, but a profusion of relational, bound, unequal dyads, each signifying women's relations to parents, husbands and parents-in-law" (Barlow 1994: 177). In Confucian Korea, for example, a *chŏngbu* (eldest daughter-in-law) was unequally related to her mother- and father-in-law. Likewise, she was distinguished in rank and behavior from the other daughters-in-law within the household unit (those women married to second or third sons), who in turn were unequal with regard to her. Far from being merely hierarchically binaried (as the current cliché would have it), "the yin/yang logic of human relations in Confucian philosophy produced a dynamic world of subject positions named mother, father, husband, wife, daughter-in-law, brother, elder brother, etc." (Barlow 1994: 176).[5]

When Yi Kwang-su invented the image of the Korean "new woman" (*sinyŏsŏng*), he did so by subverting the authority of Confucian tradition by subtly changing the terms that had once defined her: chaste wife, obedient daughter-in-law, and so on. Yet far from merely abandoning these social conventions, Yi also reappropriated them within new sets of definitions of ideal (modern) femininity. Thus reconstructed, the "new woman" becomes something that is repeated, relocated, and translated in the name of a "tradition" that is not necessarily a faithful representation of the past. By thus viewing women as cultural constructs that are continually being revised, rewritten, and re-appropriated, and not as static, essentialized biological entities, we can begin to treat the woman's question in nationalist discourse on its own terms (in all its ambivalences and contradictions) rather than as part of a totalizing theory of oppression.

Translated Modernity: Yi Kwang-su's *Mujŏng* and the *Tale of Ch'unhyang* Revisited

The idea of woman as an ontological category was imported to Asia by Westerners, mainly American missionaries, about the time that Korean Enlightenment thinkers used it to promote modern literature (Barlow 1994). In the ensuing debate between Korea and the West about the intrinsic role of women in the national imaginary, there emerged a new type of woman that radically subverted the Confucian production of gendering. Very much like China in the mid-nineteenth century, there was a rash of masculine interest in the universal sign of woman. This pro-feminine writing, which advocated such things as female education, the abolition of child marriages, and the promotion of "enlightened" relations between women and men, sought liberty for women on nationalist grounds. By appropriating woman as a transcendental sign for the "nation," early-twentieth-century Korean writers described the political conditions of Japanese colonial oppression in terms specifically related to the traditional oppression of women by men.

Yet this appropriation of woman was not without its inherent contradictions. One of the many curious features about Korea's early modern fiction writings, and *Mujŏng* in particular, is that although they distanced themselves from the traditional canon (and the social norms and subjectivities associated with proper Confucian gender/familial protocol), they often drew upon its narrative conventions. In *Mujŏng,* for example, Yi Kwang-su re-tells (and in the process thoroughly transforms) the *Tale of Ch'unhyang*, Korea's most renowned love story. Thus, even as Korean tradition (and traditional female subjectivities) came under attack, the narrative strategies and plot structures that promoted that tradition were never entirely abandoned. On the contrary, similar stories about abandoned women, virtuous wives, and absent husbands in the Confucian moral canon simply reappeared in modern Korean literature, albeit in altered form. Thus, even though they often spoke in the language of Western (female) self-enlightenment, modern Korean writers like Yi Kwang-su still used many of the major tropes from earlier literary traditions. Far from merely importing from the West, unchallenged, the idea of universal womanhood, *Mujŏng* was actively engaged in a discursive struggle over the subject of the "modern Korean woman" as she interacted with the local narrative traditions. My own reading of *Mujŏng* will explore these tensions by focusing on the way traditional Confucian ideologies of gender became simultaneously made and unmade in the context of the Korean national imaginary. My aim is to explore how the tensions between the home and world (tradition and modernity) were worked out in the context of literary translation: the "re-lation" between Yi Kwang-su's *Mujŏng* and the *Tale of Ch'unhyang*. This back-and-forth movement between these two texts offers yet another example of how the motif of travel in Yi's early work, discussed in detail in chapter 1, acquired its significance through the discursive possibilities opened up by the translated term *munhak*.

Failed Manhood

Like much of Korean literature, *Mujŏng* is a story about irreconcilable love.[6] Indeed, the central problematic around which the novel is focused has to do with the seeming inability of husband and wife (or fiancé and fiancée) to reconcile their love, and hence the woman's continual preoccupation with consummating it. In this sense, *Mujŏng* mirrors many of the same plot structures found in Korea's canonical romance tales: the loss of love (or loved one) by the wife and her struggle to overcome that loss by faithfully awaiting the return of the absent lover/husband. Nowhere do these classic themes come together better than in the *Tale of Ch'unhyang*. As discussed briefly in the previous chapter, the *Tale* begins when Yi Myong-nyong, the son of an upper-class family, and Ch'unhyang, the daughter of a socially despised *kisaeng* (female entertainer)[7] meet and fall in love at first sight. Soon after their romance begins, Yi Myong-nyong is called to the capital. Shortly thereafter Ch'unhyang is sent to prison after she refuses the advances of the evil governor. Finally, her lover returns, rescues her, punishes the evil governor, and they live happily ever after.

Not surprisingly, the principle female protagonist of *Mujŏng* is also a faithful *kisaeng* (re-named Wŏl-hyang) who, like the beautiful Ch'unhyang, remains true to her betrothed despite tremendous hardship and suffering. And like the irresolute boy Yi Myong-nyong, who visits Ch'unhyang to announce that his mother has "said that if a gentleman's son comes to the province with his father, then goes out and takes a mistress, and the fact gets known at court, he never stands a chance of being accepted. There is nothing for it, we must be parted" (Rutt 1989: 285), *Mujŏng*'s Yi Hyŏng-sik is also irresolute, weak, and indecisive. Yet, while Yi Myong-nyong redeems himself at the end of the *Tale* by returning to his betrothed, the protagonist of *Mujŏng* never returns, choosing instead to marry another woman in her place. Furthermore, unlike Yi Myong-nyong, who declares his newfound "manhood" and punishes the evil governor (which in turn leads to renewed marital bliss and the restoration of benevolent leadership), it is Hyŏng-sik who, far from punishing his betrothed's offenders, is himself punished by them. In Yi Kwang-su's modern version of the traditional tale, then, the absent husband never returns and the faithful wife's hardships are suffered in vain. Until, that is, she is saved by another woman. The "enlightened" Pyŏng-uk is the "new woman" (*sinyŏsŏng*) who comes to the rescue of the faithful wife Yŏng-ch'ae (also known as the *kisaeng* Wŏl-hyang) and by so doing, usurps the privileged place of the returning (powerful/punishing) male. I have provided a sketched diagram of the plot structures of the two narratives (opposite page).

The obvious parallels of the narrative paradigm of *Mujŏng* with the *Tale of Ch'unhyang* are striking. But far more revealing, as I have shown in different contexts, is the way in which this "master narrative" continues to shape Koreans' thinking about the history of collective suffering (e.g., colonialism and the national division) in terms that are strikingly gendered (see Chapters 5 and 6). Yi Kwang-su's refashioning of the absent husband into the modern image of the weak and impotent male no doubt struck a chord with his readers, who had witnessed their nation become a colony of Japan. Furthermore, the national subject/reader's increasing sense of frustration with Hyŏng-sik's impotence also sets the stage for Yŏng-chae's "awakening" to (modern) womanhood/nationhood.

The Tale of Ch'unhyang

husband (Yi Myong-nyong)	absent husband	return of husband
wife (Ch'unhyang)	suffering wife	saved by husband (retains chastity)
evil governor (Pyŏng Hak-to)	punishment by husband	restoration of benevolent patriarchal leadership

Mujŏng

husband (Yi Hyŏng-sik)	absent husband	does not return/engaged to another woman (Sŏn-hyŏng)
wife (Pak Yŏng-ch'ae/ Wŏl-hyang)	suffering wife (loses chastity)	saved by "new woman" (Pyŏng-uk)
evil schoolmaster/ (Bae Hak-gam)	punishes husband	"liberation" of nation by enlightened womanhood

By exploring how the absent husband/loyal wife trope found in Korea's canonical literature was revised in *Mujŏng,* we will see just how Yi Kwang-su simultaneously invoked and undermined the traditional conventions of Korean manhood (much like Sin Cha'eho, discussed in chapter 1), and by so doing, set the stage for the rise of the modern Woman.

Steadfast Wives, Filial Daughters

Female anguish because of loss is a predominant theme in Korea's canonical literary works. For the most part, male characters functioned either as the object of womanly suffering (like Ch'unhyang's husband Yi Myong-nyong, who appears only briefly at the beginning and end of the tale) or as the instigators of suffering (like the "evil" governor who beats Ch'unhyang for her steadfast loyalty to her absent husband). In each of these cases, women suffer as a consequence of men.

Like the prototype absent husband, male characters in Korea's traditional canon were also portrayed as dream-like, inhabiting the world of irreality and fantasy. *Nine Cloud Dream* by Kim Man-chung (1637–1692) is a prime example of this type of male character. Renouncing the harsh realities of the real world, the male protagonist finds consolation in the dream-world of utopian romance and riches. Likewise, in the canonical *Tale of Sim-chŏng,* also from the Chosŏn dynasty, it is the blind father who expresses the trend for dreams while the heroine (the filial daughter Sim-chŏng) grasps the realities of the world and must sacrifice her own life for her father's foolish desires.

This view of male impotence in the world of reality plays an important part in the narrator's construction of male subjectivities in *Mujŏng.* The male protagonist Yi Hyŏng-sik (like almost every male character in the novel) is impotent because he cannot act.[8] Throughout the text, he is described as "indecisive" (*chujŏhada*), "hesitant" (*mŏmch'itgorida*), "confused" (*ch'angnanhada*), "weak" (*yakhada*), and "ineffective" (*muryŏkhada*):

> Even when Hyŏng-sik spoke with ardor about something as if it were some great truth, he was unable to move his audience. His four years as a teacher were, indeed, a failure. Although at school he expressed various opinions on this or that, they were never taken seriously. His teachings and guidance were never warmly received by his students and, of course, no one ever attempted to implement them. (Yi 1996: 203)

While female characters suffer and become mature, the male characters represent the various plot spaces or obstacles which the principal female character must pass through or emerge from in order to prove her loyalty and virtue. In *Mujŏng,* it is Hyŏng-sik's symbolic absence that sets the stage for Yŏng-ch'ae's "reawakening" modernity. Like the loyal wife Ch'unhyang, Yŏng-ch'ae longs to be reunited with the (imagined) husband (of her dreams). But Hyŏng-sik never manifests himself in any real way:

> That Hyŏng-sik followed Yŏng-ch'ae to Pyŏngyang and didn't bother to find out whether she was dead or alive, that he came back and just a few days later got engaged, that he thereafter completely forgot about her, all this made him think as if he had committed some great crime. Hyŏng-sik was, indeed, a man with no feeling [*mujŏng*]. (Yi 1996: 300)

The plot of the novel thus makes an ironic tribute to the *Tale of Ch'unhyang* by continually exposing Yŏng-ch'ae's love as mere "fiction." ("You've been living a dream all this time," says Pyŏng-uk to Yŏng-ch'ae. "A husband one doesn't know is unthinkable. Therefore think of your past as only a dream" [1996: 257].) Her idealized love for Hyŏng-sik is characterized as the stuff of imagination and literature. Hence the repeated juxtapositions in the text of the real and the ideal, action and thought, deed and intention, reality and literature. "Real" love between a man and a woman requires manly "presence," not literary "absence."

By subverting the Ch'unhyang master-narrative, Yi Kwang-su rewrites the traditional plot form of separating and reuniting couples into a story of male betrayal and female self-empowerment. Instead of redeeming himself, punishing the "evil" baron, and returning to his beloved, Hyŏng-sik instead becomes engaged to another woman. Likewise, the betrayed woman overcomes her loss, breaks with "tradition," and asserts her newfound modern womanhood in the name of the nation.

Interestingly, this strategic undercutting of the idealized image of returning masculine power also turns failed patriarchy into a forum for male self-humiliation and shame. Throughout the novel, male shame is associated most frequently with male impotence. Unable to act, Hyŏng-sik cannot consummate his desires (sexually or otherwise) and thus must rely on other men to consummate them for him. Hence the link between Hyŏng-sik's obsession with other men's possession of Yŏng-chae's body and the state of its real or imagined "purity." His failure to rescue Yŏng-ch'ae from the lascivious hands of the evil schoolmaster thus turns Hyŏng-sik's rage into symbolic male impotence. Furthermore, Hyŏng-sik's own heightened sensitivity to perceived slights and insinuated insults only add to the perception of Hyŏng-sik's latent insecurity about his manhood. Passive in the face of false rumors about his illicit affair with the *kisaeng* Wŏl-hyang (Yŏng-ch'ae), Hyŏng-sik simply flees. Painfully aware that his father-in-law no longer believes Hyŏng-sik is a good match for his daughter, Hyŏng-sik nevertheless remains silent. Even in the face of his fiancée's growing coldness and aloofness, Hyŏng-sik is unable to speak up and defend himself against an increasingly hostile and inhospitable world: his students scorn him, his fiancée doubts him, his future father-in-law loses respect for him, even his friends disdain him. Instead, he consoles himself, in the way of many male protagonists of Korean fiction, in the "dream-world" of irreality: his future life in America.

Significantly, at the end of the novel when the three principle female characters come together and put on a concert for the victims of a flood, Hyŏng-sik is conspicuously absent. The progressive female image of authority (Pyŏng-uk) thus replaces the traditional dominant image of returning patriarchal power. By drawing upon traditional conventions of Confucian manhood as they appeared in Korea's canonical literature, Yi Kwang-su both rewrites and undermines the ideal of redeemed manhood in a scathing criticism of public male authority under whose (loveless) leadership the nation had succumbed to colonial dependence and despair. Hence the allusion to Yŏng-ch'ae's tears in the narrator's description of the flood at the end of the novel and the havoc it has created among the people. Just as Yŏng-ch'ae yearns for manly "presence" (so that she can realize her ideal of modern romantic love), so too the nation yearns for manly leadership to realize its people's liberation. The project of modern romance thus appears as a critique of traditional Confucian patriarchy; it is Pyŏng-uk, after all, who "liberates" Yŏng-ch'ae from tradition by feeding her with new ideas from the West and who entices her into the project of modern love. By drawing on the *Tale of Ch'unhyang* as the discursive platform upon which "tradition" is condemned, Pyŏng-uk reveals the absurdity of Yŏng-ch'ae's steadfast loyalty to a man she does not love (Yi 1996: 255).

Needless to say, the repeated allusions to the *Tale of Ch'unhyang* throughout the novel are an ideological ploy. *Mujŏng* recycles the traditional plot form of female suffering and loyalty, separation and reunion, but it uses this traditional romance tale to represent the political struggle. In this narrative device, public and private spheres merge. Yŏng-ch'ae is saved not because she relinquishes her private loyalty to Hyŏng-sik, but because she is able to successfully transfer that loyalty onto a new object of public affection: the nation. Moreover, her transformation from loyal wife to loyal patriot is made by stripping her subjectivity of familial content and replacing it with a political subject construction. The suppression of the private beneath the political is one of the many consequences of the appropriation of a general category of "Woman." The evocation of the abandoned heroine in *Mujŏng* is not about private/familial suffering. It is about public, national humiliation in the context of Japanese colonialism. Yŏng-ch'ae's "rebirth" at the end of the novel gets mixed up with the political myth of national redemption and resurrection. The channel of Yŏng-ch'ae's idealized relation to the nation thus allows her to emancipate herself from the sphere of the domestic and private order. Thus, the problematic relationship between woman and man disappears, having been subtly replaced by the enlightened female image and the (liberated) nation-state.

The Female Body and the Enlightened "New Woman"

In Korea, as in many other colonial and semi-colonial countries, women's bodies became a particularly privileged site of contested meanings about modernity. As I have shown elsewhere, the raped and wounded female body in contemporary Korean nationalist discourse has figured widely in representations of the division of the nation (see Chapter 5). In *Mujŏng,* Hyŏng-sik's (and the narrator's) obsession with the state of Yŏng-ch'ae's body and its ambiguous purity is a central focus of the novel and plays a central role in Hyŏng-sik's struggles with his (and the nation's) identity. By repeatedly stressing the plight of the female body with regard to its real or imagined physical contamination, the narrator locates the meaning of national suffering—poverty, ignorance, patriarchy, Confucianism, and so forth—in the figure of the exploited female body. Yŏng-ch'ae, after all, becomes a *kisaeng* in order to pay for the exorbitant legal costs involved in freeing her (weak/ absent) father from prison. Through the ordeals Yŏng-ch'ae endures in selling her body by becoming a *kisaeng,* the reader becomes aware of all sorts of social and political injustices visited on that body.

But in Yi's modern rendering of the tale, Yŏng-ch'ae's bodily sacrifices are not recognized and her father (like traditional society) scorns her instead. Twice scorned, first by her father and then by Hyŏng-sik, Yŏng-ch'ae turns to women for solace instead. Thus, whereas Hyŏng-sik is unable to recognize women apart from their bodies (his constant preoccupation with Sŏn-hyŏng's "chaste body" is also significant in this regard), the female characters in the text relate to each other purely in terms of the mind. Rejected by the father, Yŏng-ch'ae finds solace in Wŏl-hwa, another *kisaeng,* who introduces Yŏng-ch'ae to the world of books, ideas, and poetic reflection. Likewise, in the second half of the novel, it is the "enlightened" Pyŏng-uk, not Hyŏng-sik, who heals Yŏng-ch'ae's wounded body by teaching her the value of female education and "enlightenment" (especially in the context of marriage). Significant in this regard is Yŏng-ch'ae's own transformation from her perception of herself as a mere "body" to a person with a "heart," capable of thought and, most importantly, of love.[9] In her farewell letter to Hyŏng-sik after her rape, Yŏng-ch'ae portrays her intended suicide in purely corporeal terms: the defiled female body that must be destroyed in order to "purify" itself:

> I have protected the chastity of this body for you as much as I have upheld the teachings of the ancient sages and as fervently as I have devoted my body to caring for my father when he was alive. With my death, I now can release the burden my body has borne to protect its chastity.
> But this body has been violated. Ah, dearest, this body has been violated [. . . .] This body is now a badly scarred sinful thing that cannot be looked upon with approval either by the heavens or the earth or the gods.

This body is a great sinner for it has injured its father to whom it is a child, harmed its brothers to whom it is a sister and broken the vow of chastity sworn by all women to their husbands.

Dearest, this body now departs this world. This body departs after enduring numerous sorrows and sins suffered in its nineteen short years of life. Every day that this dirty and sinful body exists in this world fills me with shame before all living things and dread before the Heavens.

I am throwing this dirty body into the blue currents of the Taedong River, that place which is so full of hope and yet so full of rage. I want the river's currents to cleanse this body of its sins. I want the river's fish to devour this body's unclean flesh. (Yi 1996: 147)

But shortly after conversing with Pyŏng-uk, Yŏng-ch'ae discovers that more than just a passive/sexed body, she can overcome the constraints imposed on that body and assert her newfound "womanhood" in opposition to it.[10] Though "defiled" she begins to contemplate the possibility of her own future in spite of it:

"Is a newer and truer life really possible for me? Can I really start my life over again?" Yŏng-ch'ae said, looking at her companion.

"Yes. You've been deceiving yourself so far, but now a truer life can open up to you. Happiness awaits you. Why should you turn away from it by trying to cut short your precious life?" Pyŏng-uk said, now confident that she had dissuaded Yŏng-ch'ae from suicide. "So stop your crying and smile! Yes, let's laugh!" she said, smiling. (Yi 1996: 261)

The evocation of laughter in this particular passage is an interesting one. Yŏng-ch'ae's metamorphosis from a mere "body" to a person with a "mind" capable of love and laughter is signaled by her transformation from the object of laughter (the sexed body) to the subject who laughs (desexualized mind). Likewise, at the end of the novel when Yŏng-ch'ae, Pyŏng-uk, and Sŏn-hyŏng all work feverishly together to save the sick and suffering female patient/body at the train station, all three women once again burst out in laughter (Yi 1996: 341). Characteristically, this moment of empowerment of woman signaled by laughter also signals the "rebirth" of the modern "enlightened" nation as optimistically described by the narrator at the end the novel:

The dark world will not remain dark forever; it will not remain heartless [*mujŏng*]. *With our own strength we will try to make it bright, heartfelt, joyous, abundant and strong. With glad laughter and loud hurrahs, let us close [the novel]* Mujŏng, *a farewell note to the world gone by.* (Yi 1996: 356; my emphasis)

Pyŏng-uk's defining role in defeating *mujŏng* and thus allowing for the subsequent awakening of love and laughter in women is significant. In her usurpation of the returning/punishing male role found in Korea's traditional romance narratives, it is she, not Hyŏng-sik, who rescues Yŏng-ch'ae. Moreover, it is she who persuades Yŏng-ch'ae not to kill herself by redirecting the loyalty Yŏng-ch'ae felt for the absent betrothed to the new nation. In the process of replacing male authority, Pyŏng-uk also makes herself available as the mothering adult, responsible for overseeing the birth of the nation's political infants. Like the strong virtuous mother, Pyŏng-uk speaks as a fatherly midwife, urging Yŏng'ch'ae (and readers) to push, push, push her strong self into the open air and, by doing so, she is witness to Yŏng-ch'ae's "rebirth." Revising the masculine conventions of his time, Yi Kwang-su thus integrates in Pyŏng-uk qualities of both maleness and femaleness. Neither explicitly male nor female, Pyŏng-uk's identity is decisively more masculine than Hyŏng-sik's. Yet at the same time that she usurps his manly position by becoming Yŏng-ch'ae's savior, Pyŏng-uk speaks unambiguously as a mother. Pyŏng-uk's decision to change her name is significant in this regard:

Yŏng-ch'ae remembered Pyŏng-uk telling her that she had originally been named "Pyŏng-ŏk," but that she changed it at first to "Pyŏng-mŏk" because she thought her given name was too feminine and soft for her taste. But then she felt that "Pyŏng-mŏk" was too masculine and hard so she decided to compromise and settled on "Pyŏng-uk." . . .

"I disagree with the traditional way of thinking that says a woman must be soft and feminine. But I also dislike the idea of a woman being too hard and masculine. I really think something in between the two is best." (Yi 1996: 261)

It is in her capacity as half man/half woman ("motherly" husband and "husbandly" mother) that Pyŏng-uk evokes the most fitting image to call forth the "rebirth" of the nation. Functioning as a universal and political "sign," Pyŏng-uk represents an effective critique of the traditional patriarchal order. But this critique is made without ever really sexualizing the tradition's accuser. Pyŏng-uk's ambiguous sexuality is an empty signifer because she is not a flesh and blood person, but a

political name in which everyone can identify. She condems the traditional order on behalf of "the people"—the "we" (fathers, husbands,
mothers, wives) of the nation—not on behalf of women in particular
(the call for women's emancipation in Korea was never couched in anything but nationalist terms). A desexualized signifier dislocated from its
traditional "familial" context, the nationalist category of Woman is both
impenetrable and impregnable, inhabiting not the corporeal world of
real, sexed "bodies," but an abstract zone of political signs. Recall that
Yŏng-ch'ae's decision not to kill herself and to instead live "for the
nation" was made at the moment she renounced all claims made by her
"defiled" female body. By repeatedly drawing attention to and then erasing her "sexed body," the narrator of *Mujŏng* conjures up Yŏng-ch'ae's
image as an oppressed woman, which then turns into a sign of the oppressed nation. In each case, the political code entirely displaces the
sexual (romantic and gender) code. "Woman" turns into a sign of colonial oppression (and potential liberation). By taking woman out of the
private domain of traditional domestic relations and transposing her into
the realm of the political, the public, and the universal, nationalism turns
her into an agent politicizing love, loyalty, and family bonds for the
nation. In this way, the image of the loyal wife (or virtuous mother),
now deplete of any private, familial, or "bodily" value, gets connected
to the universal myth of national liberation.

This merging of the private and the public, and the erotics of politics
that manifests itself as a consequence, lies at the heart of nationalism's
persuasive narrative power. Attachments to the nation, for better or for
worse, are globally recognized forms of love that derive their particular
appeal from very localized narrative traditions. In the case of Korea, the
loyal wife was written into the narratives of the nation in a way that
drew upon traditional notions of Confucian womanhood (and manhood).
Likewise, the familial story of love, loss, and return gets re-worked in
the political code as patriarchal (colonial) oppression and (longed-for)
national liberation. Either way, it was upon the political unconscious of
these classic Confucian narrative configurations about women, gender,
and kinship that the nation was constructed. The transfiguration of woman
into "sign" thus varied according to particular cultural productions. Yi
Kwang-su's narrative intervention in the past in the name of the nation
thus makes Woman a privileged site of negotiation between, on the one
hand, the exigencies of modernity, and on the other, the local demands
of tradition.

4

Devoted Wives, Divided Nation

On June 30, 1989, at around one-thirty in the afternoon, a young woman made an emotional descent from the uneven steps of a Soviet passenger airliner toward a crowd of well-wishers who had gathered together to welcome her to Pyŏngyang, North Korea. Rising just above them, in bold neon letters, read this anachronistic sign, which served as a reception banner of sorts:

> Let the world's youth and students unite firmly under the banner of anti-imperialist solidarity, peace, and friendship.

Wiping away her tears, the woman stood still for a moment to gaze at the scene before her. It had taken nearly three days to set foot on North Korean soil. In spite of a South Korean government ban against allowing students to participate in the thirteenth annual World Festival of Youth and Students, Chondaehyŏp (National Council of Student Representatives), student leaders in Seoul had surreptitiously devised a scheme to send Im Su-gyŏng, a senior French major at Han'guk University of Foreign Studies, to the festival via Japan and Germany. Violation of the strict South Korean National Security Law carried with it a penalty of up to life in prison, and in some cases was punishable by death.[1]

If she had been frightened of what awaited her upon her return to South Korea, she certainly did not show it. The moment was too important to waste on idle fears. Chosen by the student leadership in Seoul to show the world that the two Koreas must be reunited, she was sent to Pyŏngyang as a messenger of peace. With such grand things to accomplish in such a short time, how could she be bothered with such trifles?

And yet one cannot help but wonder whether, behind the proud mask of patriotic devotion, her tears betrayed an emotion of a different kind. Did she feel a pang of remorse over the grieving parents she had left behind? And what about her fiancé, whom she might never see again?

The figure of the anguished, lonely female, unduly separated from family and friends, is a ubiquitous presence in Korea. She appears as far back as the Koryŏ dynasty (918–1392) (McCarthy 1991); later, after the founding of the Chosŏn dynasty in 1392, she was incorporated into many of Confucian Korea's most renowned love poems and instructive literature (Kim Yun-sik 1982; Kim Young-jik 1986). By the late eighteenth century, this lonely and virtuous heroine was widely celebrated in the public sphere. The *Tale of Ch'unhyang* was especially responsible for popularizing this Confucian ideal of woman, who, in spite of tremendous hardship and suffering, remains steadfast in her devotion to both husband and home.

This chapter examines this image of woman and the central symbolic role she came to play in contemporary dissident reunification politics. Since the 1980s, there has emerged in South Korea a new generation of nationalist historians whose writings have challenged the state's hegemonic claim over nationalist discourse. I hope to show that the narrative strategy adopted by these dissident historians relied on a traditional canon of Confucian morality tales about womanly virtue and female chastity. My aim is to show how contemporary Korean nationalism, in demarcating a political position opposed to the division, took up the woman question as a way of addressing the perceived crisis of Korean self-identity. Insofar as these dissidents tried to assert themselves and gain some control over the terms by which their divided world was ordered, they actively called upon this idealized image of woman as a means of retaining and strengthening the distinctive spiritual "core" of Korean national culture, which had been weakened by the division. Represented invariably as an unnatural affliction transmitted to the social body by the West, the division was perceived as a threat to the survival, prosperity, and identity of the Korean nation. Indeed, concurrent with the dissident reunification discourse was a rhetoric of crisis over the danger of contamination by "Western" values, variously depicted as individualism, consumerism, and hedonism. As we shall see, the search for the changeless inner "core" of Korean identity required the simultaneous strengthening of traditional values and mores against the West, a condition that was largely accomplished by the "virtuous" female in her capacity as loyal wife.

This nationalist preoccupation with feminine virtue, and the traditional Confucian polarization and fixity of masculine and feminine identities, particularly as it concerned the relationship between husband and wife, reveals the intrinsic relationship between love and national politics in Korea. In voicing their opposition to the division, dissidents variously linked marriage and reunification as the essential condition of Korean national survival.

Chuch'eron and the Romance of History: A New Nationalist Historiography

It was after the brutal suppression of the Kwangju Uprising in May 1980 that the beginnings of this "romance" narrative about the divided nation first emerged. The magnitude of state violence, and the complete devastation of the democratic forces in South Korea after Kwangju, drove young intellectuals to search for the origins of their predicament. They sought to explain the causes for the succession of authoritarian regimes that had emerged in the aftermath of the Liberation period (1945–1950). And they achieved this by rewriting the history of modern Korea.

Broadly speaking, this new nationalist historiography (or *chuch'eron*) has resurrected the problem of *chuch'e* (self-reliance) and questioned whether South Korean official historiography has contributed to engendering a slavish mentality in the Korean people by its association with American "imperialists."[2] Indeed, as Em (1993: 450–85) has pointed out, the central dilemma of Korean historiography since colonial times involves the polemical opposition between *chuch'esŏng* (autonomous spirit) and *sadaejuŭi* ("Serving the Great"), the latter being the official policy of the Chosŏn dynasty with respect to China. This opposition has allowed South Korean historians to address the problem of South Korea's *chuch'esŏng* (or lack thereof) and its dependent relationship to the United States.

By stressing the inherent *sadaejuŭi* relationship that exists between South Korea and United States, *chuch'eron* challenged South Korea's official claim that the Korean War was essentially an external conflict over Korea's strategic position initiated by the North Korean Workers' Party, which was acting as a puppet of Soviet expansionist policies. Rather, the real culprit in the national tragedy that was the Korean War was U.S. "imperialism." During the early years of the post-Liberation period, American backing of the KDP (Korean Democratic Party), a party which, according to *chuch'eron*, enjoyed little popular support and legitimacy, led to the establishment of a small pro-American base in the south. From this minority base of support, Americans began to set up separate executive, police, judicial, and military organs in southern Korea, which ultimately led to the creation of the separate states and the permanent division of the peninsula. Had the conservatives not had American backing during this critical period, a communist-nationalist coalition would have won control of the entire peninsula in a matter of months (Cumings 1981; Kang 1982, 1984; Pak 1988).[3]

By rewriting the history of the Liberation period in terms that allowed for a critical look at the U.S. role in Korean domestic politics, *chuch'eron* thus views the primary contradictions in the interwar years (as well as during and after the Korean War) as being mostly between the Korean nationalist revolutionary subject and U.S. "imperialism." It is a view that also implicates South Korea's ruling class in the events leading to the creation of separate states by stressing its historically "insidious" relationship with the United States.

During the mid-1980s, when students became openly familiar with the *chuch'e* thought of Kim Il Sung[4] and the cultivation and expression of anti-American sentiment became de rigueur within the mainstream of the student movement, *chuch'eron*'s impact upon dissident intellectual thinking was significant. Indeed, during this period *chuch'eron* became the principle guiding ideology behind the national student organization Chŏndaehyŏp (now known as Hanch'ŏngnyŏn, or Korean Youth Federation). Its influence on dissident intellectuals was manifest in two distinct ways. First, *chuch'eron* challenged and subverted decades of Cold War rhetoric that portrayed North Korea as *the* enemy of the South. The officially accepted relationship between friend and foe that had been part of the established nationalist rhetoric of state-sponsored historiography—a historiography that demonized North Koreans, literally, as devils—was turned upside down in *chuch'eron*. Here, the real enemy of the people (*minjung*)[5] was the United States, not North Korea; *chuch'eron* saw the U.S. decision to divide, occupy, and establish a military regime in southern Korea as a direct expression of American imperialist ambitions in the Korean peninsula. By challenging the hegemonic discourse of the South Korean state that constituted North Korea as Other, *chuch'eron* attempted to create an alternative nationalist tradition through a reexamination of the interwar years. As Em (1993: 462) has once again pointed out, "it [*chuch'eron*] not only exposed the rather inglorious origins of the South Korean state, but it also reshaped the discourse of nationalism in South Korea by positing as nationalist the resistance to the UN-sponsored election in 1948, on which the ROK claims its legal basis." Furthermore, whereas state-sponsored histories saw the North Korean menace solely in political and ideological terms (i.e., North Korean communism), *chuch'eron* argued that the "new" enemy posed a threat that was much more radical and fundamental: for students, like most dissident intellectuals, American capitalist culture represented an invasive cultural force that threatened to undermine the very core of Korean national identity. The decadent individualism of the West, which these dissidents associated with consumerism, sexual promiscuity, and crime, required the formulation of a nationalist strategy to combat this Other, external threat.

Second, the rejection of the state-sponsored view of North Korea as an "enemy" brought about the creation of a new "romantic" narrative strategy. In this new story of the divided nation, the Korean people are portrayed as heroic romantics, struggling against American "imperialism" in order to achieve the vision of what Korean history should have been. Here, the longing for national reconciliation was identified with the romantic urge to come together as one people, one family, much like a wife who wishes to reconcile with her lost husband. Indeed, to think of North and South Korea as lovers, struggling to overcome the division, challenged decades of Cold War rhetoric that portrayed communist North Korea as the South's foreign foe. The "master-code" that gives this romantic story its revolutionary appeal is the creation of a new type of patriot-lover who struggles to overcome the division by actively resisting the "evil" powers that seek to separate him/her from his/her loved one.

Thus we find that the division was often compared, in the literature of South Korea's dissidents, to a break in the relations between husband and wife, brought on and perpetuated by outside "evil" forces. Mun Pyŏng-ran, for example, likened the division of the two Koreas to the celebrated love story Gyŏn-u and Chik-nyŏ[6] about two lovers who were forced by the malicious orders of the King of Heaven to live at opposite ends of the galaxy (1990: 74–77). Similarly, images of two lovers about to fall into each other's embrace or of a happy couple triumphantly running across the demarcation line reveal the familial connection between conjugal union and a reunified nation (see Figures 4.1 and 4.2). In Min Chŏng-gi's *P'oong* (The Embrace), this theme reappears once again as

Figure 4.1 **North and South Korea, *Korea Report*, August 1990**

Figure 4.2 **Overcoming the Division, *Mal*, March 1988**

Figure 4.3 **Min Chòng-gi, *P'oong* (The Embrace)**
(Courtesy of Yolwhadang Publishers, 1981)

Figure 4.4 **Illustration from *Sahoewa Sasang*, February 1989**

the force of love overcomes the division, and man and woman are reunited in passionate embrace (see Figures 4.3 and 4.4). In each case, the
metonymic association between romance and patriotism is mutually reinforcing. The allegorical relationship between them invites a double
reading of narrative events: the promise of national reconciliation that,
in turn, becomes the expression of hopeful fulfillment of conjugal reunion (Figure 4.5). The exhortation to drive them together to achieve

Figure 4.5 **From a Seoul National University Student Pamphlet, April 1988**

통일로 가는길
-올림픽, 농민 그리고 통일

some sort of romantic reconciliation thus becomes the secret theme behind Korean nationalists' reunification project.

The significance of this romantic narrative strategy, over and beyond
its efforts to create a new enemy (and vindicate an old one), derives
from its vision of the Korean people not as passive victims of history but
active redeemers of it. The possibility that the *minjung* could achieve
the reconciliation of the two Koreas plays an intrinsic part of *chuch'eron*'s
revolutionary appeal. By limiting the idea of failure in Korea's modern
history—for example, the failure of the Korean revolutionary subject to

achieve what Korean history should have been—*chuch'eron* argues for a vision of potential success. That is, it advocates the possibility of national reunion through love.

In the sections below, I consider the important socio-symbolic role of women in this romantic story of national struggle and redemption. As we shall see, the image of the virtuous wife awaiting the day of reunification mirrors similar themes about separation and reconciliation, suffering and redemption found in Korea's traditional literary canon. In each case, women emerge as symbols of resistance: in the face of loss, loyal wives reign triumphant over evil governors, and chaste widows dutifully repulse lecherous (foreign) suitors.[7] Indeed, the drama of romance and resistance in South Korea's reunification discourse comes together in very fruitful ways, with the lonely, virtuous female always playing the leading role.

The Politics of Romance

In the vast majority of Western love stories, marriage is the reward for having overcome certain challenges. For example, a hero, in order to show himself worthy of the girl, must go to great lengths to win her heart. Likewise, a poor heroine is able to win the rich man over less noble women only by virtue of her unwavering goodness and persistent faith. In Korean love tales, however, the romantic challenge—if we can call it that—does not culminate in marriage per se; rather, the challenge begins *after* the marriage vows have already been taken.[8]

In a country where polygamous marriages were the custom, women were required to put aside their domestic jealousies and petty rivalries in order dutifully to serve their husbands. Likewise, custom demanded that a woman remain faithful to her husband even in the event of his death. Thus, the plot of the vast majority of Korea's romance tales revolved around the sufferings and frustrations of women *already* bound by the marriage vow. As Kim Yun-sik has observed, the majority of images and themes in Korea's Confucian literary canon repeatedly return to these feelings of female anguish, particularly during periods of loss and forced separation (Kim Yun-sik 1982; Hwang Tong-gyu 1989). Longing provided the context for the expression of *"han"* (grief), *"aesu"* (sadness), *"ibyŏl"* (sorrow at parting), and *"ch'enyŏm"* (resignation), all expressions that were traditionally associated with the ordeals of women. The great works of Korea's romantic fiction are all about suffering women who nevertheless remain true to the conjugal bond and are rewarded for their loyalty and steadfastness with the return of their husbands, which, in turn, sets the stage for a renewed life of marital bliss.

Let us consider once again the most famous love story in Korea, *Tale of Ch'unhyang* (Tale of the Faithful Wife, Spring Fragrance)[9] discussed in some detail in Chapters 2 and 3.

Unlike Yi Kwang-su's version, which "re-wrote" the story according to the romantic and nationalistic requirements of *chŏng,* Ch'unhyang's refusal to submit to the advances of the evil governor was not viewed as the expression of her subjective desires; rather, it was her strict adherence to her prescribed role as faithful and loyal wife that earned her respect as Korea's most cherished heroine of the Chosŏn dynasty.

Confucian ideology devised for women "roles that called for specific behavior ('virtuous wife,' 'obedient daughter-in-law,' 'chaste widow') and women were remembered either for their perfect embodiment of these roles or for their rebellion against them" (Deuchler 1992: 280–81). Ch'unhyang's devotion to Myŏng-nyŏng, then, is woven into a didactic tale about good and evil, not a romantic tale about love and abandonment. During her beatings, Ch'unhyang does not lament her fate as an abandoned lover; instead, she recites the cardinal five relationships of moral imperatives that guide Confucian interpersonal philosophy:

> The five relationships remain unbroken.
> Husband and wife both have their stations;
> Our fate was sealed by the five elements,
> Sleeping or waking, I cannot forget my husband. (Lee 1981: 262)

Likewise, at the beginning of the story, she resists the evil governor not on emotional grounds, but because an alliance between them would violate her principles: "A subject cannot serve two kings and a wife cannot belong to two husbands; that is my principle. I would rather die than do as you say, however many times you ask me. Please allow me to hold to my ideal: I cannot have more than one husband" (Lee 1981: 259).

The deeper implications of this tale, however, become clearer when we discern its underlying political message. Ch'unhyang remains true to her husband by defiantly resisting political authority. Instead of succumbing to the advances of the governor, she stands firm in her devotion to her absent husband. This structural opposition of confrontation and resistance is built into the story itself. There is the obvious confrontation between the loyal Ch'unhyang and the evil governor, Pyŏng Hak-to. There is also the confrontation between mother and daughter. Wolm'ae, Ch'unhyang's mother and an ex-*kisaeng,* prods her daughter to accept the governor so that both women can live handsomely off the match. And finally, there is the confrontation between the people and the evil governor. Ch'unhyang's resistance, reflected in all these situations, can thus be read as a political tale of struggle between the people and an illegitimately imposed authority. "The governor is the father of the people," she cries out during her beating, "but he ignores the four social classes; he rules by power and force and has no love for the people" (Lee 1981: 262).

By representing political struggles in terms of sexual conflicts, the author of this romantic drama effectively translated political problems into a sexual scandal brought about by the breakdown of moral authority. Thus we can read the tale from two distinct vantage points. On the one hand, the lascivious impulses of the intruding male threaten the sacred bonds of marriage. On the other, the wayward governor threatens the social fabric of the (national) community. In each of these perspectives, Ch'unhyang's virtuous resistance is rewarded by both the return of her husband and the restoration of benevolent leadership.

By "translating" this dominant narrative strategy in their own terms, student dissidents, like Yi Kwang-su before them, used existing symbols and practices and merged them to fit a *new* story of the (divided) nation. Such a process reveals just how the "original" meanings (about female loyalty, virtue, *chŏng,* and love) become (re)appropriated and dispersed to construct alternative representations of the nation and of history. In both versions, love overcomes separation, and suffering is rewarded by domestic (national) prosperity. The patriotic struggle for the lost (unified) nation becomes a *variation* of the same romantic story of faith and loyalty in the recovery of loss. The link between conjugal romance and patriotism is thus more than a suggestive coincidence; each had a direct investment in the other.[10] Together they mapped out the context for what constituted proper feminine behavior. The attainment of conjugal reunion, achieved by women's "virtuous" resistance to evil governors (and foreign imperialists), thus underscores the patriotic goal, which in turn also becomes the microcosmic expression of nationhood. Thus, embedded within the narrative strategy of *chuch'eron,* and of dissident reunification discourse more generally, are related themes about feminine resistance and proper womanly conduct with regard to men. Conjugal reunion and, by extension, national consolidation, could be achieved only if women adhered to the principles of Confucian virtue, that is, by faithfully awaiting the arrival of their (absent) husbands and resisting other (Western) men's sexual advances. As we shall see in the section below, resistance to the division, and the virtuous struggle for reconciliation that it implied, took the allegorical form of resistance to the foreign male.

The Politics of Sex

The allegorical relationship between romantic reunions and national reconciliation (reunification) was grounded upon women's adherence to certain codes of social conduct that defined their proper attitude toward their husbands ("loyal wife," "chaste widow"). Women's adherence to these codes was essential for the growth and prosperity of the family–household. This is because the regenerative survival of the agnatic line and of paternal power depended upon the successful conscription and discipline of female reproductive sexuality within the hierarchical structure dominated by men. In a Confucian-style society, the implementation of the agnatic principle was accomplished through the activation of an agnatic consciousness within a descent group. This explains why ancestor worship still plays such a central role in both the domestic and public realms of contemporary Korean society. Men's place in the ritual hierarchy of agnates "determines the individual's rights and duties within the descent group and allocates him a corresponding standing within the political sphere" (Deuchler 1992: 129).

This also explains why women's adherence to strict codes of sexual conduct was so important. Confucian moralists at the beginning of the Chosŏn dynasty were convinced that unrestrained interaction between the sexes jeopardized the integrity of the social structure. Deviation by women from prescribed sexual mores (men were not bound by the conjugal bond) would lead not only to the disruption of the agnatic line and paternal power but would undermine the foundation of the national sphere as well. Illicit sexual relations committed by, or forced upon, women thus constituted a threat to both the stability of the family and the continuity of Korean patriarchy. Female chastity and virtue were not so much a private issue between couples as a public one that involved the well-being of the state.

The significance of these traditional ideals of gender differentiation, particularly as they concerned women, becomes clear when one considers that the images that most frequently emerged in the context of the divided peninsula were those of the Korean woman despoiled. Indeed, the breakdown of the relations between husband and wife came to stand symbolically for the nation at war with itself. Sexual metaphors of rape and violation were repeatedly elicited as an icon of a dislocated world used by dissident intellectuals in their portrayal of the division of their homeland. In keeping with the *Tale of Ch'unhyang* genre tradition, the woman-as-nation-body was represented as being ignobly confronted with the violation of her body by an intruding "evil" outsider (like the lecherous governor) who would steal the chastity and honor she was virtuously preserving for her lost lover and husband. The division of the peninsula was construed as violence against the female-nation-body, an illicit intrusion into the sacred relations between husband and wife, a lascivious act of domination by the (foreign) male over the (indigenous) female.

The portrayal of the division as rape, however, more than just a suggestive metaphor, had actual basis in the Korean historical experience. In tracing the usage of this metaphor in history, we find that the violation of women as a symbol of national humiliation and shame first appeared during the first half of the twentieth century when Korea became a colony of Japan. It was a symbol, moreover, that was rooted in the real-life experiences of thousands of Korean women. At the height of Japanese militarism, thousands of "healthy Korean virgins" were forcibly and systematically recruited by the Japanese government to serve as prostitutes (euphemistically referred to as "comfort women") for Japanese soldiers during the thirties and forties, soon after the Nanking massacre of 1937, in order to restore order and discipline to the troops and provide them with disease-free sex slaves (Hicks 1993, 1994).

Not surprisingly, the image of rape to describe Koreans' experience under colonial rule was also widely used by contemporary dissidents in their portrayal of the division. The appeal to the feminine in the language of resistance in contemporary Korea, much like in colonial times, carried with it the values of purity against filth, and of chastity against contamination, evoking the explicit sexual implication of the division as rape. In Kim Nam-ju's poem "Pulgamchŭng" (Frigidity), for example, prostitution and violence are interrelated themes in its representation of the division:

Frigidity

My elder sister
is our liberated country's lady of the night.

To borrow one highly venomous tongue,
She is a widely gaped vulva like a
chestnut burr under the boots of the U.S. Eighth Army.
My little sister is our modernized country's new woman.
To borrow an expression of a common boy,
She is a widely open tourist vulva under the Jap's yen.
How deep did we lapse by rotting,
Not awakening no matter how much [we are shaken]
Not feeling no matter how much [we are pinched]
Ah, my half-piece country,
After 36 years of broken waist, when will you open your eyes from
Your long, long, humiliating sleep. (1989: 3)

The poem's title "Pulgamchŭng," which refers to frigidity caused by a woman's guilt or fear of becoming pregnant or contracting a venereal disease, further emphasizes the link between rape, the division of the peninsula, and the loss of female (sexual) reproductive power. Rape constituted not only a threat to the conjugal bond; it also posed a crisis of maternity and (social) reproduction. The danger of Western—and specifically American—cultural contamination, formulated in terms of related themes about rape, frigidity, and the loss of female reproductive power, had to do with what many perceived as the West's potential threat to the regenerative survival of Korean national identity. The retrieval from the West of the superior, inner "core" of Korean culture, required that women band together and resist the advances of the lascivious foreign male.

The reality of American military presence in South Korea merely exacerbated this perceived crisis. The threat of miscegenation posed by the foreign soldier challenged the very foundations of Koreans' self-identity as a pure and pristine people whose racial integrity has remained identifiable throughout the centuries. As we saw in chapter 1, this connection between race and nation (minjok) was first made by the historian Sin Ch'ae-ho. In order to create a new history that could serve as a starting point for building a strong national identity, Sin "translated" the modern concept of race in (local) genealogical terms, and thus came up with the interpretation of the origins of the Korean people in which lineage loyalties now became linked to a fictive biological cohesion. Despite repeated attacks on the nation's sovereignty by foreign powers, an identifiable racial and spiritual "core" had remained intact throughout the ages ever since the founding of Tan'gun Chosŏn nearly five thousand years ago.

This fact alone, according to Sin, was testament to the strength of the original ancestors of the "race-nation."[11] Only by resurrecting this "original" strength of the people-nation-ancestors, which had been purposefully obfuscated by Korean and Chinese *sadaejuŭi* ("Serving the Great") scholarship, could the basis for a new sense of identity—an autonomous spirit (*chuch'e ŭi chŏngsin*)—be laid. These same ideas about race and nation were in turn re-appropriated by contemporary dissidents in their efforts to build the foundations for their version of a reunified national community. Indeed, from the point of view of *chuch'eron*, which resurrected Sin's work and gave it relevance in contemporary Korean historiography, nationalism was the creation of an identity that uncovered this autonomous racial feeling and made it self-conscious. Locating the core identity of Koreans in an unchanging, unique racial *essence* allowed for an idealized reading of Korean culture and history as a seamless narrative of continuity and cohesion. The belief in the unique and immutable core—the ethnic origins—of the Korean people was thus an endeavor loaded with deep psychological and political implications. To be assured of the ethnic uniqueness of the Korean people provided a past that was ageless and secure; it also served as a basis for an autonomous national identity that had to be maintained through constant struggle. Thus, *chuch'eron* resurrects Sin's idea of history as the struggle between national and anti-national forces. Only through struggle could a race-nation (*minjok*) maintain its identity and autonomy. Like Sin, *chuch'eron* sees the entire history of the Korean people as an epic struggle to overcome foreign domination and feudal oppression. The historian's task, in other words, entails the examination of the experience and legacy of the Korean people's struggle to preserve their "core" identity.

Given this highly racialist reading of Korean history, it is not surprising to find that miscegenation became a central issue in the reunification discourse of contemporary dissidents. Perceived as a significant threat to this core identity, miscegenation became associated with a whole host of related themes about the defense of the social body—the retrieval of a superior "core" Korean identity in the name of a phantasmic Korean *essence*. The ability of the foreign male to penetrate (literally) the inner and inviolable sanctum of Korean women and to establish conjugal alliances with them was perceived not only as a threat to the viability of the family, but as an act that undermined the fundamental cohesion and identity of the Korean nation. Thus we find in Korea that those women who formed marriage alliances across racial lines were

Figure 4.6 **Demonstration Against the Rape and Murder of a Korean Prostitute, Seoul, South Korea** (*Stars and Stripes*, Pacific Edition) *(Photo courtesy of A/P Wide World Photos)*

popularly perceived as being women of "loose" morals: prostitutes, bar hostesses, or entertainers. In fact, they were represented as the polemical *inversion* of the idealized virtuous female associated with Korea's traditional romance narratives. By allowing themselves to be appropriated by the West, these women were simultaneously perceived as being victims of Western imperialism and faithless profiteers of American capitalism. Both pitied and despised, the whore thus became the symbol of the nation's shame as well as the rallying point for national resistance (see Figure 4.6).[12]

Concurrent with the nationalist rhetoric about miscegenation, rape, and prostitution was a deeper concern over preserving the changeless inner essence of Korean (female) identity. Borrowing from Sin Ch'ae-ho the nationalist preoccupation with racial and national autonomy, *chuch'eron* reveals the anxious relationship that exists between state patriarchy and (female) reproductive power. Out of the nationalist obsession with a changeless Korean *essence* came an idealized version of the entire history of Korean culture as a seamless narrative of regenerative fatherhood and ethnic cohesion, preserved intact throughout the ages by the vigilant virtues of the Korean female.

Directly related to the anxious fear of miscegenation and cultural "contamination" by the West was the age-old Confucian Korean concern with (male) transgenerational replication and regenerating fatherhood (Chapters 5, 6, and 7). The subsequent show of protective solicitude of women in Korean nationalist discourse derives from women's role in assuring the regenerative survival of Korean patriarchy. As the pliant conduit of paternal regeneration, women unwittingly became both the object of concern over the state of Korea's racial (inner) "purity" and the subject of active resistance to (outside) foreign "contamination." Now appropriated as a symbol of resistance against the "outerness" of the West, nationalist rhetoric also made women the "virtuous" signifiers of Korean interiority.

What all this suggests is that nationalism and sexuality are mutually reinforcing categories. Resistance to forms of imperial domination was fought as much in the private bedroom as it was in the public streets. Koreans' attitudes toward sex, and particularly the dangerous libidinous power of "unrestrained" female sexuality, thus had a direct bearing upon their view of politics. The threat to feminine chastity (and by extension, to marriage) was perceived as a threat to the integrity and "inner" (racial) continuity of the nation itself. By the same token, the promise of conjugal conciliation becomes the allegory of hope for restored national legitimacy. The search for an ideal ending for these romantic and political fantasies constitutes distinct but complementary narratives about, on the one hand, the nation's quest for reconciliation and, on the other, the woman's quest for conjugal reunion.

Part Three

Men

5

Park Chung-hee's Agrarian Heroes

*Our modern history has been a record of failures, national ruin
and confusion. Our people have lacked autonomy of thought. They
have been characterized by slavishness and subjected to the
control of foreign powers. A Japanese historian once spoke of the
"heteronomy of the Korean people," and if we reflect on our
national history, we must admit to the aptness of this
characterization [. . .] our history has been a record of a people
constantly groping in the dark. . . . The [Chosŏn] dynasty* yangban
*class, who did not have to work for a living, gave birth to a lazy
national character [. . .] and the Korean people have become, as a
consequence, passive and resigned to being
slaves. . . . What is important now is to thaw the frozen
minds of the masses. . . .*

—President Park Chung-hee (1970b)[1]

*The Saemaul Undong (New Community Movement) is spreading
like wildfire to all corners of the country. . . . By widening the
narrow farm roads, we are opening up a spiritual path for
unhindered progress of the nation. The Saemaul Undong
repudiates the diseases of inertia and indolence bred in the shade
of ease and complacency and represents a spiritual revolution to
eradicate the evil habits of waste and luxury.*

—President Park Chung-hee, 1972[2]

On October 26, 1999, about 3,000 people gathered together at the national cemetery in Seoul to pay their respects to the late president Park Chung-hee, who, twenty years earlier, had been gunned down at the hands of his intelligence chief and once intimate friend, Kim Jae-kyu. Three former presidents, Chun Doo-hwan, Roh Tae-woo, and Choi Kyu-ha, were all present at the memorial service. President Kim Dae-jung sent flowers. It was an event that had come to symbolize the increasingly positive view that Park's memory has come to play in South Korean society during the turn of the millennium. That nostalgia helped catapult Park's daughter, Park Kŭn-hye, into a sweeping victory in a parliamentary by-election in 1998, fueling widespread speculation that she will make a presidential bid in 2007.

While some credit Park's revival to the shock of South Korea's 1998 economic collapse, others see it as merely an expression of a collective yearning for simpler times. Whatever the reason, the tangible results of the Park revival have culminated in the creation of a massive Memorial Hall dedicated to the late president. First proposed by President Kim Dae-jung in 1999, the timing for completing the Memorial's construction was made to coincide with the June 2002 opening of the 2002 World Cup, co-hosted by Japan and Korea.

The coming together of these two events was not coincidental. If the World Cup symbolized the meeting of former colonizer and colonized in a shared project of industrial equals, it was President Park Chung-hee who had made this meeting possible. As Bruce Cumings has observed (a severe critic of Park Chung-hee if there ever was one): "Ever since [the "big push"] Koreans have straightened their backs and walked with confidence. . . . When the industrial sovereigns of the twentieth century are lined up— Andrew Carnegie, Henry Ford, Joseph Stalin, Chairman Morita of Sony— a Korean captain of industry will be among them" (Cumings 1997: 325).

The aim of this chapter is to explore the conceptual vocabulary and narrative coherency that informed this "captain of industry" in his quest to modernize Korea. Park's vision for creating a new and strong Korea in many ways was informed by the same Self-strengthening ideology of Korean nationalists at the turn of the century. Indeed, as we explored in detail in chapters 1 and 3, the nationalist treatment of the effete and effeminized *yangban* as symbolic of all that was wrong with traditional Korea also formed the basis for Park's efforts to transform Korea into an "enlightened" and "civilized" nation. My interest is to explore how the appropriation of these early nationalist and colonial images of effete manhood was resurrected within postwar Korean domestic politics and served as the primary means by which a new military elite legitimized its hold on power. This chapter considers how the military—and the idealized images of martial manhood—became the new "subject" of the authentic Korean national culture and how these earlier colonial and nationalist representations of Korean "backwardness" were co-opted in this revisionist project.[3]

Nowhere was this discourse about self-reliant, martial manhood more evident than in the rural modernization campaign called the Saemaul Undong (New Community Movement), which was initiated by President Park in April 1970.[4] Indeed, as we shall see, the spiritual transformation of Korea's "lazy" and backward farmers into industrious, modern, and forward-thinking patriots was the primary aim of the movement, and as such, the Saemaul Undong serves as a particularly revealing example of the character and function of Park's appropriation of early nationalist and colonial discourse in promoting his martial nationalism.

Writing a New History of the Nation

The "May 16 Revolution," as Park Chung-hee named the 1961 military coup d'état, marked the beginning of South Korea's extraordinary path toward economic development. In his eighteen-year reign, from the military coup he led in 1961 until his assassination in 1979, Park is remembered less for his successive waves of political repression than as the father of his country's remarkable economic progress (Oberdorfer 1997: 33). In his account of the May 16 Revolution entitled *The Country, the Revolution and I*, Park expressed a profound sense of fulfillment of a promise to write a new chapter in the history of Korea and redeem the nation of its "shameful" past:

> This Revolution was not simply a change of regimes. It was a new, mature national debut of spirit, marking the liquidation of the continuation of the ancient and medieval times of schism and strife. It marked, too, the end of 500 years of stagnation of the Chosŏn dynasty (1392–1910), the oppression and bloodshed of 35 years of Japanese rule and the nagging chronic diseases bred by the residue of the Liberation. It was a national debut, inspired by the courage and self-confidence of a people determined never again to be poor, weak or dumb. This resolution is the turning point in the history of modern Korea. It is our third start after Liberation. It is our last chance for national renaissance. (Park 1962: 22)

In building the groundwork for a "national renaissance," Park believed that a national reconstruction movement aimed at improving the spirit and character of the Korean people was necessary to bring about genuine economic progress. While the national reconstruction movement attracted little support in 1962, Park's obsession with the need to create a "spiritual revolution" as the basis for economic construction did not decline. After the successful execution of the First Five-Year Economic Plan, President Park brought up the idea again in his speech about a "Secondary Economic Movement" (Hahn 1981: 106–7). At his press conference on January 15, 1968, he opined, "Spiritual posture is no less important than the external and material one. Genuine modernization is achieved only when material reconstruction is made on the basis of healthy national morality and social ethics" (Hahn 1981: 106).

Later that year, the Secondary Economic Movement once again became the subject of Park's speech at a national rally on September 18, 1968:

> The Secondary Economic Movement . . . aims to intensify our social solidarity and add impetus to our economic reconstruction by means of a new spirit and brighter vision of our future. . . . We must discard the mental habit of dependency and explore a brighter future image of the fatherland by uniting our strength. Therefore, the leading core of this movement is not simply a small part of the population, but the whole nation . . . if every individual examines himself and removes all the old conventions and distorted attitudes, the flame of the secondary movement will continue to burn. (Hahn 1981: 106–7)

Interestingly, the term Secondary Economic Movement suddenly disappeared after January of 1969, and was replaced by Saemaul Kakkugi Undong (New Community Cultivation Movement) on April 22, 1970. The following year, *kakkugi* was dropped from the title, and the Saemaul Undong was officially launched as a nationwide movement. Its official aim was to promote and accelerate rural development which had lagged significantly behind the rapidly rising living standards that were being achieved in the cities. Ideologically, the Saemaul Undong became a catch phrase to denote "a new way of living," a "spiritual revolution of the people," the start of a "new history of the nation."

The launching of the Saemaul Undong (New Community Movement) in April 1970 has been recognized as one of Park's greatest achievements and is considered to be a watershed event in the history of Korea's rapid economic progress. While the nation had made rapid economic strides during the 1960s, Korea's rural communities had lagged far behind the remarkable growth that was being achieved in the cities. Korea during this period was still overwhelmingly rural—70 percent of its estimated 30 million people lived in small villages. Genuine national progress could not be made, reasoned Park, without similar developments occurring in Korea's rural areas.

In 1971, the government began to subsidize extensive projects in villages around the country. Roughly 300 bags of cement were distributed to each village under the condition that it be used for communal and not individual projects (Figure 5.1). The result of the first year showed that out of 35,000 villages, 16,000 responded positively (Park 1979: 2–3). The following year, villages that had successfully participated in the movement were rewarded with 500 additional bags of cement.

The allocation government funding was conditional, however, upon the community's ability to raise matching funds by themselves. In addition, farmers were not reimbursed for any private lands or labor donated for community projects. It was believed that by adhering to these conditions, farmers would not only make the best use of government funding, but would also learn the values of diligence (*kŭnmyŏn*), self-help (*chajo*), and cooperation (*hyŏpdong*) which had become the hallmarks of the movement. "Acting under this stimulus," observed Park, "our farmers are finally awakening from their long slumber and lethargy and opening their eyes. They are rising up and are beginning to work for themselves. They are beginning to have a sense of confidence: 'I can do this!' . . . Today we have the confidence that there is nothing in this world that we cannot accomplish if we work hard in unity and mutual cooperation" (Figure 5.1).[5]

The ideals of diligence, self-help, and cooperation were repeatedly contrasted to the "inferior" cultural values of *sadaejuŭi* ("Serving the Great," or dependence on China),[6] indolence (*anil*), and factional strife (*tangjaeng*) that had come to epitomize the values of Korea's past civilian leaders under whose reign the nation had fallen into colonial dependence and under whose leadership the people had experienced the devastations of war, poverty, and corruption. According to Kim Joon, the director of the Suwŏn Saemaul Leadership Training Institute in Suwŏn, the Saemaul movement's primary aim was to "cure the sickness of our minds in order to regain the pure traditions of our ancient forefathers" (Kim 1983: 24). It was about "establishing a new and venerable image of Koreans who have rid themselves of corruption

Figure 5.1   **Farmers Participating in a Road Development Project,
Yongpan Village, 1977** *(Saemaul Research Archives, Saemaul
Institute, Songnamsi, Korea)*

(*pup'ae*), indecisiveness (*chujŏ*), and divisiveness (*punyŏl*), and who
instead value diligence (*kŭnmyŏn*), self-help (*chajo*), and cooperation
(*hyŏpdong*)."[7] The problem of national recovery was therefore linked to
the shedding of certain accretions of an unproductive "middle" age in
order to resurrect the true spirit of the nation. As the journalist Kim Il-
chi put it,

If a nation is to rise above its national humiliation and write a new chapter in its history, it must begin from the unique principles its people have developed. If this is not done, the slave mentality of *sadaejuŭi* will obliterate its national spirit of independence and self-reliance. . . .

Given the fact that China imported weapons from Korea 4,300 years ago, it is clear that the Chinese were well aware of Korea's great military strength. Korea was a highly developed and self-reliant military power.

During the Chosŏn dynasty, however, Korea's *sadaejuŭi* historians ignored Korea's true history and instead revered the works of Chinese historians. In this way, they fostered the dependence of the Korean people on China. As a result, the Korean people's true national spirit was repressed.

A fundamental goal of the Saemaul Undong is to rewrite the untold history of Korea's independence and self-reliance. The Saemaul Undong must become a movement that can push aside antiquated notions of *sadaejuŭi* and foster the growth of a new spirit of independence and self-reliance [*chaju charip*]. The movement must establish an historical perspective of Korea that can encourage a national spirit of independence and self-reliance by correcting the outdated notions of *sadaejuŭi*. An objective of the Saemaul Undong is to reconstruct the corrupted national spirit by writing the true history of the Korean people.[8]

As the locus for the nation's reconstruction, the countryside thus became associated with both the "corrupt" legacy of Korea's Confucian past and the renewed hope of national/martial revival. The years of stagnation associated with the Chosŏn dynasty had been, according to Park Chung-hee, the legacy bequeathed to Korea's farmers so that "the impression gained from a visit to the farming village was one of a total lack of progressive mentality and, of course, stagnancy (*ch'imch'ae*)."[9] Farmers were pervasively characterized as "lazy," "uncooperative," and "obsessed with extravagant lineage rituals." Over the course of the "past few centuries, the rural communities have been mired in corrupt customs and traditions. Stagnation is the word most often to describe these villages."[10] While they "might work hard during the summer days, once the harvest was in, they would stay home and play cards and drink."[11]

Under the influence of the Saemaul Undong, however, Park and the Saemaul Undong leaders believed this "corrupt" (*pup'ae*) outlook had, at last, begun to change. Whereas farmers "used to be wholly lacking in the ambition or the will to rise up and put in a real effort to improve their lot,"[12] the Saemaul Undong has enabled them to "gradually extricate themselves from this yoke of traditional lethargy."[13] As Park observed, "the real national image of the great man was not that of a weak pendant, but rather, of a great patriotic fighter who would readily die on the battlefield in defense of his country" (Park 1970b: 96). Koreans' "awakening" nationhood, in other words, was construed as a process of "reawakening" self-reliant manhood. The ability to inculcate the values of self-reliance in a community that was, by Park's own definition, backward, lazy, dependent, and passive thus became a key focus of the Saemaul Undong and, indeed, of Park's modernization effort as a whole:

> The Confucian Chosŏn dynasty destroyed . . . the patriotic of the *hwarang* of Silla who were dedicated to patriotism and national defense. Our lofty national dignity as once upheld by King Kwanggaet'o of Koguryŏ disappeared and our nation was continually invaded by foreign aggressors. But this national spirit, the spirit of the *hwarang*, flared up from the people's roots whenever the country was threatened with foreign invasion, although the ruling (Confucian) class remained weak and helpless. Its golden example is the achievement of Admiral Yi Sun-sin. The scholar Yi Su-kwang, a contemporary of Admiral Yi, experienced the Japanese Invasions of 1592 in person and saw in the Korean people the rebirth of the *hwarang* spirit. In his book *Chibong Yusŏl*, Yi Su-kwang points out that the *hwarang* were national heroes and banded together in groups known as the *hyangdo*. During the Japanese Invasions of 1592, patriotic young men formed into *hyangdo*, inspired by Admiral Yi Sun-sin's leadership, thus reviving the tradition of the *hwarang*. (1970b: 95)

The allusion to Admiral Yi Sun-sin, which resonates throughout the Park regime, demonstrates an interesting corollary to the exceedingly negative representations of Korea's traditional farming communities. If Park and the Saemaul Undong leaders took aim against Korea's traditional culture as embodied in the country's rural communities, they offered in its place a "revised" warrior tradition, embodied in the person of Admiral Yi Sun-sin.[14] As Park observed in his commemorative address on Admiral Yi's 424th birthday:

> At a time when the nation was plunged into a period of confusion and the people's lives were miserable and distressing due to the vicious repetition of factional feuds and the disease of idleness . . . only Admiral Yi foresaw the future of the nation ten years thence, and urgently pressed for building up a strong armed forces in order to achieve a "rich nation, strong army" [*puguk kangpyŏng* 富國強兵].[15]

More than simply a movement to enhance the economic growth of Korea's rural communities, the Saemaul Undong was conceived in relation to the problem of national security summed up in the dictum "rich nation, strong army" (*pukuk kangpyŏng*).[16] As Park related, "When all our farm villages are transformed, the foundations of our nation will be reinforced and strengthened. Only a nation that is strong and whose villages are prosperous and full of vigor offers no foothold to Communists."[17] Park's determination to defend the nation against communist North Korea was thus made to parallel the same defensive nationalism exhibited by Yi Sun-sin in his struggle against the Japanese during the late sixteenth century. Like Yi, who strengthened the nation by energetically building up the country's armed forces against the enemy, Park worked to strengthen South Korea's rural communities in the same defensive spirit. In his May 16, 1972, speech, Park declared, "in continuation of the glorious tradition of our righteous army [*ŭibyŏng*] handed down to us from our ancestors, we have pledged our firm resolution to depend on ourselves with our own strength and to safeguard our villages against all forms of aggression."[18] Moreover, Park's so-called "persecution" by his own civilian critics—in this case leftist students and intellectuals—was juxtaposed with the story of Yi Sun-sin's persecution by the same "backward" Confucian literati nearly four hundred years earlier. In his commemorative speech on the occasion of Yi Sun-sin's 424th birthday at Hyŏngch'ung-sa Shrine, Park observed:

> Though grief-stricken and imprisoned due to the wicked slander by villainous retainers and his ill-treatment by the king, Admiral Yi Sun-sin nevertheless went to sea to battle the enemy without official insignia, in order to save his Fatherland. Only a real patriot could achieve such a feat. . . . I would like to stress that the way to respect and venerate Admiral Yi does not simply mean constructing this shrine for him; rather, we must reaffirm and intensify our determination and effort to overcome the difficult circumstances of our fatherland and faithfully follow the precious teachings he has left behind.[19]

More than simply appropriating Yi Sun-sin's heroic narrative to strengthen Park's own image as a *hwarang* warrior incarnate, the Admiral's life-story became part of a larger subtext of the Park regime's heroic nationalism.[20] In the case of the Saemaul Undong, Yi Sun-sin's story was made to resonate with the personal lives of Korea's newly enlightened farmer-heroes who had to overcome their own personal struggles against idle village leaders, backward traditions, and lazy neighbors in order to save their communities and the nation from destitution and destruction.

We can better understand how Korea's warrior past—and the heroic narratives of the nation's warrior heroes—functioned in this movement by examining the training of Saemaul Undong leaders themselves. Korean backwardness, in habit or in spirit, was continually evoked as something that had to be overcome through the resurrection and cultivation of the "authentic" martial spirit.

From Confucian Farmers to Agrarian Patriots

Training Confucian farmers to become patriotic leaders of their community and the nation at large was not a simple task. From the beginning of the Saemaul Undong's inception in 1970, the Park government not only encouraged farmers to better themselves and their communities materially, but also encouraged a select number of rural folks to undergo a period of "spiritual" training. Following the initial success of the cement distribution campaign that was begun in 1971, the training of village leaders began in various institutes on different levels. The Saemaul Leadership Training Institute in Suwŏn was best known for its unique program and effectiveness.[21] In January 1972, 150 villagers (one from each county) entered the Institute as its first trainees. Local administrative offices recommended leaders in those villages that had successfully participated in the cement distribution program; matriculation at the Institute was supposed to be voluntary.[22] Although the duration of the program varied, most trainees spent two weeks at the Institute. Furthermore, while the course content was not fixed, there was uniformity in both the methodology and the structure of the training, for men as well as for women.[23]

In addition to familiarizing the farmers with new and modern agricultural techniques and equipment, the purpose of the training was to "motivate them in a desired way and also to modify their mode of behavior for a better performance of their roles regarding social and/or organizational goals" (Cheong 1981: 555). Whereas Korea's farmers had been steeped in *sadaejuŭi,* were thought to be lazy, and lacked will or ambition, the Saemaul training sought to bring about a "revolution in spirit." To become modern leaders of society, in other words, required the cultivation of certain "progressive habits" aimed at undercutting the

Figure 5.2 **Trainees Signing In at the Saemaul Leadership Training Institute, Suwŏn, South Korea**

lingering traditions of a backward age. As Kim Joon, the first director of the Institute, commented:

> The subject of the movement is the human being. A true *saemaul* [new community] can be built and a new history created only when the human being is reborn. . . . Our obsolete thinking should be refreshed; when this is done, our behavior will change. (*Korean News Review*, 9/8/79)

When trainees entered the Institute, they were asked to give up all personal belongings, including their clothing (Figure 5.2). Age, status, and class distinctions between trainees were forcibly erased. "All trainees wore the same gray uniform, ate at the same table, used the same facilities, and treated each other on just the same level" (Cheong 1981: 560). Cleaning was done cooperatively; all trainees were responsible for making their own beds. Those sharing the same room (usually about eighteen) divided up cleaning chores among themselves to ensure that their living quarters were kept neat: "At the Institute, everything is 'do-it-yourself style.' Trainees, some in their 50s and 60s and with respectable social positions, sweep and mop their rooms, toilets and corridors by themselves" (*Korean News Review*, 9/8/79). One story relates how an

Figure 5.3 **Saemaul Trainees Going About Their Daily Chores**

older trainee, a man in his fifties, had at first been reluctant to sweep and clean alongside his younger roommates. Days later, "awakened" by the Saemaul spirit, the same man was not only performing his cleaning duties enthusiastically, but had even taken it upon himself to clean all the toilets as well (Figure 5.3).[24]

Punctuality was also rigorously enforced to contribute to the atmosphere of equality and uniformity. "Every session starts exactly on time and finishes on time. No one expects or receives special treatment" (Cheong 1981: 588). Saemaul songs woke the trainees at 5:50 A.M. every morning and, shortly thereafter, everyone was required to assemble outside for the daily exercise routine followed by a two-kilometer jog (Figure 5.4, p. 90). A general daily schedule of the training program is provided below:

Activities	Hour
Wake-up	5:50
Roll-call and physical exercise	6:00–6:30
Cleaning and washing	6:30–7:00

Breakfast	7:00–8:00
Morning sessions (success case-studies)	8:00–12:50
Lunch	12:50–14:20
Afternoon sessions (success case-studies)	14:20–18:10
Dinner	18:10–19:10
Group discussion	19:10–22:00
Evening roll-call	22:00–22:30
Sleep	22:30

This regimented schedule was supposed to foster a sense of discipline and orderliness "so as to train participants to cast off their selfish habits and make them understand that they cannot wake, eat and sleep whenever they feel the need or want to."[25] Furthermore, table manners aimed at promoting an ethic of self-reliance and responsibility were also actively enforced. All trainees served themselves, on a cafeteria-style "self-serve" basis. "Here, they learn table etiquette, particularly related to group eating. After the meals, they carry their trays and plates to the designed place for proper disposal" (Cheong 1981: 561) (Figure 5.5). The day ended with an evening roll-call (Figure 5.6), and bedtime was promptly set at 22:30 (Figure 5.7).

Physical exercise was also heavily emphasized throughout the training period. In addition to the two-kilometer run every morning, all participants were "required to use the stairs when going from the ground floor to the living quarters on the 9th floor." Likewise, few comforts were allowed to ease the strain of this routinized existence:

It is a common principle that the trainees are collected at the campus with no connection or communication with the outside permitted. . . . Each trainee gets up early in the morning, makes his own bed, salutes to the national flag, sings the national anthem together [with others], jogs a few miles [with others], and carries and cleans his own dishes. Through this strenuous and routined existence, the trainee recognizes the true history of the nation and discards the corrupted national spirit. By listening to lectures presented by earnest instructors, including poor and ill-educated living heroes from the bottom class of society, by visiting the real sites of ardent struggle against hardships, and above all, *by fighting against one's own corrupt self* by becoming a dedicated contributor to the common welfare, the trainee learns the real meaning of patriotism (my emphasis). (Ministry of Government Administration and Home Affairs [MOGAHA] 1975: 42)

Figure 5.4 **Saemaul Trainees Doing Their Morning Exercises**

Figure 5.5 **Saemaul Trainees Eating in the Cafeteria**

Figure 5.6 **Bedtime Roll-Call**

Figure 5.7 **Bedtime at the Saemaul Leadership Training Institute, Suwŏn, South Korea**

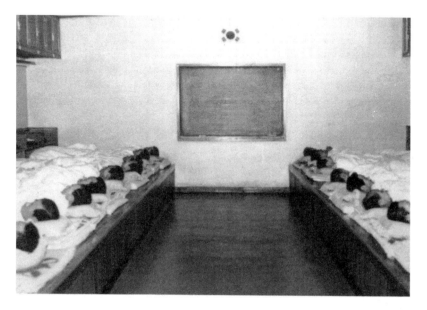

Through the creation of this atmosphere of strenuous self-reflection and self-cultivation, trainees were supposed to emerge from the program as stronger, more self-reliant, patriotic modern citizens. Spiritually reawakened through their "rediscovery" of their truer, vigorous, and more "self-reliant" selves, these new leaders were supposed to return to their farms and villages to redeem their former lives of indolence and sloth by actively building their nation's progressive future.

This same theme of spiritual redemption whereby backward farmers, now recognizing the corruption of their former lives, transformed themselves to become patriotic leaders of their communities, also formed the central focus of Saemaul classroom instruction. Classroom training consisted mainly of trainees listening to other Saemaul leaders recount their own stories of hardships in instituting Saemaul projects in their communities and how they sought to overcome them. Broadly referred to as Saemaul Undong "success case-studies," these experiences formed the most important part of the curriculum. The MOGAHA publication about the Saemaul Undong describes this unique feature as follows:

> The presentation of the experiences of successful village *Saemaul Undong* leaders (success case-study stories) is a very effective and persuasive means of educating other *Saemaul* and social leaders. Especially for a member of the social elite who makes policies for others to implement, the story of a poverty-stricken village woman who, with no formal education, has finally managed, by dint of hard work, to extricate herself from poverty and is now helping other villagers to live better, gives a long-lasting impression and makes him feel that the village woman is perhaps contributing more to society than he is. By listening to such stories, the prominent person reevaluates his past life style and begins sincerely to respect the village *Saemaul* leaders. (MOGAHA 1980: 37–38)

Rooted in real-life experiences, these stories were supposed to inspire trainees to persevere in their own endeavors, to "awaken" them from their former stupor and indolence, and transform them into enlightened, patriotic citizens. The aim of listening to these stories was to facilitate these farmers' spiritual "rebirth."

Presented in movies or slide shows, the common narrative structure underlying these struggle-and-redemption narratives involves the following themes: the Saemaul leader encounters extraordinary difficulty as he/she tries to better the community, usually struggling alone in the face of resistance by his/her elders and peers; he/she manages to over-

Figure 5.8 **President Park Chung-hee Awarding Saemaul Prizes to Selected Saemaul Leaders**

come these challenges, and finally ends up with remarkable success that results in both the betterment of the village and his or her redemption in the eyes of the community. The Saemaul leader eventually becomes a village hero (or in some cases a national hero), as his/her patriotic struggle on behalf of the community leads to the economic prosperity of the village and the nation. To honor these "living national heroes," Park established in 1973 the Saemaul Prize in which select Saemaul leaders were honored for distinguished contributions to their communities and the nation (Figure 5.8).

The Saemaul Undong thus mobilized familiar images of the embattled and redeemed hero—exemplified by the saga of Admiral Yi Sun-sin—to put forth a message of hope for national revival. Like Admiral Yi, these new agrarian heroes had to face their own uphill battles against a wayward Confucian tradition (conservative leaders, idle neighbors, communal strife, and so on) to save the nation from the enemy (in this case, North Korea) and bring about the nation's "revitalizing reforms."[26] Situated in the remote recesses of Korea's Confucian past (the traditional farm village), the farmer-hero, like Admiral Yi, battles the "backward" accretions of a corrupt and unproductive age by restoring the nation's authentic martial "essence" and thus saves the nation from certain destruction and demise. Saemaul activists were exposed to, and then repeated in their own personal correspondence, this same process of struggle to overcome the limits of a backward tradition. Spiritually reawakened through their rediscovery of their truer, vigorous, and more "self-reliant" selves, these new leaders were supposed to return to their farms and villages to redeem their former lives of indolence and sloth by actively building their nation's progressive future. Virile patriotism was thus used by the Park regime to attack "tradition" in the name of a more authentic national culture in order to promote the nation's progress.

The resurrection and celebration of an *alternative* national tradition are central to any level of understanding of the Saemaul Undong, but they also need to be discussed within a broader issue of nationalism. The Saemaul Undong was, on many occasions, criticized for its negative portrayal of the Korean character and the so-called traditional agrarian life-style of the Korean people. Critics of the movement labeled the Saemaul Undong a preposterous distortion of the actual conditions of Korea's farming communities, which were far from the lazy and backward caricatures depicted by the movement's leaders.[27] Its defenders argued, on the contrary, that the Saemaul Undong expresses a deeper and more profound nationalism—the nationalism of the *hwarang*—the very strength of which lies in the *rejection* of all the negative elements of a cultural tradition in order to better preserve that tradition. In this way, Park could still champion the image of himself as the nation's "farmer's son" without seeming to reject the values and mores of Korea's agrarian community, including his own personal family background (Figure 5.9 and 5.10).[28]

The critical point here is that Park's advocacy of a more "authentic" Korean tradition relied on early nationalist and Japanese colonial images of the effete and ineffectual *yangban* to create a cultural message put forth *against* the civil authority and hegemony that Park associated with the Chosŏn dynasty. The "inferior" Korea of Park's polemic was presented as part of a strategy for exposing the "inferiority" of Korea's traditional civil/Confucian domestic leadership. Seen from this perspective, the discursive practices of colonialism exist in a kind of paradoxical relationship to the discursive practices of the Saemaul Undong in that both shared many of the same ideological techniques and strategies

Figure 5.9 **Park Chung-hee Planting Rice, Suwŏn Saemaul Leadership Training Institute, 1973** *(Saemaul Research Archives, Saemaul Institute, Sŏngnamshi, Korea)*

PRESIDENT PARK CHUNG HEE

and both were rooted in same principles of development and modernity. Despite their similarities, however, they served very different purposes. The negative representations of Korea that were put forth by Japanese colonialists were part of a strategy employed for the regional domination

Figure 5.10 **Park Chung-hee at Harvest Time, Suwŏn Saemaul Leadership Training Institute, 1973** *(Saemaul Research Archives, Saemaul Institute, Sŏngnamshi, Korea)*

of Asia, whereas the same representations evoked by the Park regime were employed primarily as a political discourse of self-legitimization. Furthermore, while Park's conceptual vocabulary was similar to that used by Korea's early nationalist reformers like Sin Ch'ae-ho, who also employed representations of ineffective manhood as a means of nationalist self-critique to engender reform, Park's depiction of Korean backwardness was primarily used to legitimize the military's hold on political power. The image of effete Korean manhood was not offered as mimesis, but as counter-discourse, that sought to subvert the civilian hold on politics in order to sustain a revised version of Korean history in which the military—and the militarized masses—became the new and legitimate leaders of society.

6

Students and the Redemption of History

In the bright hours of a cool April afternoon on the Seoul National University campus, a group of students began to assemble in the quiet spaces of the Acropolis, the large open square of gray concrete that resembles a Greek amphitheater of sorts. Situated just in front of the university library, the Acropolis lies at the center of the campus. On this day, it became the locus of immense activity. Chairs were being arranged on the open-air stage behind a large black table where student leaders would be seated to enjoy the privileged view of the day's activity. From there, each one would have his turn at the wooden podium where he would address, like a priest before the parish, his "revolutionary" flock.

It was April 19, 1989, the day when university students across South Korea would commemorate the April 19, 1960, Student Revolution. These ritualized performances would be among the first in a series of university demonstrations that would take place during the school year. Indeed, not a semester would go by without a commemorative rally of some sort to mark the passing of an important patriotic event (the March 1919 Uprising, the Student Revolution of 1960, the Kwangju Uprising of 1980, and so on). By no means did all students participate in these rituals; but most were keenly aware of them. Since they took place at the center of the university campus, few could escape the sounds of beating drums, the shouts of anti-American slogans, or the gleeful singing of songs, all of which were punctuated by the sounds of eager speech-making.

These were public spectacles—some more elaborate than others, depending on the occasion—that involved the whole university community and often lasted an entire afternoon. During these special "holidays," students reenacted significant historical events through a highly elaborate performance of ritualized commemoration that also became an expression of their membership in the national community. Thus, more than being merely explicit movements of dissent, these demonstrations were also about memory and collective representation. In their effort to remake the nation into a vision of their own choosing, students reenacted key events of the past to guide them on the path toward their ideal of a "revolutionary" future. This future, as we shall see, entailed nothing less than the task of healing their afflicted nation of the scourge of division in order to make it whole once again.

This chapter explores the relationship between gender, history, and dissident politics during the late 1980s, a period that witnessed an explosive growth in student activism not seen since the 1960s when students toppled the Rhee regime in April 1960. I suggest that the story of Korea's modern history as told by dissidents was constructed as a seamless narrative of patriarchal continuity and cohesion. I consider how this view of the past—and in particular, of the resistance movements that have loomed so large in Korea's modern history—has been written as a patriotic narrative of ongoing transgenerational replication and regenerating fatherhood. Throughout my account, I stress that the way history is told by contemporary dissidents arises out of, and is prefigured in, the same nationalist preoccupations with manly redemption discussed in detail in chapters 1 and 5. Instead of the cult of military manhood expounded in Sin's and Park's nationalist histories, however, student dissidents were preoccupied with the "recovery" of benevolent fatherhood personified, though not always, in the person of Kim Il Sung.

Since the 1980s, a new generation of South Korean nationalist historian has emerged whose writing has challenged the state's hegemonic claim over nationalist discourse. I consider how the Confucian ideology of patriarchal succession and state fatherhood informed this new vision of history and motivated student dissidents in their struggle for national reunification. Far from rebelling against the traditional Confucian mores and values, South Korea's "radical" students often conformed to traditional Confucian (scholarly) norms of behavior, norms that also justified their "patriotic" actions of resistance.

This connection between piety and patriotism lays the groundwork for the second part of the chapter, in which I examine how the narrative conventions that informed students' vision of the past also helped to shape the agents of history.[1] As John Comaroff reminds us, "The making of historical actor is crucial to his or her actions in the making of history; the latter cannot be fully understood except in relation to the former" (Comaroff and Comaroff 1989: 661). This observation is particularly true in the case of former North Korean leader Kim Il Sung. We shall see that the way in which he was fashioned as a patriotic leader shared important features with the students' own conceptualization of themselves as "patriotic" heroes—complete with the ideal gender models associated with them—particularly in the way they saw their role in history.

History as Redemption

The vital link between manhood, history, and the nation has been made throughout Korea's modern history. This link, however, became even more apparent in the dissident writings that began to appear shortly after the suppression of the Kwangju Uprising in May 1980. The magnitude of state violence, and the complete devastation of the democratic forces in South Korea after Kwangju, drove young intellectuals to search for the origins of their predicament. They sought to explain the causes for the succession of authoritarian regimes that had emerged in the aftermath of the Liberation period (1945–1950). And they achieved this by rewriting the history of modern Korea.

As discussed in Chapter 4, this new nationalist historiography, or *chuch'eron*, has resurrected the problem of *chuch'e* (self-reliance) from Korea's colonial historiography and has questioned whether South Korea's official historiography has contributed to engendering a slavish mentality in the Korean people by its association with U.S. "imperialists." *Chuch'eron* also challenged South Korea's official claim that the Korean War (1950–1953) was essentially an external conflict over Korea's strategic position as the nexus of East Asia (a conflict that, accordingly, was not all that different from two earlier wars fought in and around the Korean peninsula: the Sino-Japanese War of 1894–1895 and the Russo-Japanese War of 1904–1905). By challenging the State's hegemonic claim, which saw Korea's division as fated by geopolitics, *chuch'eron* attacks the "official" version of Korea's modern history on two fronts.

First, *chuch'eron* charges that by treating the Korean War and the events that led up to it as being the product of the deepening conflict between the United States and the Soviet Union, the Korean people's role in history was effectively being erased. It thus attempts to highlight the internal political cleavages that had come into existence within Korean society during the interwar years (1945–1950). In contrast to the State hegemonic view that portrayed the Korean people as passive victims of geopolitical rivalries, *chuch'eron* argues instead that distinct political cleavages between the Right and the Left emerged, cleavages that developed more out of a response to Korean domestic nationalist concerns than to the international pressures of the Cold War. By portraying the conflict between the Right and the Left as the main motive force in Korea's post-Liberation politics—and taking a partisan stand on the side of the Left—*chuch'eron* argues that the revolutionary struggles of the interwar years had more to do with trying to overturn the regressive effects of Japanese colonial rule than with geopolitical rivalries between the United States and the Soviet Union (Em 1993: 457). As Bruce Cumings has observed, "when Americans entered southern Korea in 1945 . . . they found revolutionaries who posited their right to rule on the charismatic basis of resistance to the Japanese and conservatives who based their claim to legitimacy in tradition: they ruled before, they would rule now—that is to say, if the Americans would have them" (Cumings 1981: 100). By highlighting the role that the Korean Left played in trying to overturn the devastation left behind by the Japanese colonial regime, *chuch'eron* views the Korean War as essentially a civil war and faults the United States precisely on the grounds that it actively supported a political faction that sought to perpetuate the regressive effects of the colonial regime. Had the conservatives not had American backing during this critical period, a communist–nationalist coalition would have won control of the entire peninsula in a matter of months.

Second, by showing that the primary contradiction in the interwar years (as well as during and after the Korean War) was not between the Soviet Union and the United States, but between the Korean revolutionary nationalist movement and U.S. "imperialism," *chuch'eron* implicates South Korea's ruling class in the events leading to the creation of separate states and the permanent division of the peninsula. By stressing its historically "insidious" relationship to the United States (as well as its connection to the Japanese colonial bureaucracy), *chuch'eron* views the South Korean government as being nothing more than a "puppet" regime whose primary aim has been to serve foreign, not Korean, interests.

By rewriting the history of the Liberation period in terms that allowed for a critical look at the conflict between the Korean revolutionary subject and U.S. "imperialism," this new nationalist historiography casts the Korean *minjung* not as passive victims of history, but as active (albeit unsuccessful) redeemers of it. Even though the *minjung* had been denied their nation's liberation, it was not because they had not been willing to struggle for it. Indeed, each "revolution" in Korea's modern history (the Student Revolution of 1960, Kwangju Uprising of 1980, Student Unification Demonstration of June 1987, and so on) was a testament to the *minjung*'s will to make right all that had gone wrong during the post-Liberation period. *Chuch'eron* celebrates the heroic efforts of the *minjung* to redeem the past so that they can begin to build a better future. Far from being hapless victims *of* history, *chuch'eron* sees the *minjung* instead as active participants *in* history who have *yet* to fulfill their destiny.

Thus, *chuch'eron* is inherently positive in nature; its appeal derives, as Henry Em has observed, from its vision of Korean history not as failure (that is, the failure of the Korean revolutionary subject to fulfill the nation's destiny as an autonomous [*chuch'esŏng*] unified nation), but as *potential* victory (Em 1993). *Chuch'eron* celebrates the *minjung*'s struggle against adversity and by the same token suppresses and limits the idea of failure in Korea's modern history (e.g., the failure of the Liberation period to create a unified Korean nation-state) by arguing for a vision of potential success. That potential entails the reunification of the two Koreas through active resistance to both internal *sadaejuŭi* "dictatorship" and external American "imperialism." Here, the "master-code" that gives this history its persuasive power is the vision of what Korean history *should* have been. "The most important reason historical science today should make the present period of national division a major study," wrote historian Kang Man-gil, "is due to the fact that Korean historians have the [moral] responsibility to contribute to bringing an end to the present situation of national division" (Kang 1984: 3).

Far from being an exploration of Korea's modern history of division, then, *chuch'eron* serves actually to redeem that history, not to critically examine it. It celebrates the collective struggle of the *minjung* by simultaneously denying the *minjung*'s failures to achieve its purported goals. By accentuating the positive role of the Korean revolutionary subject to fulfill his/her destiny, *chuch'eron* also denies that Korea's historical failures are real. The logical difficulties of this narrative strategy are thus suppressed by *chuch'eron*'s romantic vision of what Korea's history might have been. This is because *chuch'eron* is not really interested in examining the historical past; rather, it merely wants to commemorate the past so that it can be redeemed by some "revolutionary" future. In this sense, *chuch'eron* historiography, like the commemorative ritual demonstrations of student activists, seeks only to heal the wounds of Korean history, not to critically examine them.

The narrative coherence of this "redemptive" historical paradigm is captured well in Sin Tong-yŏp's well-known poem "Kŭmgang" (Kŭm River):[2]

> . . . . We felt our hearts in March 1894
> and were amazed at their powerful beating.
> We offered them in one offering,
> and blood flowed profusely.
>
> In the third month of 1919, once again
> we bore witness to our hearts that grew,
> bearing arms and washing them in blood,
> but blood flowed less.
>
> In the fourth month of 1960, we felt again
> the power of our hearts and marched
> into the field of history and won,
> and lost, but blood flowed little.
>
> Why?
> I believe the day of peace will come.
> Bloodless, won by our long-suffering wisdom
> and our long-growing compassion,
> not to be lost again to blood-suckers.
>
> There will break a new day
> when a revolution will come and plant
> love and brotherly exchange of labor
>
> In the dark of winter spring is conceived.
> In the dark of our hearts love is conceived.
> A Revolution will gush forth
> like a fountain from the heart. . . .
> (Lee 1980: 246)

Note the reference to spring, an allusion to the cycle of seasons. The idea that Korea was in the midst of a dark winter and that the Korean people were struggling toward a blooming springtime was used repeatedly in the popular narratives of postwar Korea to evoke images of rebirth and national renewal. These images were also closely associated with national symbols such as Mount Paektu, the legendary birthplace of Korea's mythical first king, Tan'gun.[3]

All these images, with their youthful and patriotic connotations, were frequently made use of by student dissidents in their oratory and pamphlets to symbolize Korea's deliverance from the division and its rebirth as a reunified nation. In the following passage, which was recorded by the author on April 19, 1989, at the Seoul National University ceremony commemorating the twenty-ninth anniversary of the 1960 Student Revolution, spring, reunification, and Mount Paektu all appear together in this rallying cry for a "liberated" and reunified Korea:

> Youth! you who vigorously strike the bell of freedom at dawn, stomp out of the dark shadows of the Stars and Stripes with bloody cries, and with longing for the sun-shining Mount Paetku, work for the independence and reunification of this land. Only then will spring arrive joyously. Let us finish together the incomplete revolution so that we can live in a better world.[4]

But the "rebirth" of the nation was also taken literally; it signaled the arrival of new sons on the national scene, youths who would redeem their nation's past failures and so create a better future. In a world that continually stressed the continuity between the generations through the ritual observance of ancestor worship, the persuasive appeal of *chuch'eron* historiography was that it told the story of Korean history in the familiar language of Confucian family renewal. Here, the "master-code" that gives this critical historiography its power is the vision of redemption of failure by the father through his "rebirth" in the person of the son. Significant events in history (like the March 1919 Uprising, the Student Revolution of 1960, or the Kwangju Uprising of 1980) are not mere isolated happenings; they are embodied as family tradition, passed down through the generations to be acted out and replayed over and over again until they can be redeemed and given closure by a future generation. It was also a view of history that made tangible the private sufferings of Koreans as the basis for nationalist discourse. As Hwang Sŏng-yŏng (1985) observed in his *Chugŭmŭl nŏmŏ, sidaeŭi ŏdumŭl nŏmŏ* (Over

Death, Over the Darkness of the Age), the link between national history and family tragedy gives this nationalist historiography its emotional power:

> From the Tonghak farmers' rebellion through the Righteous Armies [of the nineteenth century], and the Kwangju Student Rebellion [of 1929] and other events, *there had come into existence a family-like tradition of outstanding pride and self-awareness regarding the democratization movement. Members of the younger generations, through the recollections of their families or grandfathers or great-grandfathers* who had been members of the Tonghak, or the Righteous Army, *carried in their blood the living vestiges of modern history.* Thus, in a single family might be found the personification of a full hundred years of modern history.[5] (My emphasis.)

These same familial themes and recollections were also made abundantly clear in the dedication text of the memorial monument erected for the students killed during the 1929 Kwangju Uprising. In it, the author speaks of "inheriting" (*yuchŏn*) the spirit of resistance passed down through the generations:

> With burning patriotism as their shield and a flaming sense of justice as their torch, these students, as the vanguard of the Korean nation, wrote a new chapter in our history by roaring for independence. In order to glorify their sacred and great undertaking, this monument was erected on November 3, 1953, through the blazing fire-like sincerity of all Korean citizens *who desire to inherit forever the spirit of these young students.*[6] (Text on the Memorial Monument for the martyrs of the Kwangju Student Uprising of 1929, erected on November 3, 1953, Kwangju city; my emphasis.)

Significantly, many new "nationalist" novels in Korea personalized Korean history by writing about political struggles in terms of ongoing family drama. In Pak Kyŏng-ri's best-selling roman-fleuve *T'oji* (Land), for example, the successive cycles of national struggle were linked to the temporal order of family lives, with the spirit of rebellion and resistance passed on, so to speak, at birth from parent to child: Son Ke-su is one of the founding leaders of the Tonghak movement[7] and his son grows up to inherit his father's patriotic spirit and to himself become a member of the Tonghak. This son marries and has a daughter who in turn marries a leader of the March 1919 uprising. Their daughter, in turn, marries a man who, not surprisingly, becomes a leader in the Kwangju Student Uprising of 1929.

These genealogical preoccupations with "patriotic" heritage are in turn played out in Cho Chŏng-nae's ten-volume roman-fleuve *T'aebaeksanmaek* (The Taebaek Mountains). In this "lineage" of resistance, the protagonist of the novel, Ha Tae-hi, whose grandfather was a slave and a Tonghak activist who was brutally murdered by his landlord, becomes a leader in the ten-day communist Yŏsu-Sunch'ŏn Rebellion of 1948. The Tonghak legacy, which finds its expression in the grandson, also looms over the destiny of the father as he pays with his life for his son's communist sympathies by being murdered in angry retribution by a group of landlord sons. Similarly, in Sŏnu Hwi's novella "Pulkkot" (Flowers of Fire), the protagonist is caught between the static and unchanging world of his grandfather and the progressive, liberating world of his father, a Japanese resistance leader killed during the March 1919 Independence Movement. In the end, he embraces the spirit of his father and becomes the proud successor to his patriotic heritage.

Agnatic politics, along with strong familial bonds reinforced by a Confucian ideology that stressed the importance of social relations in a man's awareness of himself, thus determined the students' understanding of history and their relationship with regard to it. As "inheritors" of a particular patriotic tradition, which they linked to the cycles of family histories, (male) students' perception of their role in history was shaped by their experience in ritual obligations to their ancestral past. Their similarity flowed from the cultural construction of time and events that was mediated by the concerns of a domestic world that emphasized the connection between descent and succession, the past and the present, the living and the dead, as one enduring cycle of interconnected (agnatic) family relations. Indeed, far from cutting its link with the past, each new struggle to reform the world becomes instead a form of dramatic narrative about the past, with each new actor spontaneously revising old roles. Each "revolution" is thus structured, in this narrative paradigm, as a single movement in the history of Korean family culture written into a patriotic narrative of ongoing (agnatic) transgenerational revitalization (father, son, and grandson).

The appeal of this narrative strategy was that it limited the idea of failure of the Korean "revolutionary" father by providing the potential for closure in the person of the son (or grandson). The recurrent metaphorical use of "springtime" and "rebirth" in signaling the attainment of a unified Korea—both metaphors associated with the beginning of new life—gives this historiography its power: it provides a redemptive vision of past failures of the father/grandfather by providing the possibility of success for the son.

In pointing to the redemptive narrative structure at the heart of *chuch'eron,* I am merely repeating what Hayden White and Paul Ricoeur have said about the intrinsic relationship between the way we experience the world and the stories we tell about it. How we choose to narrate the past thus has direct bearing on our view of our community. As David Carr put it, "A community exists wherever a narrative account exists of a 'we' which has continuous existence through its experiences and activities" (Carr 1986: 163). The stories we tell ourselves about the past, which take the form of configured sequences of beginnings, middles, and ends, derive from our shared experience of time in social life. With regard to the narrative strategy of *chuch'eron,* it tells the story of recent Korean history in terms that reflected the dissidents' own experiences of family struggle. In a published letter by student leader Chŏn Moonhwan to his father shortly after the dissident student activist Im Sugyŏng had surreptitiously left for North Korea to attend the Festival for Youth and Students, Chŏn, who had helped plan Im's journey, wrote:[8]

> As I told you before, the reason why I decided to take on the responsibility of the Pyŏngyang Festival Preparation Committee chairmanship was not merely due to my desire for unification alone, but rather because *our family's history is intertwined with the history of the war that resulted in the division of our homeland.* I wish to heal the sufferings of our family caused by the division . . . and for this reason I wanted to devote my life to the reunification of the peninsula. (Chŏn 1989: 187; my emphasis)

For students in South Korea who were bent on changing their world, "revolution" (*hyŏkmyŏng*) did not mean throwing away the past, but merely redeeming it. Thus piety and patriotism in Korea go together easily; the idealized model for the ardent revolutionary is not the executor of fathers, as he is in the West, but the filial son. In this respect, despite its highly radical political pretensions, *chuch'eron* is actually quite conservative in nature. In good Confucian fashion, filial sons are loyal patriots, or so the theory goes.

This vital link between family and nation, personal struggle and national redemption is nowhere better illustrated than by considering how Kim Il Sung was constructed in the imaginative sociology of students.

The celebration of Kim Il Sung as *the* exemplary model of Confucian fatherhood in the dissident literature of the mid-1980s challenged South Korean leaders' own claims to political legitimacy. In the context of a narrative strategy that sees the course of Korea's modern history as a series of failed struggles against foreign imperialism, Kim Il Sung alone emerges triumphant. Thus, while recognizing the recurrent setbacks in Korean history, *chuch'eron* nevertheless argues for a partial victory: Kim Il Sung's successful defense against Japanese colonialism and, later, American imperialism, a claim which South Korea's ruling class, given their link to the colonial regime and American leadership, would be hard-pressed to make.

The way in which Kim Il Sung was constructed and popularized in the narrative imagination of South Korean dissidents thus bears significant weight in the story of manly "redemption" that structures the ongoing narrative of struggle in Korea's recent history. Kim was idealized by South Korean student dissidents precisely because he was deemed the *only* revolutionary father who had been able to successfully fulfill the nation's destiny. That is, while all other leaders (and fathers) had failed, Kim Il Sung alone emerges triumphant in his struggle against the foreign foe. The shaping of this historical figure will therefore reveal much about the narrative logic of *chuch'eron.* That he was celebrated as the Confucian embodiment of the wise and benevolent father has to do with these youths' disappointment with their own fathers, a disappointment that derives from these fathers' failure to achieve the vision of what Korean history should have been.

This dissident preoccupation with fatherhood, however, went way beyond oppositional politics. The crisis of fatherhood, which dissidents linked to the crisis of nationhood, was also an issue of concern even among the more politically moderate. The rise of student dissident activity in the mid to late 1980s was seen as being symptomatic of a larger social problem that could be traced back to problems within the home. In the wake of the student activist Im Su-gyŏng's clandestine trip to North Korea in June 1989, for example, there appeared an outpouring of concern over the welfare of the father–child relationship in South Korea. "The discord between the father . . . and the daughter who has gone to Pyŏngyang," wrote the *Tonga ilbo,*

> definitely shows that the relationship between the father and the child [in this age] is sadly twisted. . . . Why can't their [youths'] actions, which

originate from what they personally believe to be right, and their love for their fathers come together instead of clashing together from opposite directions? Why does following the father's will and honoring the father have to be regarded as anti-patriotic, anti-righteous, and an act of anti-unification? (*Tonga ilbo* 7/4/89)

Other journalists more sympathetic to student dissidents, however, interpreted Im's defiant actions as being the consequence of a serious "problem in our father-image of this period." If Im had run off to North Korea leaving her family in despair, she was not the only one to blame. It was the fathers,

> not their children, [who] must take responsibility for all the social suffering that is caused by the children's rebellion toward the bad-father image of these fathers. . . . We must discover the cause of the psychological conflicts of those college students who push aside school work and devote themselves to student movements. There are many problem families where the father is utterly unconcerned about his children's welfare. In some cases, even though these children go to college with their father's money in their pockets, the child is suspicious that this money was conceived by evil means. . . . Due to this kind of image of the father, the child feels a sense of repulsion, which is the source of his twisted outlook [on life]: that disobeying his father's will is, in fact, an act of righteousness. (*Tonga ilbo* 7/4/89)

It remains to be seen how the shaping of Kim Il Sung as the idealized symbol of benevolent fatherhood—an image that sharply contrasts with the failed father image of South Korea's military leaders—worked to reinforce the "redemptive" familial narrative of history offered by *chuch'eron* historiography. The myth that was his life, while not directly addressed by *chuch'eron,* nevertheless permeates the subtext of its redemptive thinking. Indeed, it is difficult to separate *chuch'e* ideology from the life of the man who worked so hard to embody it.

In pointing to the intrinsic relationship between Kim Il Sung and *chuch'eron* historiography, I am of course positing the vital connection between the historical actor and the making of history. The celebration of Kim Il Sung as *the* great patriotic leader, and the familiarity with *Chuch'e* Thought of Kim Il Sung that became *de rigueur* within the mainstream of the student movement during the mid-1980s,[9] correspond to the idealization of him as a benevolent (and successful) father. As we shall see, the story of Kim Il Sung's life is a patriotic story of struggle by the father that culminates in the resolution of struggle by the son, a story ironically not unlike the vision of national/manly redemption implicit in the narrative structure of Park Chung-hee's nationalist historiography.

Heroic Biography

Almost all North Korean biographies of Kim Il Sung, with few exceptions, begin with an account of his formidable "patriotic" pedigree. Born Kim Song-ju on April 15, 1912, in Pyŏngyang, his paternal great-grandfather had allegedly been a leader in the attack against the U.S. ship *General Sherman* in August 1866. "Burning with patriotism," wrote Kim's biographer Baik Bong in his *Kim Il Sung Biography: From Birth to Triumphant Return Homeland* "he [Kim's great-grandfather] fought fearlessly in the vanguard of the masses and led them in the task of stretching a rope across the river to block the advance of the pirate ship" (Baik 1969). Kim's grandfather, moreover, had purportedly devoted himself to assisting Korea's "sons and daughters" in their independence movement and revolutionary activities during the 1894 Tonghak Rebellion (Baik 1969: 15). His father, Kim Hyung-jik, was also "an ardent patriot who devoted his life to the restoration of the fatherland; a vanguard fighter and a revolutionary who organized powerful underground groups to fight the enemy" (1–16).

Kim's mother was also heralded as an "ardent patriot," "a woman of strong will who spent her life in the anti-Japanese struggle" (Baik 1969: 16). She became, according to one "revolutionary's" account, "the mother of us all. Whenever we think of her great and deep affection for us, we feel that we must redouble our efforts for the revolution" (34). One of Kim's uncles allegedly was "a devoted revolutionary" who "took up arms against the Japanese imperialists" until he was arrested and "brutally tortured by the Japanese in Sŏdaemun Prison in Seoul where he died" (16). And his younger brother, Kim Chul-joo, had been yet another "devoted anti-Japanese fighter" who fought against the enemy in Manchuria where he was murdered at the youthful age of twenty (16).

Similar praise of Kim's patriotic "heritage" can also be found in official North Korean historical records. *A Brief History of the Revolutionary Activities of Comrade Kim Il Sung*[10] notes that "the family and relations of Comrade Kim Il Sung, the outstanding Leader of the Korean people—from great-grandfather, grandfather, father, mother, uncle, younger brothers to grandfather and uncle on the mother's side—fought passionately from generation to generation for the freedom and liberation of the people" (Baik 1969: 7). Not only could "such a revolutionary family record be hard to find anywhere else in the world," it continued, but "their devotion to traditional familial values" had also to be highly commended (7). Despite Kim's father's commitment to the independence movement, he nevertheless "paid special attention to the education of the children," reading to his eldest son stories about Korea's celebrated historical events as well as its most beloved patriotic heroes:

> He [father Kim Hyung-jik] told the story of Koreans burning up the American pirate ship *General Sherman* which sailed up the Daidong river to invade the country, and stories of famous generals, such as Eulgi Moon Duk and Kang Kam Chan, and Li Soon Sin who courageously defeated foreign enemies, the story of the martyr An Joong Keun, who shot and killed Hirobumi Ito, the Japanese ringleader of the invasion of Korea. These are the stories that sowed the deeds of courage and patriotism in the heart of the infant General. (Baik 1969: 39)

Kim's mother was described as particularly devoted to her son. One old man recalled that he saw Mrs. Kang Ban-suk on a particularly cold night "crouched before the cooking stove, building a fire," where she was "breaking firewood by wrapping it first in her skirt." When the man asked her what she was doing, she "put her finger to her lips to keep me silent, came out and whispered to me, 'Soon Joo (General Kim's childhood name) did not come till late. . . . He is now deep in a book in that cold *ondol* room. So I am heating it without making noise lest I disturb him'" (Baik 1969: 33).

The attempt to situate Kim Il Sung within a long family "tradition" of resistance was repeatedly emphasized to legitimize his unique place in Korea's modern history. The narrative conventions used to plot his life within four generations of patriotic achievement mirrored Koreans' own experience of modern history as one enduring cycle of family struggle. His biography was the very embodiment of a Confucian-based concept of historicality. Through repetition of certain themes, time extended beyond the life and death of the individual to his "rebirth" in the household of the next generation. The character of temporality structured by these stories was rooted in the unity of time as future, past, and present; personal fate was linked to a common destiny (the family, the nation). In this respect, the struggle of Kim Il Sung and his idealized family came to stand for the possibility of achieving the idealized nation (the "great revolutionary family"). His optimistic pursuit fused civic virtue with family ethics: filial piety, loyalty, benevolence. The pathway along which he hoped to lead his people (itself an expression of Confucian ideology) mirrored his own personal journey toward self-cultivation: from filial son to benevolent father.

Thus we find that official biographies of Kim's early childhood repeatedly make reference to his exemplary filial devotion. According to O Tak-sŏk (1980) in his biography *The Benevolent Sun: Mt. Paektu Tells,* on days when Kim's mother was obliged to wash the family's clothes outside, her fingers numb and cold, the "Great Leader" would "warm them with his breath and put ointment on them with a worried look" (O Tak-sŏk 1980: 18). And when his mother gave him money to buy himself a pair of canvas shoes, he came back instead "with a pair of woman's rubber shoes in his hand, for it hurt him to think about his mother who led such a hard life . . . and thought rather of her than his [own] worn out shoes" (18). Accounts of his great "fatherly love" and "parental caring" for the Korean people, whom he adored as his very own children, had, by the early 1960s, also become an established theme of his personality cult. The North Korean journal *Korea Today,* for example, spoke of the prosperity of the people's land, "lovingly cultivated by their Great Father":

> He [Kim Il Sung] is a Great Father to the people, who believes in the people and even turns the sea into land for them, and who moves mountains and blows up in a moment precious things, even a big factory, if they harm the people. Thanks to his benevolent love ours have become the happiest people and our country has turned into a paradise.[11]

Even ordinary language dictionaries in North Korea illustrate the meaning of words in reference to the "Great Father." Take, for example, the meaning of the word benevolent:

> benevolent: *chaaeroun.* Lead a happy life under the benevolent care of the fatherly leader.

If Kim Il Sung was celebrated for his paternal benevolence, it was because the Great Leader responded to the private sufferings of his people in a way that was both intimately familial and openly political. It was his purported ability to publicly relate to his followers as private citizens (father, brother, son) that accounts for the persuasive power of Kim Il Sung's political persona. *The Benevolent Sun,* for example, poignantly describes how the "fatherly leader" took special care of his comrades in arms during their fight for independence, "just like a caring parent." In one story, Kim sought to find the mother of one of his fallen soldiers: "The Great Leader took special care of this revolutionary family and gave her [the mother] money so that she could provide padded clothes for her children who were wearing hemp clothes even in rigorous winter." His "deep affection" and "loving care for these families," was so great that "he took the place of their sacrificed parents, sons or daughters" (O Tae-sŏk 1980: 117).

Kim Il Sung also extended his "great love and devotion" to the children of his fallen soldiers. In his *Uri ŏbŏ* (Our Parents), Kim Chŏng-suk (1987) describes Kim Il Sung's role in the establishment of the Mangyŏngdae School, founded in 1947 to house the orphaned children of "the late revolutionaries" who died "fighting for their nation's independence," in terms that were characteristically familial:

> The Great Leader told us that during the old days of their mountain battles, the comrades who had sacrificed their lives had begged him with their dying breaths that if the land was indeed liberated, the Great Leader would see to it that their sons and daughters would study hard and be raised to bring about the righteous revolution. . . . So he raised the children of the late revolutionaries energetically and with care. . . .
>   *The Great Leader's love of the young, which embraces their destiny and future together as one body, can be compared to the warm love that only parents can bestow.* The Great Leader patiently teaches even simple truths to the young of this land, and just like their parents, he wants the best for the children. When he builds a school or a children's park, *he does so just like a parent, who would want the best for his children.* And even though the children's accomplishments may be small, their achievements are highly praised by the great fatherly leader, just like a parent who would be happy and proud. Surely, the Great Leader is our true father. (Kim Chŏng-suk 1987: 88–90; my emphasis)

Films, too, became a popular medium for Kim's cult of personality. In *The Bosom of Eternal Love* (1983), he is featured visiting the students of Mangyŏngdae School and giving presents to each child personally. "He checks their bags, making sure they have pencils, erasers, notebooks and other needs. He even inspects their socks and shoes"

(Lee Manwoo 1983: 129–30). When he appeared for a surprise visit at the school, the children "came running, scrambling in to see him first,"

> But after they looked over their shabby clothes, they suddenly became shy and bowed their heads in shame. The children's eyes filled with thick tears which fell down their cheeks, and while they wanted to run to his embrace, they stopped in their steps because of their poor clothes. Our Great Father choked and couldn't move either. . . . Then one child's tearful voice called out "General!!" and he ran to the Great Father's broad bosom which embraced him. Other children came running to the general, their faces wet with tears.
>
> "General! General!"
>
> The orphaned children of the late revolutionaries sobbed with their faces buried in his chest. The Great Father, while embracing the children, also burst into sobs, and choked with emotion, he said:
>
> "Don't worry about your clothes. Don't cry. . . . Study hard . . . and everything will be all right." (Kim Chŏng-suk 1987: 92)

These stylized narratives reveal an important dimension of North Korea's national politics: the pervasive belief in the intrinsic connection between leadership and fatherhood. The image of the father as benefactor and protector came to stand symbolically for the idealized patriot. His show of protective solicitude over the national offspring thus finds expression in the changeless narrative of transgenerative replication where filial sons become benevolent fathers.

Not surprisingly, then, foreigners—particularly Americans and Japanese "imperialists"—represented a threat to self-regenerating fatherhood and to the survival, prosperity, and identity of the family-nation. In an intellectual world obsessed with notions of self-reliance and independence, Kim Il Sung's attachment to domestic values was repeatedly contrasted to the unnatural crimes that Korea's foreign enemies had committed against the nation and the family. North Korean short stories, historical dramas, and "actual" events recorded in museums and documented texts repeatedly focused on foreign violations of the Korean family (marriage, parental bonds, and so on). In particular, atrocities committed against children, to whom Kim Il Sung himself showed singular tenderness, were themes that were most often stressed. Baik Bong (1969: 42) tells us, for example, that when a young girl was waving the national flag in her right hand during the March 1919 popular uprising, a "vicious Japanese imperialist aggressor" cut off her arm. She courageously took up the flag with her other hand and he cut that off too. "The girl, even in death, kept cheering," he wrote, "and the soldier now thrust his sword through her heart." In another "historical" account, the "vicious punitive forces" of the Japanese "burned a whole village including women, young and old" during the summer of 1932 (O Tak-sŏk 1980: 327). A scene from the highly popular drama, *P'ibada* (Sea of Blood), features a young independence fighter who finds refuge with a poor widow. When Japanese soldiers are unable to obtain information about his whereabouts, they "shoot the widow's little son to death in cold blood" (1980: 286–87).

These types of violations committed against the family and children were attributed to American soldiers as well. Within the walls of the Sinch'on Museum, for example, are glass cases holding the remains of fire-charred cloth shoes said to have belonged to women and children who had been locked in a storage house, denied food and water for several days, and then burned to death by Americans during the Korean War (*Korea Today* 8/23/89). Other displays feature strands of black braided hair said to have been recovered from corpses of women weighted down with stones and thrown into a reservoir (*Korea Today* 8/23/89). Four hundred women and 102 children were said to have perished in a mass burning of two brick storehouses set afire by American soldiers (*Korea Today* 8/23/89).

While none of these reports has ever been confirmed by sources outside North Korea, and much doubt has been cast about their authenticity, their truth or falsehood seems less important than their effective ability to generate national solidarity. Such atrocities committed against the family, especially against children, were contrasted to the celebrated benevolence of the fatherly leader whose attachment to the young was particularly renowned.

Retribution for crimes committed against the family also became a popular motif in North Korea's historical works. O Tak-sŏk tells the story of Kim Jong-suk, who lost her family to the Japanese: "When she rushed down from the mountain from where she was working, she discovered that her house had been destroyed and her mother fatally burned." Her mother's last dying words to her daughter had been: "Take revenge on the enemy." Crying and stamping her feet, "she swore before her dying mother and sister-in-law to avenge their deaths a hundred times" (O Tak-sŏk 1980: 338).

A similar version of this family revenge tale is told about the "Great

Leader" himself. At the age of seven he and his mother visited his imprisoned father, whose countenance had "sadly changed from the tortures endured." After the visit his mother told him that he would never see his father again. "I want you to grow up fast and avenge your father!" she cried, whereupon Kim, hearing these words, "swore before his mother that he would avenge his father without fail" (Baik 1967: 39–40). Once again, past meets present in the future retribution of the father by the son. The narrative behind Kim's narrative is thus one of a fantasy of self-regenerating fatherhood and patriarchal power.[12] But it also offers a redemptive vision of history in which the failures of the father are redeemed by the successes of the son.

Fathers, Sons, and the Historical Imagination

The crisis of nationhood created by the division of the peninsula was, as we have seen, often expressed as the crisis of fatherhood. Weakness, impotence, and the loss of national dignity all boiled down to the same frustration, a frustration that could only be relieved by the hope that a new generation of men would continue to struggle to redeem their nation's sorrowful past. This vision of patriarchal succession, and the redemptive tale of "rebirth" that lay at the heart of this optimistic narrative, contributed to a family-state ideology that combined ancestral memory with patriotic obligation.

Within this context, it is not surprising to find that student dissidents in contemporary Korea felt themselves connected to their university community in much the same way as they felt connected to their ancestral home. Like the family unit, the university community functioned as a reservoir of tradition from which student activists could trace their "patriotic" heritage. Indeed, many of them saw their link to their university peers as an extension of domestic ties, with younger students often referring to older students as "father" (abŏji) and "grandfather" (harabŏji) (Pak Chung-ch'ŏl 1989: 120). This also explains the enormous importance placed in the student movement on the ritual observance of key "patriotic" events (the Student Revolution of April 19, 1960; Kwangju Uprising of May 18, 1980; Student Uprising of June 10, 1987). During these ritual "holidays," students performed an elaborate commemorative ritual that was almost always followed by a violent struggle (t'ujaeng) at the university gate. In Kwangju City, for example, students from campuses all across the city gathered together once a year on

May 18 to visit the burial sites of those who fell during the 1980 Kwangju Uprising, "tending to their graves as a filial son would his own father's."[13] Through these and other commemorative rites, students sought to impress upon successor generations their links to their "ancestral" past, as well as their allegiance to patriotic memory.

Thus, regardless of whether student dissidents sought to find their nationalist inspiration in Kim Il Sung's patriotic heritage or whether they looked to the family histories of their own university communities to discover their own "patriotic" roots, the Confucian family ethic set the bounds of political and moral conformity within which these filial and patriotic sons were to locate themselves. As fathers die and are reborn again, past and present meet in circular succession. The twin themes of this optimistic fashioning of the past— redemption and resurrection— thus formed the inherent logic of *chuch'eron*'s Confucian family-centered world order. Indeed, a close inspection of the internal logic of *chuch'eron* and the "redemptive" narrative strategy that it used to tell the story of Korea's modern history reveals how its construction of the past was not unlike similar colonial and "official" post-war nationalist historiographies discussed in the previous chapters. If dissidents sought to redeem their nation's past with the language of patriarchal renewal, they did so because benevolent fathers were deemed few, and filial sons had to, somehow, fill the void.

7

Monumental Histories

Our ancestors were manly men until the middle ages, but
this masculine character disappeared by the time of the
establishment of the Chosŏn dynasty. . . . Sorrow is the
only reward we can get from surveying our past history.

—President Park Chung-hee[1]

How does one commemorate a war that technically is still not over?
While the Korean War, at least for Americans, "ended" in 1953, the
discourses of commemoration about the war have not been brought to
closure in Korean society.[2] How does one bring closure to a war for
which the central narrative is one of division and dissent, a war whose
history is still in the process of being made?

In South Korea, the official commemoration of the Korean War has
always taken on an anti–North Korean stance. But this official view was
suddenly questioned in the wake of Kim Dae-jung's historic meeting in
Pyŏngyang with North Korean leader Kim Chŏng-il in June 2000. Indeed, to the surprise (and dismay) of the hundreds of veterans who had
gathered in Seoul to commemorate the fiftieth anniversary of the Korean War in June 2000, it was announced that most of the planned commemorative events, including a large city parade and an historical
reenactment of the 1950 Inchŏn landing, were to be canceled.

Of course, the singular and official historical narrative of the Korean
War, including the anti–North Korean rhetoric that was embedded within
it, has always been open to question in South Korea, although it was not
until very recently that these new views and, especially, new percep-

tions of North Korea, could be freely aired. While any commemorative act, particularly about wars, is a form of history-making that aims to promote and secure a particular interpretation of events while at the same time blocking or erasing potentially contestatory readings, in South Korea, official memory about the war has always been constituted within a discourse of national self-definition aimed to promote the legitimacy of the State. In the Korean official culture of commemoration, the Korean War has played a fundamental role in defining the masculinist language of national self-definition and State legitimacy in South Korea. Not only has this official commemorative culture perpetuated and generated a view of the past in terms of a particular masculine ideal, memories of the war have affirmed the identification of the national subject with the authority of these masculine images aimed to perpetuate the State's vision of a future reunified Korea.

The purpose of this chapter is to explore the masculinist logic of this official commemorative culture through a detailed examination of the War Memorial, a huge architectural complex located in Yongsan-gu, Seoul. Conceived under the Roh Tae-woo regime in 1988, the Memorial was opened to the public in 1994, soon after the election of Korea's first civilian president Kim Yong-sam, in over thirty years of military rule (Figure 7.1). While the War Memorial glorifies the ancient or eternal character of the nation, which it links to the lost "manly" past of a forgotten martial tradition, it simultaneously seeks to emphasize the unprecedented novelty of the modern nation, which it links to the "recovery" of ancient military values. The connection made between the military, manliness, and nationalism throughout the War Memorial thus presents us with a window through which to view not only how history was written by those who saw themselves as the privileged "subjects" of the nation, but also, and more importantly, how the gender ideals implicit in that history—in this case, martial masculinity—were appropriated by the State for political ends in order to *affirm* its legitimacy vis-à-vis North Korea. The War Memorial not only tells the story of the manly and strong nation against the plight of its war-torn past, it also advocates manliness and brotherly strength as patriotic *values* against the plight of its divided future.

The cult of virile (military) manhood that was expounded in Sin's nationalist histories and later reinforced during the Park regime is thus essential to understanding how the legacy of Korea's military past continues to influence civilian politics in South Korea today. During the

Figure 7.1 **War Memorial, Yongsan-gu, Seoul**

economic crises of 1998, for example, the recuperation of Korea's "warrior culture" was suggested by the Kim government as a way to get South Koreans out of their economic slump. Moreover, the robust efforts made by President Kim Dae-jung to honor the legacy of Park Chung-hee reveal that the narrative about manly "redemption" cultivated during the Park era is *still* being used as a solution to all kinds of problems.[3]

Sincere efforts to reproduce, memorialize, and concretize this warrior past was made, strikingly, during a period that witnessed the historic culmination of nearly thirty years of military rule in South Korea. Far from being merely a poignant reminder of State military power, however, the War Memorial is heir to the particular historical legacy of social Darwinism, militarism, and nationalism that sought to link national "progress" with martial prowess, economic "survival" with the cult of martial masculinity. Moreover, as the central locus for commemorating the Korean War, the War Memorial has played a significant role in the historization and rehistorization of the military in South Korean society by forging a consensus version of the events aimed to bring together military leaders and the "people," North Korea and South Korea. The cultural memory of the Korean War is evoked in the context of memories about other wars, so that the "healing" process associated with the division of the peninsula appears to be metaphorically related to other moments of healing in Korean history brought about by heroic soldiers and martial leaders.

The War Memorial

When the War Memorial opened its doors to the public in 1994, it created a minor, although vocal, public outcry from certain sectors of society. To dissident intellectuals and students, the opening of the War Memorial signaled the continuation of state authoritarian power through the forced celebration of a patriotic history imposed upon the public from above. Spectacular and triumphant, the Memorial was deemed nothing more than a calculated tribute designed to bolster state authority and established interests. Evoking feelings of insecurity and anxiety, the War Memorial, its critics claimed, makes the visitor "feel vulnerable" in the presence of state power (Kim Ran-ki 1994: 171; Chong Ki-hong 1994). Alternatively compared to Stalin's Soviet Palace, Hitler's Berlin Square, Mussolini's Rome, and Mao's Mausoleum, the War Memorial's severest critics unanimously deemed it "a wicked plot," "a bastard that should never have been born," "an illegitimate child that should never have seen the light of day" (Lee Sung-kwan 1997).

What is interesting about these criticisms, above and beyond their attacks on the Memorial as a vehicle of State power, is the very language the critics chose to condemn it: the Memorial as an illegitimate child. By attacking its legitimacy in familial terms, these critics unwittingly attacked the very basis upon which the War Memorial was founded: to establish a link between family and nation, ancestral lineage and State pedigree, "blood inheritance" and State legitimacy.

The idea that Korea's war heroes, from the establishment of the ROK Army during the Korean War era to its deployment overseas during the Vietnam and Gulf wars, could be traced back to a single "patriotic" (male) warrior lineage, beginning with the Three Kingdoms period, lies at the very core of the Memorial's significance as a State monument and a national museum. In this sense, the Memorial's monumentality derives from its latent insecurity; its aim is not only to "prove" its legitimacy in the eyes of the public, but also to challenge other family/national histories that might lay claim to the heroic (martial) history which the State deemed to be its very own. The timeless past of Korea's heroic history was thus presented as an unbroken warrior tradition; the intent of the Memorial is not to periodize history, but to link separated historical phases into a continuum.

The first clue of the Memorial's self-preoccupation with its own "blood-line" legitimacy can be seen at the Central Plaza. A vast open area embraced on either side by the right and left Galleries, the Central Plaza (also called the War Memorial Plaza) is an empty space except for two reliefs carved at each end facing the main stairway. They both reveal familiar scenes: on the left-hand side we see the belligerent poses of the common citizens on their way to battle the Japanese colonial oppressors. On the right-hand side, the Righteous Army itself is depicted in full battle gear, accompanied by this telling inscription (Figures 7.2 and 7.3):

> Ah, our proud Army!
> Inherit the anti-Japanese Righteous Soldier's sacrificial spirit,
> Devote yourselves to restoring our national pride,
> Hear the battle cry of the Independence Army and the Restoration Army,
> You are the honor restored by their souls!

Implied within the obvious link made between the Righteous Army (ŭibyŏng), the Independence Army (tongnipkun), and the Restoration Army (kwangbokkun) is a familiar familial code:[4] the "inheritance" of the spirit of resistance passed down through the generations. But the inscription has other key codes that link these historical phases into a family continuum: father and son form the vanguard of the people's army on the left wall, a generational continuum reinforced by the "embracing" presence of the left and the right Galleries, which house the names of South Korea's Korean War "martyrs." Thus, represented visually is the symbolic familial link between the anti-Japanese war heroes of the Righteous Army and the Independence Army, who in turn are surrounded by the anti-Communist war heroes of the modern ROK Army. Still, the reliefs in the Central Plaza contain a third code in their narrative structure: the link between the military and the people. To those who oversaw the planning and construction of the War Memorial, this link was central to the legitimizing presence of the structure itself: military heroes as the people's heroes. In fact, this link is presented as soon as the visitor first steps onto the Memorial complex. On the right-hand side of the pathway that leads toward the Central Plaza is an inscription carved in granite that reads:

Figures 7.2 and 7.3 **The Righteous Army, War Memorial, Seoul**

Suffused with the everlasting breaths of our noble and majestic countrymen,
This is the living domain of the sacred spirit of national defense,
This is where one's love of country magnificently bursts forth.

The brilliant service of the heroes,
Who protected our inherited self-respect and our land,
It is they who are responsible for the peaceful rays
of the sun and the moon over this land.

By pursuing the spirit of our martyrs who defeated invasions,
By spreading the gospel of love of country.
Here forever will be preserved the proud history of our people.

The dual purpose of the War Memorial thus becomes clear: as a museum, its function is to educate and reform; as a memorial, its purpose is to bless that newly acquired education with a spirit of reverence. Through it, the inevitable outcome was a correct and unanimous understanding of Korea's patriotic history as both intimate yet eternal; fleeting yet immortal.

The ritual honoring of "one hero every month" in the Central Hall merely reinforced this idea of familiarity within the vast continuum of "inherited" patriotic history. Chosen on a rotating basis from among the fifty or so statues represented in the Hall of Heroes, the purpose

Figure 7.3

of giving homage to a new hero every month was "to laud their ethos and achievements thereby making them a shining example to the new generation."[5] Thus honored, the hero stands between an immortalized past and glorious future ("a shining example to the new generation"). The temporal logic of this presentation of patriotic history was to forge a homogenous and continuous national subject who is both unique and yet ordinary, distinct yet indistinguishable. It is the spirit of patriotism, not the hero's particular patriotic act(s), that is being commemorated.

From this individual encounter with a single hero, the visitor walks down through the Hall of Heroes toward the darker recesses of the Memorial Hall (see Figure 7.4). The Hall of Heroes is structured in such a way that the deeper one travels down the Hall, the further back in time one finds oneself (from the Korean War period to the Three Kingdoms period). National history is told in flashback: it is a retrospective reconstruction of the past from a present vantage point of repetition. Here, Koguryŏ's struggles against the Sui in A.D. 598 become the "ancestral" predecessors of South Korea's struggles against North Korea Communists in 1950. By conceiving of the past in this way, history becomes a process of the continual development of the same (Duara 1994). The visitor thus finds himself caught between two temporalities: an ageless

Figure 7.4 **Hall of Heroes, War Memorial**

and glorious past that in turn becomes the foundation for an equally ageless and glorious future.

Here, time and space appear separated but unambiguously linked: history and nation meet as one entity born and reborn over and over again in one long genealogical sequence of fathers, sons, and grandsons. It is the "spirit" of patriotism passed down through the generations, not the individual (lost) battles themselves, that are being commemorated. And it is precisely this historical continuum, expressed visually by the repetition of column-like forms, which leads the visitor from the contemplative space of the Central Hall (present), to the long walk down the Hall of Heroes (past), and into the dark recesses of the Memorial Hall (ancient past). While the walk back into Korea's past is supposed to evoke the glorious past of Korea's triumphant history, the very monumentality of the Memorial structure itself stands for the present and future of that patriotic history.

The Exhibitions

So what exactly *is* the nation's past? And how was it supposed to be exhibited? For the overseers of the Memorial, this question had everything to do with the mythologized history of the nation's struggle against foreign domination and the pivotal role that the military had played in Korea's history of national self-defense: "The primary reason why our people have been able to turn back so many foreign invasions and maintain an unbroken 5,000-year history has been due to the patriotic [*aeguk*] and selfless [*salsin sŏngin*] service of our national heroes" (*CCKNK* 1990: 11–12). Through the sacred contemplation of past heroic deeds, the future reunification of the nation could be realized. As the exhibition manual explains:

> The aim of the War Memorial is to become a place where people can go to pledge themselves to the dream of realizing national unification, by learning from our heroes and from their pride and love of country. In order to achieve this objective, the following basic principles must be established:
>
> (a) Make people aware that only the solidarity of the people, the government and the army can help a nation withstand national suffering.
>
> (b) Remind visitors that the attainment of the present state of national prosperity has been due to the many sacrifices and tribulations of our armed forces. Through this presentation, create not only a proud image of our army but also make people realize that the army and the people are one.
>
> (c) Foster not only trust in the military, *but also firm trust in the nation by clearly showing how nations, regardless of who they are, will stand at the crossroads of fate if they allow their military to become weak.* (CCKNK 1990: 11–12; my emphasis)

The repetition of such words as "solidarity," "unity," "strength," and "trust," which either appear or are alluded to in this passage, occurs throughout the entire "master plan" for the War Memorial. This repetition itself points to a predominant theme running through Korea's modern history: the triumph of strength over weakness, solidarity over division, faith over distrust. The celebration of the nation's "strength," which could only be guaranteed by the people's recognition of the military as a legitimate force in society, would also guarantee the eventual strengthening and reunification of the nation. Just as the solidarity of the military and the people resulted in the prosperous South Korean State, so the happy unity of South and North Korea would eventually be realized by the same strength evinced by those fruitful bonds.

The Chosŏn Dynasty Exhibit and Admiral Yi Sun-sin

The history celebrated by the War Memorial everywhere portrays the force of the fundamental alliance and unity between the people and the military as *the* primary condition for a prosperous (unified) future. The nation's victories are represented not merely as the triumph of the military in battle, but the triumph of the Korean people over both internal and external adversity. The message is clear: a unified people leads to prosperity and peace; a divided people leads to national ruin ("united we stand; divided we fall"). From this perspective, the extensive exhibition space devoted to Yi Sun-sin's (1545–1598) triumphant role during the Hideyoshi invasions (1592, 1597), when Koreans were able to overcome impending national disaster by relying on the magnetism of his "unifying" force, becomes a clear metaphor for the present state of national division. In each case, the historical analogy symbolically presented by the prominent display of Yi Sun-sin's Turtle Ship is testament to a past and a present of the Korean nation and the military's vital role in both (see Figure 7.5). According to the exhibition manual, the Japanese invasions of the peninsula (1593, 1597) occurred because "the nation had fallen into distress" as a result of "a divided national opinion" (*CCKNK* 1990: 82–83). The aim of the display was to "lead the visitors to believe in the necessity of the unity of the people" as demonstrated "during times of imminent national danger by Admiral Yi Sun-sin's leadership" (*CCKNK* 1990: 82–83). The exhibition manual further relates:

> Make it a well-known fact that the source of our 5,000 years of long history and brilliant culture, as well as the force that effectively handled countless numbers of national crises, arose from the manifestations of the Korean people's unique love of country as demonstrated during times of imminent national danger under Yi Sun-sin's leadership. . . . In particular, by emphasizing the uprising of the Righteous soldiers and the many incidents of resistance, [the Memorial] will put forth the proposition *that the Korean War soldiers' self-sacrificial ethos during that tragic internecine war began with the martyrdom ethos of the Righteous soldiers who were willing to sacrifice their lives for their country during a national crisis, an ethos that was passed on to the (colonial period) Righteous soldiers and the Independence Army in their struggle against Japanese imperialism.* (*CCKNK* 1990: 82–83; my emphasis)

Figure 7.5   **Admiral Yi Sun-sin's Turtle Ship, War Memorial**

Of particular interest in this passage is the issue of legitimacy. In tracing the "blood-line" heritage of the ROK Army to the Righteous soldiers and the Independence Army, Japan's formative role in the establishment of the South Korean military is strikingly absent.[6] Clearly, if such a lineage had to be drawn, it was the DPRK Army, and not the ROK Army, that had accumulated the vast majority of anti-Japanese Independence fighters within its ranks (Cumings 1981). The obfuscation of this fact once again indicates the present-minded vantage point of the

Memorial: the possibility of laying claim to Korea's (anti-Japanese) "patriotic" past could be made only by illuminating the victorious State's *ultimate* triumph over its enemies (Japanese imperialism and North Korea communism) through the grandiose display of power and prosperity embodied by the very structure of the Memorial itself. It was precisely this assertion of *ultimate* victory that allowed the South Korean state to lay claim to Korea's patriotic tradition because North Korea (and the DPRK military) had *ultimately* failed.

Furthermore, the possibility of summarizing the past as victory clearly manifested some historical problems. In particular, the Memorial's portrayal of the Chosŏn dynasty is singularly problematic. (Not coincidentally, this period of history was given significantly more exhibition space than any other period of Korea's ancient history.) Inventing a newer, stronger, and militarily more powerful image of Chosŏn Korea, the War Memorial sought to rewrite the history of the Chosŏn dynasty from the vantage point of military strength and not of bureaucratic weakness. Because this chapter in Korean history was widely considered the most "shameful" due to the dynasty's "dependence" on China, the aim of the Memorial was to lay claim for the present a stronger, more "manly" military tradition—one that had been, in reality, nonexistent. This forging of a new history of the Chosŏn period on behalf of a "victorious" present is explicitly demonstrated in the exhibition plan:

(a) Show how generals and warriors [during the Chosŏn dynasty] possessed intellect, virtue and physical strength by explaining the Chosŏn period military system. . . . *Show how the national defense posture improved during the Chosŏn dynasty* as a result of the soldiers' going to battle with a strong military spirit and a firm belief in the nation. . . .

(b) *Organize the exhibit to wipe out the stereotype that the Chosŏn period had a weakened national defense as a result of bureaucracy (munch'ijuŭi)* by displaying various actual and replicated weapons.

(c) Make it possible to directly experience our ancestors' "providing is preventing" philosophy of national defense, *and their progressive and active will to expand our territory* by exhibiting how the Chosŏn dynasty conquered Tsushima Island, a Japanese den, and how it drew the northern barbarian Jurchens out and established outposts along the Yalu River and garrison forts along the Tumen River. (*CCKNK* 1990: 82; my emphasis)

The Chosŏn dynasty is portrayed not merely as a military power able to defend the nation from external threats but also as one bent on territorial expansion. The aim of the display was to rewrite the history of the dynasty in terms that marginalized the prominent role played by the Confucian high literati culture during that period. Furthermore, the portrayal of the "Great Taehan Empire" (1897–1910), which marks the end of the dynasty, was accomplished in such a way as to draw a comparative link between Korea and other contemporary "great" imperial military powers. This connection was made in the striking visual connection posed between Korea's military uniforms and those of Britain, Germany, Japan, the United States, and China.

Ironically, the display of "The Military Uniforms of the Great Taehan Empire" starkly contrasts with the actual events of that period of Korean history: it was during this "Great Empire," after all, which lasted a mere thirteen years, that the Korean people witnessed the collapse of their nation as a sovereign state and the colonization of the peninsula by Japan (1910–1945). Indeed, Japan's colonization of the peninsula is hardly discussed at all, becoming instead a mere blank period in the genealogical line of commemorated battles and celebrated military "victories." (Significantly, what is highlighted is the battle of Ch'ŏngsa-ri in October 1920—entitled "The Great Battle at Chŏngsa-ri"—which represents the Independence Army's first major military victory over the Japanese in Manchuria.)

If Korea's colonization by Japan was given only passing mention in the history of Chosŏn Korea, its triumph over Japan four hundred years earlier was celebrated as one of Korea's greatest achievements. Not only is Yi Sun-sin's victory over Japan in 1592 and 1597 allotted extensive exhibition space, the strategic position of Yi Sun-sin's Turtle Ship within the museum, situated in the center Left Hall, was designed in such a way that the visitor cannot help but come across it several times during the course of a visit. As one "travels" through the course of Korea's ancient history, the triumphant figure of Admiral Yi's Turtle Ship becomes testament to a past that is both heroic and triumphant. The strategic placement of Yi's Turtle Ship was thus meant to create a past that could give meaning to both present and future: Yi's triumph over foreign adversity and domestic strife becomes an analogy for South Korea's (eventual) triumph over North Korean communism and national division. By holding up this period in the nation's history as an example for future generations, the War Memorial sought to legitimize the State as Yi Sun-sin's "filial" successor.

The Korean War Exhibit

The second main exhibition area after the Chosŏn period rooms is the Korean War exhibition, located on the second and third floors. Although the exhibition downplays anti–North Korean propaganda ("Quickly get over the fact that the Korean War was an act of provocation by North Korea," *CCKNK* 1990: 342), the visitor is nevertheless presented with clear evidence that the war was instigated by the North ("Present clearly with actual evidence that the Korean War was an illegal attack by North Korean communists who received support from the Soviet Union," *CCKNK* 1990: 342). Divided into four main rooms, the exhibition is presented in the following chronological order: (1) the background of the Korean War; (2) the North Korean invasion; (3) Defense Operations at Nakdong River; (4) the Inch'ŏn Landing; (5) Northward Advancement of the Armed Forces; (6) Intervention by Chinese Communists; (7) Stalemate Battle Phases; and (8) the Armistice. The last room, created almost as an afterthought, is devoted to the UN participation in the Korean War (which merely displays uniforms worn by UN soldiers), wartime life, and weapons. Indeed, one of the more striking features of the Korean War exhibition is the attempt to highlight the South Korean army as the *principle* (heroic) subject of the war, so that the conflict is portrayed as being fought chiefly between the South Korean Army and North Korean *and* Chinese Communist forces (with little reference given to the vital role that the UN forces played in the conflict). Moreover, unlike the strategic role played by UN forces in the war, Chinese aid to North Korea is emphasized. The exhibition manual explains:

> Although the early period of the invasion was disadvantageous for our army, *present the fact that even in such a situation, our brave soldiers displayed a self-sacrificial patriotic spirit that arose from their love of country and the people.* . . .
> By vividly showing the Battle of the Hills during the Armistice talks, where both sides struggled to take a little more of the land, *convey our brave soldiers' spirit of national defense and make the visitors feel grateful toward our heroes.* (*CCKNK* 1990: 342; my emphasis)

Two points are significant here. The first concerns the idea of history as a righteous struggle to overcome adversity. The narrative is a familiar one: Yi Sun-sin's struggle against the Japanese in 1592 and 1597; the Independence Army's struggle against Japanese colonialists; South Korea's struggle against North Korean Communists. Like similar wars witnessed in the preceding exhibition spaces, the Korean War is treated like part of a *continuum* of righteous struggle. The second point concerns the idea of "gratitude" ("make our visitors feel grateful toward our heroes"). Not only are the visitors to the Memorial urged to honor their war dead, the very idea of honor was written into the history of the post-1945 liberation period itself. The Expeditionary Forces Room, which follows the Korean War exhibition and displays artifacts dealing with South Korea's involvement in Vietnam, the Gulf War, and peace-keeping operations in Somalia, West Sahara, and Angola, shows "how we South Koreans helped our friends in the cause of freedom" (Chang Chŏng-dŏk 1997).

Rising from the ashes of the Korean War, South Korea thus emerges to be an internationally recognized power, a loyal friend, a trusted world partner fighting side by side with other world powers for the cause of freedom. A nation that has fought for freedom within its borders, South Korea also fights for freedom in the world. As an honored member of the international community that shares its "righteous" cause, the military once again becomes the subject of honor by the people.

The Armed Forces Room and the Outdoor Exhibition Area

So how exactly did the planners of the War Memorial attempt to reinforce the inherent link between the military and the people, and between military power and national prosperity? The first step was to reemphasize the historical link between the modern ROK Army and its "original" predecessors. The visitor is confronted with the same "historical" chart, accompanied by this explanation of sorts:

> When the military forces of the Chosŏn dynasty were forcibly dissolved by the Japanese in August 1907, Righteous Armies arose in defiance all across the nation. Upon the Japanese annexation of Korea in 1910, the Righteous Armies were organized in the Independence Army to continue their anti-Japanese struggle.

Righteous Army (*uibyŏng*)
↓
Korean Independence Army (*tongnipkun hwaltong*)
↓
Revival Army (*kwangbokkun*)
↓
National Constabulary (*kukbang kyŏngbidae*)
↓
ROK Army (*yukkun*)

The idea of the ROK Army as *the* subject of the linear (patriotic) history of the Korean nation exposes one of the most persistent splits in nationalist histories: that between the atavism of the nation and its telos of modernity (Duara 1995). Here, the ROK Army is conceived as the end product of the "natural" evolutionary process of the Korean nation, so that what is considered the "authentic" warrior spirit of the nation is now "atavistically recovered" as something new and entirely modern. Hence Duara's point that "as the subject of History, the nation must daily reproduce the project of recovering its national essence—to secure its transparency as the already-always of the nation-space—especially to external challenges to this claim" (Duara 1995: 29). In the case of Korea, this "essence" became affiliated with a largely mythical military culture that came to serve as the "master subject" of the nation. And with this assumption of national continuity came other claims, to history, tradition, and culture for all of "its" nation's past and future. Hence the War Memorial's attempt to privilege the military as *the* principal agent defining the national community and "the people." The modern period is thus conceived as a period of renewal—with the "recovery" of a lost past even as one forges into the future. By positing the military-people (the "people's army") as the new subject of national history, the planners of the War Memorial sought to "recover" the continuity of culture and the people even as they fashioned the people's "future":

> The Army has performed its duties as the army of the people during those times when the nation faced difficulties and its people suffered misfortunes. . . . *The army became the foundation of today's nation and society because, not only did it provide direct support to various (civil) construction projects, but because military training became closely connected to normal day-to-day social education.* . . . The Army is the object of terror and threat to the enemy, *the symbol of trust and devotion to the people, and the buttress of the nation's prosperity and its [goal of] reunification.* The army builds its image as a fresh and progressive institution that is *fulfilling these roles as the army of the people.* (*CCKNK* 1990: 202; my emphasis)

If the "people's army" emerged in the name of the "people," the implication is that the people-nation had always been present historically. But who exactly were the people? As the basis of the nation's sovereignty, the people were supposed to be very old. And yet, in order for the people to partake of the "fresh and progressive" future—and particularly the future of national reunification—they also had to be remade to fit their newly acquired "modern" status. In order to serve as a source of legitimization of the new nation of the "people's army," the "people" themselves had to be remade. To this end, the planners of the War Memorial undertook the pedagogy of the people in which the military now assumed a new and vital role in the lives of the people. Serving both as a repository of traditional authentic Korean "values" *and* as the vehicle of the "people's" modernization, the people's army becomes synonymous with the people-nation itself. The "awakening" of the spirit of national self-defense was thus conceived as a "reawakening" of the original people-army-nation.

We can now understand the importance that the Memorial's organizers attached to the physical bonding between the people and the military of the "new" people-army-nation. The Large Equipment Room and even more so the Outdoor Exhibition Area invite the visitor to actually touch the machines of war, to roam freely among them, to interact with them (Figure 7.6). The merging on a geographically symbolic plane between the army and the people, the people and the patriotic history of self-defense, would also give credence to the legitimacy of the military as "the army of the people." The goal was to bring together the State power and the public in a familiarly intimate way. This familiar (and familial) demonstration of military strength was calculated to illustrate the continuity of an "authentic" core culture rejuvenated within modern South Korean society.

Reverence and Embrace

As much as the visitor's freedom is encouraged in the Outdoor Exhibition Area, however, it is severely restricted in the enclosed spaces of the Central Plaza area. This vast open space leading up to the entrance of the War Memorial was designed to promote a "feeling of reverence" (Lee Sungkwan 1997b). It was within this space that the "petty" concerns of everyday life "were supposed to be brushed aside so that the visitor can confront the extraordinary meaning of war, sacrifice and patriotism" (Lee 1997b). Enveloping the Plaza with its "arms," the visual effect of the galleries on this space was "to imbue it with a sense of inclusiveness, warmth, and even love" (Lee 1997b). It was within this inclusive space that the heroic past and the glorious present, the people and the nation, the individual and history, were supposed to come together in the staged dramaturgy of national unity, reverence, and shared memory.

Figure 7.6   **Outdoor Exhibition Area, War Memorial**

The repetitive placement of columns and tablets (inscribed with the names of over 100,000 Korean dead since 1945) within the space of the Galleries themselves merely accentuates this temporal preoccupation with national history and memory. The historical continuum expresses itself in the repetition of forms. This space was supposed to evoke "a quality of reverence and remembrance" "enhanced by the calm shadows which lengthen with the changing position of the sun, thus evoking the passage of time" (Lee 1997b). This movement of shadows, "formed by the columns and the tablets inscribed with the names of the dead interspersed with sunlight which shines through the empty spaces in between them" was designed to produce "a revelatory and repetitive sequence of death and life, anger and repose, past and present" (Lee 1997b) (see Figure 7.7).

But the idea of "embrace," associated here with the meeting of the people and their history, offers still another interpretation: the embrace of *all* Koreans (including North Korea) by the nation's southern Korean War martyrs. The brotherly magnanimity of that visual embrace—accentuated here by the building's triumphant celebration of "manly" strength—was supposed to underlie the War Memorial's significance as a "monument devoted to the peaceful reunification of the land" (Lee

Figure 7.7 **Galleries, War Memorial**

1997b). The outstretched and open "arms" of the Galleries, which are visually reinforced by the statue of embracing brothers to the Memorial's left, denote forgiveness as well as triumph, love as well as victory. The story of national reunification is written as a narrative of brotherly reunion. Significantly, the meeting between brothers—one strong and one weak, one older and the other younger—is portrayed in such a way that the genealogy of the ancestral blood "line" was never questioned: South Korea is the older son, the legitimate "heir" of Korea's patriotic warrior tradition, whose forgiveness of his weaker, wayward brother becomes the condition upon which North Korea is finally allowed to return to the "arms" of the family/nation fold.

Fraternal Embrace

The *Statue of Brothers* was conceived after the plans for the War Memorial had already been approved; nevertheless, its message of reunion through "manly" strength merely reinforces the masculine celebration of national triumph evinced by the War Memorial structure itself. Located on the left-hand side of the Memorial complex, the first thing to strike the viewer about the *Statue of Brothers* is the enormous discrepancy in the size between the two figures (see Figure 7.8). Embracing his smaller brother to his heart, the South Korean soldier's emotion-laden face stares intently at his younger North Korean brother while the latter looks up at him with admiring, grateful, and (one imagines) tearful eyes. The contrast between these poses is further enhanced by the fact that only the older brother wears a weapon; the younger one is as defenseless as he appears weak. According to Choi Young-jeep, the statue's sculptor, the "forgiving" embrace of the South Korean soldier is "enhanced by the weapon which points outwards in a non-threatening manner" (Choi 1997). Yet the very fact that he wears a rifle at all signifies that the "South is prepared for war should the nation be ever provoked again. It is only when nations are weak that wars become inevitable." Furthermore, the portrayal of the younger brother as weak and defenseless was designed to show "the defeat of communism and the victory of South Korean democracy."

The legitimacy of the State, which became inextricably linked with this narrative of triumphant (or failed) manhood, was therefore couched in very familiar terms: one brother was heroic and virtuous, the legitimate "heir" of Korea's victorious "manly" past. The other brother was weak, effeminate, and, by extension, illegitimate. The rhetoric of fraternity was therefore not incompatible with an extremely strict sense of familial hierarchy. This is because the unity of the nation could be secured only by acknowledging the true "blood-line" descendants of the original ancestors: South Korea as the eldest brother and, hence, the *only* legitimate heir.

Reunion and Rebirth

Given this reading of the *Statue of Brothers*, what are we to make of the circular dome that forms its pedestal? According to Choi, the pedestal is

Figure 7.8 **The *Statue of Brothers*, War Memorial**

modeled after a Silla Kingdom tomb mound. Given the Silla's role in the unification of the Three Kingdoms in A.D. 668, the historical analogy between the ancient past and the divided present becomes strikingly apparent. Rising up out of the "tomb," a reunified peninsula is reborn again as a nation of brothers. The cracks at the bottom of the pedestal become smaller as the two figures, standing on two sides of a divided dome, embrace each other to form one single entity. As Choi Young-jeep remarked: "My idea of using a [Silla] tomb as a pedestal was not intended to evoke the idea of death. On the contrary, it was intended to

Figure 7.9 **Stele to King Kwanggaet'o the Great Memorial**

evoke ideas of hope and rebirth, the cycles of history, so to speak. The two brothers are reborn out of the womb of the past to be one again in the future" (Choi 1997).

The notion of national rebirth was also enhanced by the strategic placement of the *Statue of Brothers* in relation to the other objects within the War Memorial complex. Standing to the right of the Memorial at the opposite end of the *Statue of Brothers* is a reproduction of the large memorial stele to King Kwanggaet'o the Great (the original stands in Jian City, Jilin Prefecture, China), perhaps the most celebrated king of the kingdom of Koguryŏ. Engraved on all four sides is the mythical story of the founding of Koguryŏ, the meritorious deeds of Kwanggaet'o the Great, and the rules for the care of the tomb (see Figure 7.9). Erected in A.D. 414 by King Kwanggaet'o's son, King Changsu, to commemorate his father's great national achievements, the stele takes on a newly significant role at the War Memorial. Although it stands for Korea's heroic national past, the stele also announced the nation's glorious "rebirth." Likewise, in its celebration of a "victorious" present, the War Memorial creates both a past and a future of a mythologized Koguryŏ history that becomes as much a tribute to the heroic dead as it is to the

Figure 7.10 **Spatial Relationship of War Memorial Monuments**

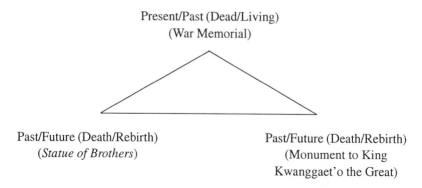

Present/Past (Dead/Living)
(War Memorial)

Past/Future (Death/Rebirth)   Past/Future (Death/Rebirth)
(*Statue of Brothers*)   (Monument to King
                                                    Kwanggaet'o the Great)

living and the unborn. The triangular placement of these objects within the Memorial complex links them thematically, each in its own way standing for both past and present, past and future, history and national "rebirth." Figure 7.10 shows the symbolic structure of the War Memorial complex.

The triangular scheme of this monumental complex demonstrates the State's vision of history and the nation on a geographic plane. Just as the future of a unified Korea finds its legacy in the Silla (left), so the future of the vigorous ("manly") nation-state is modeled after the Koguryŏ (right). Past meets future in the moment of a victorious present.

The trope of brotherhood thus served the State well to fuse its two primary concerns: the need to construct a racial community of (warrior) men who are the "authentic" (legitimate) descendants of the original ancestors, and the need to establish a modern society. In order to recover the "lost" past of a glorious (primordial) military tradition and hence forge a homogenous and continuous national subject, the War Memorial had to search for alternative traditions to Confucianism within Korean history. In the process, North Korea was symbolically subsumed by the Memorial's appropriation of Koguryŏ's history as its own. This history, as we have seen, was the story of a Korean military heritage that had, for the most part, ceased to play a vibrant role in the last five hundred years of Korean history (1392–1910). The problem of "recovery" thus also becomes the problem of shedding certain accretions of an "effete" middle age. What began as a project of commemorating the past thus turns into the familiar project of reconstructing the nation's (reunified) future.

War and Peace

If the painful memories of the Korean War have been temporarily over-
shadowed by the startling images of Kim Dae-jung and Kim Chong-il in
brotherly embrace, what role will the War Memorial play in this drama,
I wonder, in the minds of future generations? Will its monumental tribute to the dead and future soldiers of the nation still be read as an official
testimonial to peace or as an ominous prelude to yet another war? Will
the *Statue of Brothers*—the submissive gaze, the manly posture, the forgiving embrace, the ready rifle—signify hoped-for reunion or future
conflict? Will the monument to the military be read as a reminder of the
violent excesses of past military regimes, or will it be viewed as a symbol of inclusion and peaceful transition to democracy? The ambiguity
of these conflicting possibilities offered by the War Memorial has, of
course, everything to do with the ambiguity of the Korean War experience itself, a war that has not yet ended and for which no closure has yet
been reached. Couched within the powerful monumentality of its masculine gaze is an equally powerful offering of reconciliation and peace,
although it is a peace that can only be represented by a memorial to war.

Epilogue
Kim Dae-jung's Triumph

I began this book by tracing how the ideal of martial manhood first began to take hold in Korean national discourse through an examination of the thought of Sin Ch'ae-ho and later Park Chung-hee. Although my discussion of Yi Kwang-su and student dissidents focused on the role that women played in the national imaginary, it was by foregrounding the "failed" men associated with Korea's Confucian past that women emerged as the enlightened and stalwart defenders of the home and, by extension, the nation. What I have hoped to show is that the emergence of the nation as linked to the rise of the global economy of the modern capitalist world system transformed the ways in which Koreans perceived themselves as gendered beings. The creation of new forms of masculinity (and to a lesser extent, femininity) in Korea was conditioned by the global demands of the modern world system and the nation-state.

Of course, these observations are not completely new. George Mosse has said as much in his pioneering work *Nationalism and Sexuality,* although his focus, like that of many contemporary theorists of the nation, has been to discern the ways in which the nation-state has inhibited the expression of one's (natural) sexuality and gender through its mechanisms of power and control, while I have emphasized, quite to the contrary, the creative power of the nation to *produce* new identities.[1]

Indeed, it is this fascination with the creative power of nationalism to transform itself in diverse contexts and settings, all the while creating *similar* modern paradigms and oppositions (home/world; tradition/

progress; female/male; barbarism/enlightenment, and so on), that has led me to analyze a number of seemingly unrelated texts and events in Korean history. In doing so, I have also tried to call into question the claims of an all-encompassing theory of history whose aim is to reconstruct the putative past of the nation as a narrative of progression. While the nation-state, as Duara and others have pointed out, works to create the myth of a continual story-line that moves toward some predetermined destination, whether this be modernity, progress, and civilization, the focus of this book is, by contrast, to problematize the myth of historical progression. This has been accomplished by making explicit the uncanny connection between seemingly disparate texts and events in order to locate in them a forgotten or repressed "memory" that joins with the experience of the present reflections about the past. My aim is to reveal an alternative historical temporality of the nation-state as a *collection* of moments/texts rather than their linear development through time.

This concluding chapter on President Kim Dae-jung lays the final groundwork of this project.[2] I want to show how Kim Dae-jung has consistently utilized and creatively reworked the "tropes" of manhood that have been so far explored in the preceding chapters. In particular, I am interested in analyzing how Kim's ideal of manliness, borrowed from Christian sources, has influenced his vision of the (reunified) nation and is intimately related to his image of himself as a national (manly) leader. As we shall see, Kim's idea of manhood grew out of his conformity with, and opposition to, previous forms of manliness.

A New Kind of Man/Nation

The "rise" of Kim Dae-jung to the office of president is a remarkable story and one that Park Chung-hee, Kim's one-time nemesis, would probably have much appreciated: a poor provincial boy with little formal education struggles against all odds to oppose the (corrupt) powers that be, stalwartly overcoming assassination attempts, house arrests, and political intimidation, to become the nation's first oppositional president since national liberation in 1945. "The struggling hero redeemed at last," or simply, "The righteous leader's moral (democratic) victory," are familiar narratives in Korea's national rhetoric that have also been widely applied to make sense of the extraordinary life of this extraordinary man.[3] Indeed, much of the reason behind Kim's personal appeal is that his story resonates with the story of the entire nation. As one editorial put it in the wake of Kim Dae-jung's selection as the recipient of the 2000 Nobel Peace Prize: "Kim Dae-jung's political struggle shared the same path as the Korean people's historical struggle toward democracy. In this way, his Nobel Peace Prize is not only an individual honor but an honor shared by the entire nation" (*News People* 2000: 10.26).

Kim also put his life's story to good use, using it as an allegory of inspiration to spur the Korean people forward out of the nation's worst economic crisis since Liberation:

> My life over the past 40 years was full of difficult challenges and hardships, but I have overcome them. I know I will live up to your expectation to overcome our national hardship. I have utmost confidence in your potential because you have persevered through trials and tribulations of industrialization and democratization. . . . The sacred spirit of fallen patriots will watch over us—the patriots who gave their lives for national liberation, for democracy and for the Republic. United in hand, let us all rally under the banner of the "Second Nation Building." Let us all take the reigns of our glorious destiny. Then we will be able to pass it on to our children and grandchildren with pride. (*Chosŏn ilbo* 11/3/98)

This same narrative of struggling and redeemed manhood/nationhood was further reiterated in Kim's February 25, 1998, Presidential Inaugural Address, where the allusion to Admiral Yi Sun-sin's battle "to save the country from its enemies" is similarly employed to inspire the people in their "fight" for economic/national recovery:

> Let us take powerful strides forward and overcome the trials that are obstructing our path. Let us open up a new age . . . *just as our forefathers saved the country with indomitable will whenever they met with national ordeal, let us write a great chapter in our history by overcoming today's difficulties* and undertaking another leap forward. Let us turn today's crisis into a blessing. (*Tonga ilbo* 2/26/98)

Yet, despite these allusions to battles and struggles, the distinctive feature of Kim's politics, unlike those of his military predecessors, is its *selective* repudiation of the forms of (martial) manliness that were idealized by Sin Cha'e-ho and the Park regime. In this sense, the idea of struggle for Kim takes on an entirely different meaning than it had in the past, becoming much more allied with the Christian idea of suffering and redemption rather than with social Darwinian notions of progress.

Few foreign observers of Kim's politics have given much credence to the ways in which his faith as a devout Catholic has influenced his world view and has deeply impacted his vision of himself as a man and as a national leader. Yet Kim Dae-jung's fervent religiosity, based upon the ideals of Christian forgiveness, is the source and ideological foundation that has shaped his politics and actions.

Take, for example, his proposal to erect a memorial hall to the late president Park Chung-hee.[4] Recalling the former president's persecution of him, Kim Dae-jung has said time and again that he bears no grudge or ill-will against Park or Park's predecessors Chun Doo-hwan and Roh Tae-woo (one of Kim's first presidential acts was to pardon the two former presidents), stating: "Without a spirit of forgiveness the leader can no longer look after the interests of the people and society. Instead, he becomes caught up in the embarrassing cycle of vengeance that calls for an eye for an eye, a tooth for a tooth." And he further relates:

> Only a courageous leader knows how to forgive. Only a leader who fears nothing but his own people, only a leader who holds the conviction that the righteous will always prevail, only such a leader can show true courage. *He who holds the conviction that forgiveness is the ultimate victory can forgive with confidence.* . . . (Kim 1998: 116; my emphasis)

What is interesting about this passage, and about Kim's philosophy in general, is the extent to which his view of "victory" is grounded in the ideals of Christian forgiveness and not in the Darwinian world view of struggle ("true forgiveness is being able to forgive the unforgivable, an ultimate act of human triumph" [1998: 64]). Indeed, throughout his autobiographical writings, Kim makes a point of repudiating this world view, stating that "from the beginning, I was neither a fighter nor tough. Rather, I come from a family with an artistic disposition" (1998: 164). If Park Chung-hee had idealized Napoleon during his childhood, Kim Dae-jung had "creatively modeled myself after Christ who bore the cross" and President Lincoln, "who showed me how to forgive the enemy" (1998: 173):

> Jesus Christ said: "Forgive us our trespasses as we forgive those who trespass against us."
> This saying was [indirectly] looked down upon by Friedrich Nietzsche, who viewed Christianity as the religion of the weak. When one considers his absurd philosophy that says that it is acceptable to mercilessly trample

down upon ordinary people and women, because only heroes and super-men matter, it is possible to understand how such a perverse view of Christianity could have arisen. But what became of Hitler who supposedly inherited Napoleon's philosophy that was also worshipped by Nietzsche? Furthermore, we have witnessed the ruin of communism, which called Christianity the opium of the masses that weakened the people's resistance against exploitation by their rulers. *History only honors those who confess their sins before God, who forgive their enemies and who look after their neighbors.* (1998: 173)

The form of manliness that emerges from Kim Dae-jung's politics is one that idealizes neither the fighter nor even the "fittest," but rather someone who "simply endures": "While it is important to win a battle," Kim observes, "the principle aim is to win the war. What does it matter to win a battle if the war is lost?" (1998: 182). For Kim, this war involves the battle of higher moral principles rooted in the virtue of Christian forgiveness: "without forgiveness, one may win the battle, but one will lose the war" (1998: 182). Indeed, as Kim relates, "with such lofty goals in mind, we will be able to endure anything":

Those who have to endure will endure. One fails to endure not because one's suffering is too unbearable, *but because there is no higher purpose that gives meaning to this suffering.* (1998: 182; my emphasis)

In this sense, Kim's view of history, although propelled by seemingly related ideas about struggle and manly/national redemption, is actually quite different from the nationalist vision promulgated by his military predecessors. If history is the record of the "progress" of human endeavors toward some secular "victory" (e.g., enlightenment, civilization, nationhood, and so on), Kim's version of history is the record of progress toward some transcendental goal: the *universal* triumph of democracy, mercy, and forgiveness for all people.[5] In his acceptance speech of the Philadelphia Liberty Medal on July 4, 1999, for example, Kim relates that in his pilgrimage toward freedom, two forces sustained him. The first "is the Christ which I believe in," and the second "is my understanding of history." This version of history is one marked by struggle and redemption in which the righteous ultimately prevails: "Throughout history and the world, those who fought for liberty and justice ultimately prevailed. Too many times, the reality was grim. *But I was always certain that history would make me a winner*" (my emphasis, *Korea*

Figure E.1   **Chairman Kim Chŏng-il Meets President Kim Dae-jung, Pyŏngyang, June 12, 2000**

Herald 10/14/00). Of course, what Kim meant by this statement had nothing to do with the idea of "victory" as defined in purely secular terms, but victory in the spiritual sense of having lived one's life according to one's higher principles "through the realization of God's justice in the world" (Kim 1998: 144).

Not surprisingly, it is precisely the "higher calling" of Kim's politics that most worried his adversaries. If love and forgiveness became the catchwords for Kim's attempts to reconcile with his former enemies, these same ideas became the mantra of his Sunshine Policy toward North Korea. Indeed, the poignant scene of "brotherly reunion" between Kim Dae-jung and Kim Jong-il following the former's arrival in Pyŏngyang for the historic June 12–14, 2000, summit, made the reconciliation between the two "enemies" look easy (Figure E.1). Kim Chŏng-il, it appeared, was not crazy after all, but quite sane, and even witty and funny. Kim Dae-jung was treated with reverence and respect (as an older brother should) and even appeared to be enjoying himself. And if this initial scene of reconciliation was not enough to thaw the ice between the two countries, there were many more scenes that followed which did, so that when Kim Dae-jung returned to Seoul two days later to a hero's welcome, it appeared that his politics of forgiveness had actually worked.

Although it is still far too early to assess the success or failure of Kim's visit to North Korea in the long term, the point that I would like to emphasize here is how the mythology of national struggle and redemption (reunification) was reworked by Kim to create yet *another* version of nationhood/manhood that sharply contrasted with the ideals of masculinity set forth by his military predecessors. While Kim has made clear his respect for the value of Park Chung-hee's accomplishments, he nevertheless revised the latter's notions about male identity and male power to accommodate his own views about Christian virtue and forgiveness. Although beaten down countless times by the powers that be, this "new" man rises up time and again, not to slay the enemy *but to forgive him.* Indeed, quite in contrast to the ideal of manhood advocated by Sin Ch'ae-ho and Park Chung-hee, Kim's idealized man is indomitably strong *at the same time* that he is also vulnerable and weak; his strength derived not from his physical prowess but from his spiritual might. As Kim put it, "No matter how strong we are, we are also weak. One does not go forth because one has no fears. Rather, one goes forth despite those fears" (1998: 37). This understanding of strength in weakness is summed up by Kim's nickname, "*indongch'o,*" referring to a vine that bears red fruits during the winter months (Figure E.2).[6] As Kim himself has observed of this affectionate appellate, "the frail *indongch'o*'s strength to endure the winter comes from its belief that spring will eventually arrive. Likewise, I have also survived with the belief that if I can endure the winter, spring will also come" (1998: 317). The "triumph" of Kim Dae-jung thus lies not in his physical strength, associated with such masculine ideals as aggressiveness, physical prowess, and/or virility, but in the force of his spiritual convictions: "genuine inner growth of human beings is possible only through hardship. The prophets and the saints who attained the highest spiritual summit of history of mankind are the ones who, when confronted by outer and inner challenges, daringly rose up, responded and overcame" (Kim 1987: 253).

What implications these newer versions of manhood/nationhood will have on the future reunification of the two Koreas has yet to be seen. What is clear, however, is that the forms of manliness cultivated by Kim Dae-jung to enhance the legitimacy and authority of his government and the future reunification of the nation have derived from previous ideas about manhood. While this transition appears to affirm the same evolutionary paradigm that accompanies the logic of inevitable historical progression—in this case, the apparent transition from an authoritar-

Figure E.2 **President-Elect Kim Dae-jung Shortly after Winning the 1997 Presidential Election** (In *Chugan Chosŏn* 1/1/98)

ian form of government to a democratic one—my point throughout the book has been to show that such a progression is a myth. Far from distancing himself from the past (and from Park), Kim Dae-jung actively posited his engagement with it. Instead of disavowing the past, Kim drew his inspiration from it to re-create new representations of manliness that both reiterated the major themes and representations of the Park era while locating in them their concealed connections with the present and/or alternate future.

As we enter the twenty-first century and reflect upon the failed promises of an all-encompassing theory of history which never moved beyond the conception of transition to address the relationship between the past and the present, the challenge remains to write a history of the nation-state without falling hostage to its dominant paradigms. The result of such a strategy cannot simply entail the rewriting of the dominant culture through an act of difference and resistance, nor by eschewing historical narratives altogether. Rather, by returning to the tradition of an earlier critique of progressive history, we can begin to rethink our conceptualizations of the nation in terms of what Benjamin (1968) calls the "dialectic image"—the moment of awakening when otherwise concealed or forgotten connections with the past are revealed by their unexpected emergence within the present. The task of the historian, therefore, is to peel away the various layers of meaning revealed by the juxtaposition of texts, events, and images so as to (re)capture the infinite, unexpected, or subterranean connections that exist between them.

Notes

Introduction

1. Bhabba uses the concept of colonial mimicry to describe the relationship between the postcolonial subject and the nation-state, relating that "mimicry emerges as the representation of a difference that is itself a process of disavowal. . . . The effect of mimicry on the authority of colonial discourse is profound and disturbing. For in 'normalizing' the colonial state or subject the dream of post-Enlightenment civility alienates its own language of liberty and produces another knowledge of its norms" (1994: 86). The notion of "mimicry" and "alienation," according to Bhabba, also produces a profound ambivalence on the part of the postcolonial subject by the knowledge that this replication is always "partial" and "incomplete."

2. What are we to make of the religious and cultural "contamination" of China, Japan, and Korea brought about by Buddhism that developed in India, or for that matter, the political ideology of Confucianism that originated in China and later took root in Japan and Korea?

Chapter 1

1. General Lea fought against the Boxer Rebellion and became an advisor to Sun Yat-sen. Quotations are taken from Hofstadter (1992: 170, 190).

2. From *Hsin min shuo* (Towards a New People) (1903), quoted in James Pusey (1983: 261).

3. Schmid (2002): 122. Schmid relates that while Korean nationalism and Japanese colonialism had diametrically opposed political agendas, they nevertheless were committed to similar goals since both were invested in the modern promise of *munmyŏng kaehwa*. Styles of nationalist self-critique by Korean nationalists could thus be easily co-opted by Japanese authorities to justify their colonial exploitation in the name of the same principles as Korean nationalists—civilization and enlightenment.

4. As Duara (1995), among other scholars, has noted, the circle of Social Darwinist discourse in the nineteenth century not only enabled nations to be imperial powers,

but it also justified imperialism and aggression as the battle of (natural) principles: of modern civilization against barbarism. Social Darwinism represented the underside of Enlightenment ideology for it was in the name of enlightened civilization that the hierarchies of "advanced" and "backward" nations were sustained and colonial exploitations justified (Duara 1995; Stocking 1987). But just as importantly, notions of the "survival of the fittest" (*chŏkcha saengchon*) and "struggle for existence" (*mulgyŏng*) that were couched in the linear progress of history, connected the attainment of civilization with the ability to wage war and do battle. Such was the basis of Japan's assertion of its rights over Korea, Taiwan, and parts of Southeast Asia. Indeed, as the only non-Western imperialist power to colonize a non-Western nation, Japan displayed not only its military and industrial prowess, but also justified that military prowess on the basis of racial/cultural superiority. The conquest of the recently barbarianized Chinese in the Sino-Japanese War of 1894–1895 was thus seen, in this newly appropriated narrative paradigm, as the mark of "civilized" status.

5. I have relied upon a number of edited compilations of Sin's work for this essay. The most comprehensive of these is the 1962 edition in four volumes, including the *Separate Collection*, but I also include several other modern compilations of Sin's work.

6. Im Kyŏngŏp and the Knight of Ch'anghae are two historical figures, the first documented and the second probably mythical, who demonstrated an aggressive martial spirit in defense of the Korean national polity or interest. Im was a Chosŏn dynasty government official who served during the Manchu invasions in the seventeenth century. He advocated conducting aggressive attacks against the Manchu Qing dynasty (1644–1911) in retaliation for the invasions. The Knight of Ch'anghae was a semi-mythical figure supposedly from the Korean peninsula (before there was any state polity in Korea) who was hired by the Chinese Qin dynasty in the third century B.C. to take revenge against the Han dynasty, which had conquered them. He was said to have used a long heavy iron pole as his weapon. The Knight of course failed in his attempt as the Han dynasty unified China and provided its first emperor.

7. For a good treatment of the aims and philosophy of the cultural national movement in colonial Korea, see Robinson (1988) and Wells (1990).

8. The term *minjok* is a neologism first invented by Japanese intellectuals in the early Meiji period. As Schmid (1997) has pointed out, the term was used as a powerful conceptual tool by Korean, Japanese, and Chinese scholars to reconceive the nation and rewrite its historical past. In Korea, the term first appeared in the editorials of a number of daily newspapers, but its usage was not widely accepted until the publication of Sin's *Toksa sillon*. This work provided the fundamental critique of conventional Confucian historiography and, "by setting the bounds of the neologism, moved to establish a vision of the nation as a historically defined racial entity" (1997: 31). The term *minjung*, on the other hand, refers to a broad political grouping of oppressed and exploited masses. As Em reveals, Sin Ch'ae-ho's use of the term was more amorphous than Marx's *proletariat*, but it was not synonymous with the Korean people as a whole (Em 1999: 360).

Chapter 2

1. The theme of female enlightenment and conjugal love that appeared throughout in Yi Kwang-su's nationalist imagination also figured prominently in almost all

the nationalist and literary writings of the early colonial period. The promotion of women's education, the call to reform traditional marriage practices, and the "uplifting" of women's social status, were central to the political debates of the time. See Wells (1990); Robinson (1988); Kim T'ae-jun (1994); Kim Yun-sik (1986).

2. Michael Robinson (1988) notes that many of Korea's early modern writers and intellectuals who came of age in the last years of the Chosŏn dynasty (1392–1910) had studied in Japan. Waseda University alone "produced many Korean graduates who later became prominent in colonial intellectual circles," including Ch'oe Nam-sŏn, Kim Sŏng-su, Yi Kwang-su, Chang Tŏksu, and Hyŏn Sang-yun, all of whom were important members of the journalistic, literary, and academic circles of the time (Robinson 1988: 56–57). It was toward the end of Yi Kwang-su's years in Japan that he began to embark upon his literary career. One of his first published literary endeavors, "Saranginga" (Is It Love?) (1909), was written in Japanese. Other Korean authors writing in the genre of the new novel (sinsosŏl) began their literary careers translating Japanese works (including Japanese translations of Western novels). They include: Yi Hae-ho's (1869–1927), Ch'ŏl segye (World of Iron) (1908) by Jules Verne, translated from the Japanese version; Yi Sang-hyŏp's (1893–1957), Haewangsong (Sea King's Star) (1915) from the Japanese translation of Alexandre Dumas's Count of Monte Cristo (1845); and Ch'oe Ch'an-sik's (1881–1951) Ch'uwŏlsaek (Color of Autumn Moon) (1912) from Ozaki Koyo's Konjiki yasha (Golden Demon) (1902).

3. Hwang has described how the use of the Japanese term bungaku coincided roughly with the establishment of English literature departments at Tokyo University's College of Arts and Sciences, which also marks the period when modern literary criticism in Japan began to flourish, heralded by the publication of Tsubouchi Shoyo's The Essence of a Novel (1885) (Hwang 1999: 14–15). Williams (1976) tells us that the development of a national literature first appeared in Germany in the 1770s (under the new term Nationallitteratur) with the publication of Johann Gottfried Herder's Über die neuere Deutsche literatur (1767). Emphasizing the variety of national characteristics, literature became another means for the aesthetic expression of the Volksgeist. In this sense, the idea of a "nation" having a "literature" is a crucial social, cultural, and political development that happened not only in Europe, but in East Asia as well through the translated term bungaku. While it is beyond the scope of this chapter to examine the history and usage of this term as it developed in Japan, I will refer the reader to two Japanese sources, that Korean literary theorists have frequently cited in their work on modern Korean literature: Fukuchi Ochi, Meiji bungaku zenshu (Tokyo: Chikuma Shobo, 1966); and Isoda Koichi, Rokumei no keifu: kindai nihon bungei shiji (Tokyo: Bungei Chunjusha, 1983).

4. Yi Kwang-su's belief that the national language was the means through which a people can express their national "essence" coincided with the development of a new thinking about the relationship between the (Chinese) writing system and the nation. Exclusive usage of the Korean vernacular han'gul, according to Yi, would enable the people to become aware of their "Korean self."

5. For a good discussion of the sinsosŏl (new novel), see Kim Yun-sik (1986). In this work, Kim discusses a range of novelists, including Yi In-jik and Kim Tong-in, but also devotes a great deal of time to the development of ŏnmun ilch'i (correspondence of written and spoken language), which derived from the same movement that had appeared in Japan (genbunitchi).

6. For a good discussion of these themes see Andre Schmid (2000), who observes that by naturalizing the link between the written word and the nation, "writers simultaneously undermined the claim of the [Chinese] character to national transcendence" (p. 93). For the first time since Chinese characters were introduced into Korea in centuries past, they were highlighted as foreign and "Chinese."

7. Yi Kwang-su (1979a).

8. Yi Kwang-su (1979b).

9. The traditional Confucian understanding of *chŏng* is derived from the doctrine of *sŏngchŏngron* (性 情 論), which was first formulated by Mencius. According to this doctrine, "the state of absolute quiet is nature (性 *sŏng*), while the state of being acted upon and immediately penetrating all things is feeling (情 *chŏng*)" (Chan 1986: 62). In other words, *chŏng* comes into being only when "nature is aroused." By the fifteenth and sixteenth centuries, Korean intellectual discourse was deeply involved in a philosophical discussion and debate over the metaphysical question of the primacy of *li* (principle; or nature [*sŏng*]) over *ch'i* (material force; or physical principle [*chŏng*]) and their reciprocal relationship to one another. For a good discussion of the "Four-Seven Debate," see Julia Ching (1985).

10. This doctrine is explained in detail in Yi's "What Is Literature?" (1979b).

11. Interestingly, Yi Kwang-su seems to have discounted all Korean literature written in Chinese. Although he does include the vernacular genres, *sijo* and *kasa* as being distinctly Korean, he states that outside of these genres and the *p'ansŏri*, *Tale of Ch'unyhang* and the *Tale of Simchŏn*, there is "little to show for Korean literature from the past" (1979b: 555).

12. Generally speaking, the basic tenets of cultural nationalism advocated the idea that the spiritual regeneration of the people was required to achieve national liberation. Advocates of cultural nationalism, including Yi Kwang-su, An Chang-ho and Yun Ch'i-ho, worked to encourage the spiritual changes within the Korean people, by instilling in them new and modern ideas. Education, of course, was essential as the nation's rebirth could not be achieved without first bringing about the moral and spiritual regeneration of the people.

13. Scenes of traveling and studying abroad are a predominant theme of Korea's new novels (*sinsosŏl*), including Yi In-jik's *Hyŏlŭi nu* (Tears of Blood) (1908) and his *Ŭnsegye* (Silver World) (1908); Yi Hae-cho's *Chayujŏng* (Freedom Bell) (1910), and Ch'oe Ch'an-sik's *Chuwŏlsaek* (The Color of Autumn) (1912), among others.

14. As Karen Wigen has noted, "travel and the literature of travel contributed to a hallmark of Japanese early modernity, national integrity" (1999: 1195). Indeed, as many scholars of Japan have noted, although *kikōbun* (travel writing) was a time-honored pursuit that had existed in Japan (in both prose and poetry) since the early middle ages, it preserved its popularity into the modern period. Kojin Karatani (1993) has noted, however, that while the *kikōbun* genre remained vibrant into the Meiji period, its focus changed. Citing from Yanagita Kunio's *Kikō bunshu* (Travel Essays), Karatani suggests that this transformation consisted of the "liberation of travel literature from the literary" and from the conventions of what Yanagita himself had described as "a string of poems and essays" (1993: 52). What emerged was what Karatani describes as the "discovery of landscape," a development that was not unlike the *genbunitchi* (writing in conformity with speech) movement that was occurring in modern Japanese literary practice. For a good discussion of these ideas, see

Wigen (1999); Karatani Kojin (1993); Vaporis (1998); and Joshua Fogel (1996).

15. Yi Kwang-su (1972: 442–46). Translated from the Japanese into Korean by Kim Yun-sik.

16. In *Mujŏng* (1996 [1917]), for example, it is on the train that the principle female character of the novel, Yŏng-ch'ae, becomes spiritually "awakened" both as a new woman and a patriotic subject (see Chapter 3).

17. Yi Kwang-su (1993a: 82–95).

18. Yi Kwang-su (1993b).

19. Kim Yun-sik makes a similar point about the nationalist implications of the story, which focus on the fulfillment of *chŏng* (or lack thereof) as a specifically Korean, not an individual, problem. See Kim (1999: 255–56).

20. Written by an anonymous hand sometime during the latter half of the eighteenth century, this story begins when the son of an upper-class family and the daughter of a socially despised *kisaeng* (female entertainer) meet and fall in love at first sight. Soon after their romance begins, Ch'unhyang's lover, Yi Myong-nyong, is called to the capital. Shortly after his departure, an evil provincial governor, enraptured by the beauty of Ch'unhyang, demands her services. When she refuses his advances, she is sent to prison, where she endures beatings and other pitiless atrocities with tremendous fortitude. Finally, her lover returns, rescues her, punishes the evil governor, and they live happily ever after.

21. Unlike some scholars of *mujŏng*, including Ann Lee (1991) and Jin-kyung Lee (2000), who maintain that the principal male protagonist of the novel, Hyŏng-sik, is "awakened" through a brief erotic encounter in Pyŏngyang, I am much more in agreement with Kim Tong-in's (1959) assessment of Hyŏng-sik as a "failed character" precisely because he is unable to relate to women outside of the bounds of the sexual and the physical (see Chapter 3 in this volume). Indeed, as the narrator himself points put, "Hyŏng-sik was, indeed, a man of no feeling [*mujŏng*]" (1996: 300), this being a critical assessment of him that is made throughout the novel:

> Hyŏng-sik's conception of love had not evolved and was still primitive. It was the kind of love that children experience when they like each other and don't want to be separated. It was the sort of love that only uncivilized people feel when they fall in love with a pretty face. If there is a difference, the concept of love experienced by uncivilized peoples is quickly transformed into simple physical lust, but Hyŏng-sik's concept of love did take into account an emotional element. Nevertheless, his understanding of emotional love was in name only as he did not really understand what it meant. He did not know that true love comes from mutual empathy. Hyŏng-sik's concept of love was, in fact, no different from the view held in ages past, an era in which people had not yet found enlightenment. (1996: 305)

22. In the largely autobiographical work "To My Young Friend," the hero, who is married, writes this letter to his lover. Its themes no doubt mirrored Yi Kwang-su's own predicament:

> Is this really a crime? Is it a crime for a married man to love another woman? My heart tells me it is and yet that it is not, that it is natural [for me to love you]. I was not responsible for my married status. I was married even before I knew what marriage was, what men and women were. My parents simply made a contract on

their own and society approved. My marriage was not of my own volition. I don't feel legally or morally bound toward my marriage because it was forced on me by a third party who took advantage of my young innocence. (1993b: 297)

23. Chapter 4 will explore the trope of separating and reuniting couples as it applies to student nationalist discourse of the late 1980s. It should be pointed out, however, that this trope was not restricted to students, but was also used in organizing the perception of the national division in the mass media. As the phenomenal success of the blockbuster film *Swiri* (1999) reveals, the trope of separating and reuniting couples had deep political implications that colored the way Koreans responded to the division of the two Koreas. A short synopsis of the film can be found in Chapter 4.

Chapter 3

1. Gayatri Spivak (1989: 227).

2. Yi Kwang-su, "The Benefits Which Christianity Has Conferred on Korea," *Korean Mission Field* 14, no. 2 (1918), 34.

3. Yi Kwang-su (1996). Because of Yi Kwang-su's ambivalent relationship with nationalism, his "canonical" status in modern Korean nationalist literature has been controversial. My reading of his work does not aim to improve his status as a Korean patriot. What concerns me here is simply to read *Mujŏng* within the specific historical and cultural confines in which it was written.

4. At the turn of the twentieth century a new social formation arose calling itself the Enlightenment Movement (*kaemŏng undong*). Its members, many of whom were also Christian converts, were among the Western-educated offshoot of a small but influential intellectual class who monopolized the appropriation of Western ideas, signs, and discourses. In particular, they sought to transform their society through (national) spiritual renewal. For Christian reformists like Yi Kwang-su, this philosophy of change embraced Protestantism's teachings of the Word, and the inherent relationship between literacy and self-improvement that these teachings implied. As bearers of the Book, these early Christian nationalists put great faith and effort into teaching Koreans how to read. By transforming the individual from within him/herself through the medium of the printed word, these nationalists argued that the written text could accomplish much the same political goals as public, armed struggle. Literacy, in other words, would lead to liberation.

5. In Chinese Confucian thought there cannot be the one without the many. As the Chinese sage Chang Tsai wrote: "The Great Harmony is called the Way. It embraces the nature which underlies all counter processes of floating and sinking, rising and falling, and motion and rest. It is the origin of the process of fusion and intermingling, of overcoming and being overcome, and of expansion and contraction" (Chen 1969: 159). The Way is therefore not an undifferentiated continuum but a unity full of clear albeit asymmetrical distinctions.

6. A brief summary of the main plot of *Mujŏng* is as follows: The school teacher, Yi Hyŏng-sik is torn between two women. The first is Yŏng-ch'ae, a virtuous daughter of Hyŏng-sik's former schoolmaster and to whom he was betrothed early in life. Due to family circumstances, however, Yŏng-ch'ae has becomes a *kisaeng* to help support her father and brothers and after many years of not seeing each other, Yŏng-

ch'ae suddenly reappears in Hyŏng-sik's life. The second woman is Sŏn-hyŏng, the beautiful daughter of a rich church elder who is also Hyŏng-sik's English language student. Sŏn-hyŏng's father has arranged for English lessons for his daughter because he views Hyŏng-sik as a potential son-in-law and plans to send them both to the United States to study. The promise of marriage to the beautiful Sŏn-hyŏng and his desire to study in America is so attractive to Hyŏng-sik that he begins to contemplate breaking off his previous engagement with Yŏng-ch'ae. However, before he can decide what he will do, Yŏng-ch'ae is raped by an evil schoolmaster, Bae Hak-gam, and in desperation, she heads to Pyŏngyang where she plans to commit suicide. Hyŏng-sik follows her but then returns empty-handed, having decided to marry Son-hyŏng after all. On the way to Pyŏngyang, Yong-ch'ae meets Pyŏng-uk, an "enlightened" woman, who befriends her and persuades her not to kill herself. At the end of the novel, all four characters meet up by chance on a train, but rain has flooded the tracks, making it impossible to go any further. All four characters therefore decide to organize a benefit concert for the flood victims. After the concert is over, they promise each other to work for the betterment of the nation as they each embark upon their respective voyages to study abroad.

7. Much like the Japanese *geisha*, the Korean *kisaeng* were women of low social standing who were nevertheless well educated. They provided men of wealth and nobility intelligent, lively conversation and entertainment.

8. In a scathing critique of *Mujŏng*, Kim Tong-in berates the author for creating "such a weak and amoral" character as the novel's principal male protagonist:

> At the very least, Hyŏng-sik is a weak and amoral man. It must have been very difficult for the author to use such an amoral character as a venue to elucidate his concept of love and the new life perspective [*insaenggwan*] and to explain the new morality [*sin todŏk*]. The novel is, from beginning to the end, full of contradictions which derive from the fact that the author chose the wrong type of character to be its central protagonist. Of course contradictions will arise when such an amoral character without any real political convictions of his own becomes the vehicle for expressing such great and deep concepts as love. The author's use of Hyŏng-sik as a vehicle to convey his ideas can be likened to a man who strikes a bamboo pole with a stick. (Kim 1959: 33)

9. The moment of Yŏng-ch'ae's "awakening" also coincides with the recognition of herself as an artist-*kisaeng*, not a *kisaeng*-prostitute (which is Hyŏng-sik's view of her) or mere "body." This epiphany causes her to relinquish her plans to kill herself and live happily with Pyŏng-uk:

> A *kisaeng* is a type of artist. But it is said that her art is used for vulgar purposes. In the olden days, famous *kisaeng* were all artists. They were all musicians and they also knew how to sing and dance, write poetry and draw. Therefore, we consider them today to be artists. If this is true, she [Yŏng-ch'ae] thought, then she too must be an artist. She thought perhaps that her calling in life was to become an artist. Like Pyŏng-uk, she thought perhaps she should also study music? She thought that dancing and singing, which she had so despised, had meaning. Before she knew it, Yŏng-ch'ae ceased thinking about death and thought instead about striving to live happily with Pyŏng-uk. She felt a gleeful joy stir within her heart. (Yi 1996: 264)

10. In Confucian thought, the body was conceived not as one's own individual possession, but as a sacred gift from one's parents to be preserved and cared for in their name. "The body is that which has been transmitted to us by our parents. Dare anyone allow himself to be irreverent in the employment of their legacy?" (Tu Wei Ming 1985: 118). Hence the rich reservoir of body-related language in the Confucian classics. Proper body etiquette and ritualized practice allowed people in the present, through their physical actions, to "represent the splendid world of the Confucian past" (Barlow 1994: 178). Barlow points out that women's adherence to strictly observed protocol affected "gender" relationally by "linking good behavior to current enactments of Confucian texts that inscribed kin difference" (Barlow 1994: 178). Likewise, taking care of one's body was taken as a sign of filial piety. As Ming observes: "In the *Saying of the Confucian School*, Confucius instructs the filial son to endure only light physical punishment from an enraged father. To run away from a severe beating, the argument goes, is not only to protect the body which has been entrusted to him by his parents, but also respects the fatherliness of his father that may have been temporarily obscured by rage" (Tu Wei Ming 1985: 120).

Chapter 4

1. Im Su-gyŏng was released from prison in South Korea after president Kim Young-sam took office in 1992. She graduated from Han'guk University of Foreign Studies.

2. *Chuch'e* can literally be translated as "autonomy" or "self-reliance." "Ron" literally means "doctrine" or "treatise." Michael Robinson (1984: 124) traces the idea of *chuch'e*, which is the most important tenet of the *Chuch'e* Thought of Kim Il Sung, to the historian Sin Ch'ae-ho (1880–1935). Although it is hard to prove (given the difficulty of North Koreans to credit alternative sources of inspiration for their own dogma), it is clear that Sin's use of the concepts of *chuch'e* served as important precedents for the development of the highly nationalistic strain in the *Chuch'e* Thought of Kim Il Sung. The *chuch'e* idea as defined by Sin literally means "self-reliance" or "independence" in politics, economy, defense, and ideology. But it also encompasses other meanings in the way equivalent expressions—"*chachusŏng*" (self-reliance) or "*tongnip*" (independence)—do not. *Chuch'e* connotes not only an idea, but a "Korean way of being" that is very much similar in meaning to the Japanese *kokutai* (*kukch'e* in Korean). "*Chu*" can be roughly translated as "master" or "main," so that "*chuch'e*" is something like the "master" or "main" ethics or principles by which Koreans are expected to lead their lives. Opposing Korean reliance on foreigners (*sadaejuŭi*, or "flunkeyism" as North Koreans translate it), Sin Ch'ae-ho, like Kim Il Sung after him, advocated complete economic, political, and cultural independence for all Koreans. Ideas of "racial essence" and "bloodline" (*hyŏlt'ong*) also played an essential part in this nationalist philosophy. For both Sin Ch'ae-ho and Kim Il Sung, the immutable racial core passed on through generations was viewed as *the* key characteristic defining the Korean nation. In this way, nationalism was the "creation of an identity that uncovered this autonomous racial feeling and made it self-conscious" (Robinson 1984: 133–34). South Korean *chuch'eron* has incorporated all these ideas in developing its new nationalist historiography. For a good discussion of Sin Ch'ae-ho's work and its historical link to the *Chuch'e* Thought of Kim Il Sung, see Robinson (1984).

3. Popular suspicion of the KDP can be traced to KDP members' former relationship to the Japanese colonial regime. The early association of American officers with the KDP thus set in motion prejudices that persisted throughout the Occupation and cast doubt on the legitimacy of KDP leadership. Even after the postwar period, South Korea's leaders were still hard-pressed to expunge themselves from their "tainted" past. The first president of South Korea, Syngman Rhee, while himself heralded as an anti-Japanese patriot, still presided over a bureaucratic and military structure that had been trained almost entirely by the Japanese, as did Chang Myŏn, who ruled briefly in 1960–1961. (Chang Myŏn also took a Japanese name during the latter part of the colonial period.) Park Chung-hee had been an officer in the Japanese Kwantung Army. The taint of these foreign alliances was thus handed down after liberation in 1945 to a new generation of Koreans who had left the Japanese bureaucratic system in South Korea virtually intact. For an excellent discussion of these issues see Cumings (1981, 1984).

4. Marx and Lenin, along with intellectuals of the Frankfurt School and Third World theorists like Samir Amin, were required reading throughout the 1970s. After the Kwangju massacre, however, the reading list was narrowed, and works about or relating to the *Chuch'e* Thought of Kim Il Sung gained in currency among student dissidents. Furthermore, Kim Il Sung's ideological emphasis on the centrality of the living subject as the active motivator of history, a view not shared by Marx or Lenin, allowed the movement to adopt an unabashedly nationalist stance.

5. Roughly translated as "oppressed people" or the "oppressed masses," *minjung* is actually a political term that broadly refers to those who are peripheral to the existing power structure. Within the capitalist relations of production, the *minjung* is made up of the urban poor, peasants, and the working lower and middle classes. The *minjung* also make up that portion of society that is adversely affected by the division and by South Korea's "subordinate" relationship to the United States.

6. In this story, the farmer Gyŏn-u and the princess Chik-nyŏ fall in love at first sight. But when Gyŏn-u's father realizes that his daughter is in love with a commoner, he banishes them to opposite poles of the galaxy. Unhappy to be separated from her lover, Chik-nyŏ cries day and night, threatening the earth with huge floods. In sympathy, magpies gather from all over the earth and make a bridge where the two lovers can meet one day of every year, on the seventh day of the seventh month. This story explains why the rainy season begins shortly after this date; Chik-nyŏ is weeping once again for the lover she misses.

7. The ritualistic portrayal of evil and chaos suffered by the nation at the hands of treacherous rebels appears in *Yongbi ŏch'ŏn ka* (Songs of the Flying Dragons), which was written to celebrate the ascendancy of General Yi Sŏng-gye to the throne in 1392. As in other early histories of Confucian Korea, the nation is portrayed as being torn between good and evil forces, with the final restoration of goodness fulfilled by the dynastic founder, in this case Yi Sŏng-gye. Furthermore, women emerged as decisive instruments in the restoration of goodness. By their diligent pursuit of unfailing loyalty, sagacity, courage, and piety, these women were portrayed as vital to the foundation of the new dynasty. Anecdotes extolling the virtues of Lady Min, for example, become the subject of cantos 108 and 109 in the *Songs*. Cited for her role in moments of national crisis, she is praised for her strategy in devising a plan to ensnare an evil official who threatened to block the foundation of the new kingdom. Lady Min's heroism is compared, in this canto, with similar heroic deeds performed

by the wife of Wang-Kŏn, the founder of the Koryŏ dynasty, "whose cogent arguments and encouragement were held to be responsible for Wang's decision to oppose his tyrannous master and found his own kingdom" (Lee 1975: 82). As embodiments of chastity and wisdom, these women were praised not only for their constancy of affection, but loyalty in deed. Themes of loyalty and loss also frequently appeared as the subject of Korean *sijo* and *kasa* poetry, particularly those written by exiled officials. Chŏng Ch'ŏl's sixteenth-century *kasa, Sa miin kok* (Hymn of Constancy), for example, composed at a time of factional strife when he was forced from the court to spend several years in exile, likens the poet's loyalty to King Sŏngjo to that of a distant wife longing for her husband. Likewise, declarations of devotion for one's lost husband also became the standard theme in the poetry of the 1920s and 1930s. In the works of Han Yong-un, Yi Kwang-su, Kim So-wŏl, and Yi Sang-hwa, the analogy between "lost love" and the "lost homeland" was used to evoke their experience of Japanese colonialism. Thus, the idea of loyalty in separation took on a new and political significance to express these poets' patriotic devotion to liberating Korea from (evil) colonial rule.

8. In Chosŏn Korea (1392–1910), when the bride entered her husband's house, she was forced to make a place for herself in a female world in which status and authority were determined by the man to whom a woman was attached. In particular, the mother-in-law/daughter-in-law relationship was a source of great friction. Also, in the case where several married brothers lived together, there existed latent tensions between the sisters-in-law. Human relationships within the female sphere were further complicated by the presence of secondary wives. These potential domestic conflicts and jealousies created a stressful, and oftentimes unhappy, existence for the young bride. When she was mistreated by her mother-in-law and other older female members of the domestic household, she could hardly expect sympathy from her husband. Because the relationship of the son to his parents took precedence over that to his wife, the young bride was often unable to seek her husband's protection against injuries inflicted upon her by his family. For a good discussion of these ideas see Mattielli (1977) and Deuchler (1992).

9. A translation of this work can be found in Lee (1981: 257–84). The theme of loyalty, loss, and reunion can also be found in the *Tale of Ong-nang*. Composed by an anonymous hand in the late eighteenth century, it tells the tale of a young woman, Ong-nang, whose fiancé is imprisoned for murder. Disguising herself as one of her fiancé's school friends, Ong-nang visits her husband-to-be in prison. After convincing him to run away while she takes his place, she remains to face almost certain death: "I am not educated, but I have heard about the conduct of loyal wives and virtuous maidens of old," she says to her lover. "There are many who substituted themselves for their husbands and faultlessly carried out their duties. I intend to follow their example. I may not be an exceptional person but my love has been constant from the beginning." In the end, however, the youth is pardoned for his crime "on account of his wife's exemplary behavior," and the happy couple is reunited. For a good translation of this tale see Baker (1976).

10. The 1999 blockbuster movie *Swiri* (referring to a kind of fish found only in the fresh waters of the Korean peninsula) also takes up this romantic theme in its portrayal of the North–South conflict. The central characters of the film are a North Korean female spy and a South Korean male government official. Sent to South Korea on a mission to disrupt a planned friendly soccer game between the two Koreas,

the female spy is set up with the South Korean official, who is unaware of her true identity. She eventually falls in love with him, as he does with her. The climax of the movie is when the two confront each other at the soccer stadium. Although they love each other desperately, their passion ends in tragedy when the North Korean woman dies at the hands of her lover.

11. The story of Korea's first founding father, Tan'gun, goes something like this: before Tan'gun's birth, his mother, who was a bear, wanted to be transformed into a human being. The God Whanin heard her wish and, together with a tiger, the bear was shut up in a cave for twenty-one days with nothing to eat but some garlic. The tiger lost patience and so he fled; the bear, however, emerged from the cave as a woman. Whanin's son, Whanung, fell in love with her and she bore Tan'gun out of that union. Tan'gun then allegedly founded the first Korean "state," called "Tan'gun Chosŏn," nearly five thousand years ago, in 2333 B.C.

12. When it was reported that a Korean prostitute was tortured to death by an American soldier in November 1992, national outrage sparked citywide demonstrations and protest in Seoul. Taxi drivers refused to serve American soldiers for nearly two months after the incident, and older Korean citizens (mostly women) gathered in downtown Seoul to shout anti-American slogans for at least a week after the incident. See *Stars and Stripes* (Pacific Edition), November 19, 1992.

Chapter 5

The presidential speeches of Park Chung-hee are printed in a 16–volume collection entitled *Pak Chŏnghui taet'ongnyŏng yonsolmunjip* (President Park Chung-hee's Collected Speeches), vols. 1–3, 5–16 (Seoul: Taet'ongyŏng pisŏsil, 1965–79); vol. 4 (Seoul: Tonga ch'ulp'ansa, 1967). The collection will be referred to below as *PTOC*.

1. This quotation can be found on pages 118–21 of Park (1970b).

2. "5.16 hyŏngmyŏng chae 11 chunyŏn mit chae 7 hoe 5.16 minjoksang sisangsik ch'isa" (Address Commemorating the 11th Anniversary of the May 16 Revolution and the May 16 National Prize Award Ceremony, May 16, 1972), *PTOC* (vol. 9, 181).

3. As we saw in Chapter 1, Sin Ch'ae-ho had also embarked upon a similar project. Lydia Liu (1995) has persuasively argued that the often assumed relationship between the subject and the object in contemporary East–West cultural criticism is not particularly useful in unraveling the complex dynamic between Japan, China, and Korea. For one thing, the same discourse that had justified Japan's imperialist ambitions in Korea during the early twentieth century were later employed and adapted within the internal Korean debate on national character. Far from merely reproducing Japanese imperialist representations, Korea's nationalist elites used them to justify Korea's new relationship toward China, including a complete reassessment of the nation's Confucian past, which paved the way for the rise of a new military elite in North Korea. In this way, Japanese imperialist discourse was put to a variety of "unintended" usages that present us with a different set of problems from the Orientalist problematic that Said has treated in another context (Liu 1994: 60).

4. In a recent poll conducted in 1998, more than two-thirds of South Koreans responded that Park Chung-hee was the country's greatest president. The same poll

named the Saemaul Undong as their country's greatest achievement in the last fifty years, followed by the hosting of the 1998 Seoul Olympics and the construction of the Seoul–Pusan Highway. See *Chosŏn ilbo*, July 15, 1998.

5. Message delivered at the National Saemaul Incoming-Boosting Skill Competition (*Saemaul Undongŭl sodŭk chungdae ch'ukchin taehwa ch'ishi*), May 18, 1972, in *PTOC* (vol. 9, 186). A translation of this speech appears in Park (1979), 156–57.

6. *Sadaejuŭi* ("Serving the Great") referred to the Confucian tributary relationship between Korea and China practiced throughout the Chosŏn dynasty. In Korean nationalist writings during the colonial period, it became associated with Korean dependence, weakness, and lack of autonomy, and hence, was directly connected to all the negative elements of Korea's traditional society that had contributed to the nation's fall into colonial dependence.

7. *Sin a ilbo*, March 24, 1972.

8. *Seoul Sinmun*, April 8, 1972.

9. New Year's Press Interview, January 18, 1974, *PTOC* (vol. 11, 64). See also Park (1979: 217).

10. New Year's Press Interview, p. 64.

11. Ibid.

12. Ibid., p. 65.

13. Ibid.

14. Admiral Yi Sun-sin was naval commander of Cholla Province and is most renowned for his role in defeating the Japanese during the Invasions of 1592 and 1597. Before the Invasions, Admiral Yi had keenly felt the need to strengthen the country's naval forces and had energetically set about building warships and training their crews. The most famous warship of this period, the "turtle ship" (*kŏbuksŏn*) was his invention. Later, Admiral Yi was dismissed from his post as naval commander due to a political intrigue against him; he was later imprisoned. When the Hideyoshi launched a second invasion of the Korean peninsula in 1597, however, the new commander-in-chief of Naval Forces of the South, Wŏn Kyun, was sorely defeated and the distraught Korean government hastily reinstated Admiral Yi to his former post. With a mere dozen warships, Admiral Yi won a resounding victory, thus saving the nation from further attack.

15. See "Commemoration Speech on the Occasion of the 424th Birthday of Admiral Yi Sun-sin," April 28, 1969, *PTOC* (vol. 6, 64).

16. The slogan "rich nation, strong army" (*puguk kangbyŏng* 富 國 強 兵) was also widely used to sum up Japan's early industrialization efforts, which were led by Japanese military industrialists to enhance national security by "catching up with the West" (*oitsuke, oikose*). Park no doubt became familiar with the slogan when he was a Japanese military cadet studying at the Manchurian Military Academy in the early 1940s. While it is way beyond the scope of this essay to examine the link between the military power and the modernizing activities of the Kwantung Army, it is clear that Park's modernizing reform and ideology were heavily influenced by his experiences in Manchuria and that it was there that Park first witnessed the intimate connection between military power and modernizing reforms on a grand scale.

17. Park Chung-hee, April 4, 1972, *PTOC* (vol. 9, 164). See also Park (1979: 148).

18. Park Chung-hee, May 16, 1972, *PTOC* (vol. 9, 183). The official English version of this speech uses the word "militia" to translate "*ŭibyŏng*" (righteous army), which fails to demonstrate the historical/genealogical relationship that Park was trying to convey in linking the Saemaul leaders with the patriotic guerrilla bands that rose up against the enemy during the Japanese Invasions of 1592 and 1597. The *ŭibyŏng* also waged an armed struggle against Japanese troops during the late nineteenth century shortly after Queen Min's assassination in 1895 and continued its struggle throughout the colonial period.

19. Park Chung-hee, "Commemoration Speech on the Occasion of the 424th Birthday of Admiral Yi Sun-sin," April 28, 1969, *PTOC* (vol. 6, 64). See also Park Chung-hee (1970: 242).

20. It should be noted that one of the first symbolic acts Park performed after taking over as president in May 1961 was to undertake the project of rebuilding the Hyŏnch'ung-sa Shrine at Onyang, Chungch'ŏng-do Province, the ancient birthplace of Admiral Yi, which was completed in 1969. Converting the ancient ruins into a national shrine, Park invested heavily in Hyŏnch'ung-sa, commodifying this past for the hundreds of schoolchildren who were sent there to imbibe the patriotic spirit of Yi Sun-sin. Around the same period, another tribute to Admiral Yi Sun-sin was undertaken with the erection of a bronze figure of the Admiral, which still stands smack in the middle of the main boulevard in downtown Seoul.

21. The Saemaul Leadership Training Institute in Suwŏn was the most well-known training center in Korea and Saemaul training at other institutes generally followed the same curricula. As the brainchild of Park Chung-hee, both the curricula and training guidelines were carefully reviewed by the president and he visited the Institute frequently.

22. In the dozens of letters and personal accounts that I examined, the vast majority of farmers who had participated in the leadership training program at Suwŏn apparently did so voluntarily, despite the fact that their absence from their farms often put a severe economic strain on their families. Whether or not these letters were censored can only be guessed at. The point is, however, that Park Chung-hee and the Saemaul Undong leaders wanted the Saemaul leadership training program to *appear* as if matriculation was completely voluntary. These accounts are currently housed in the archives of the Saemaul Institute Research Center in Sŏnggnamsi, Kyŏnggi-do, South Korea.

23. Both men and women participated equally in the movement. Although it is beyond the scope of this chapter to investigate the gendered implications of the Saemaul Undong, in principle, the movement was conceived as a "genderless movement" and the government's policy guidelines did not automatically segregate male and female roles as planners and beneficiaries of specific projects. For example, a basic textbook for Saemaul projects published by the Ministry of Government Administration and Home Affairs (MOGAHA) in 1975 contains detailed information about various types of projects and how they should be executed without *any* reference to the division of labor by sex. Saemaul activities recognized women's important contribution to national development by ensuring girls and boys equal access to education. As for the training of Saemaul leaders, women participated in leadership training programs, although men and women did not attend these events together. The course of instruction, including the emphasis on physical fitness, exposure to "success case-studies," group discussions, and training methodologies, was identical.

Although gender differentiation in men's and women's roles obviously did exist, in no way were women perceived as the "bearers of tradition" as was the case in other postcolonial nationalist movements. This is because the aim of the movement was to "reinvent" a (warrior) tradition in which hard-working, strong-willed, and enterprising individuals of *both* sexes were cultivated and valued. Indeed, to the extent that peasant women had always worked in the fields and in their communities means that their image and role did not change that significantly with the introduction of the Saemaul Undong. It remains to be seen how the masculinized discourse of Park's nationalism affected women's lives and how their participation in the Saemaul Undong altered their perceptions not only of themselves but of their "redeemed" and "re-masculinized" husbands.

24. The "spiritual transformation" of the wayward farmer into a Saemaul leader was the central tool of Saemaul indoctrination. The same theme of redemption also frequently appears in the private correspondences of Saemaul leaders who consistently describe their patriotic "reawakening" in terms of a "spiritual transformation" (*chŏngsinchŏk kaksŏng*).

25. Kim Tae-shin, unpublished letter, 1975. Much of my information about the training program at the Suwŏn Institute relied on trainees' unpublished correspondences. These correspondences, as well as a vast majority of other unpublished sources, including many photographs, are housed at the Research Center at the Saemaul Institute, Songnam-si, Korea.

26. On October 16, 1972, Park declared martial law, junked the existing constitution, disbanded the National Assembly, and prepared a plan for the indirect election of the president. Park called his new system *yushin*, or "revitalizing reforms." While *yushin* was the philosophical blueprint of Park's views on national Self-strengthening, the Saemaul Undong was its concrete realization. See Park Chung-hee, *Uri minjokŭi nagalgil sahoe chaegonŭi inyŏm* (Our Nation's Path: Ideology of Social Reconstruction) (Seoul, Kwangmyon chulp'ansa, 1978), translated in Park (1970b).

27. This has been the position of contemporary dissident students as well as dissident farmers' groups who have cited Park's training as a Japanese military officer as evidence of his anti-nationalist credentials. Likewise, critics of the Saemaul Undong have taken issue with Park's portrayal of Korea's traditional farming communities as "lazy" and "unprogressive." Although much of this dissent was suppressed during the Park years, the *Wŏlgan ssiŭlŭi sŏri* (The Voice of the People) published articles that were extremely critical of the Saemaul Undong and in particular, questioned the Park regime's characterization of Korea's traditional farming communities. See for example, Kim Kyŏng-chae's "Tonghakhyŏkmyŏnggwa nongminŭi maekpak" (The Tonghak Revolution and the Pulse of the Farmers) (1979, 2:26–35); and Pak Hyŏn-ch'ae's "Nongminundongkwa nongminŭisikhwa" (Farmers' Movement and Changing Farmers' Consciousness) (1979, 2:45–54). (Note: *ssi* in *ssiŭlŭi* refers to "seeds," or the "source." The title appears to be a play on words because "ssi" in this context refers to the "original people," meaning farmers who work with "seeds.")

28. Official photographs of Park Chung-hee frequently showed him dressed in farmer's garb, eating and working with local farmers. In addition, official biographies of Park always played up his agrarian upbringing. As Kim Chŏng-sin (1970) writes of Park's triumphal return home: "The villagers, old or young, thronged as far as the trail to welcome the great man who was born and grew up in their own village.

. . . President Park also met his old childhood friends late that evening . . . the President inquired after the health of those who were not present. . . . The President turned to look at us correspondents with a grin. He was no longer the President but 'a farmer's son' who was drinking with his old friends. They drank and talked almost endlessly" (218).

Chapter 6

Kim Il Sung passed away after this chapter was written. This chapter is based on the materials available before Kim's death.

1. The link that I hope to show between narrative and the social/political community will reveal that narratives are more than mere reflections of social reality; they are part of the consulting mechanism that makes "reality" real. Far from originating externally and imposing a story on what was previously a mass of unrelated facts, narratives—and particularly narratives concerned with nation-building—act to construct our experiences of time and space in the lived reality of our political community. For an excellent discussion of these and related ideas, see David Carr (1986); Robert Canary and Henry Kozicki, eds. (1978); Lionel Gossman (1990); and Paul Ricoeur (1984).

2. Despite its being written in 1967, this poem is still very popular among contemporary student dissidents and is often cited in student pamphlets.

3. Tan'gun, according to legendary sources, was born from a she-bear and fathered by the god Hwanung, and founded the ancient kingdom of (Tan'gun) Chosŏn in 2333 B.C.

4. These student speeches were recorded on April 19, 1989, at Seoul National University and were delivered in commemoration of the April 1960 Student Revolution.

5. This book is a depiction of the 1980 Kwangju Incident, and was listed on a sales ban until the early 1990s.

6. This monument is located in Kwangju City. The piece is a nonfictional account "compiled" by the South Cholla Social Movement Association. Although published under Hwang's name, it was actually written by Lee Jae-ui.

7. *T'oji* was published over a period of thirty-five years, from 1960 through 1994. In 1894, the Tonghak ("Eastern Learning") Movement erupted in a revolutionary peasant struggle. It owed its success to the peasantry's deep hostility and resentment toward the *yangban* (scholar-bureaucrat) class and its resistance to the inroads made by foreign powers within Korea. Unable to put down the uprising by itself, the Korean government appealed to China for military support. China's response was immediate, but within a few days Japan also sent troops. This set the stage for the events leading to the Sino-Japanese War of 1894–1895.

8. In spite of a government ban to let South Korean students participate in the thirteenth annual 1989 World Festival of Youth and Students in North Korea, Chŏndaehyŏp (National Council of Student Representatives) student leaders in Seoul had surreptitiously devised a scheme to send Im Su-gyŏng, a senior French major at Han'guk University of Foreign Studies, to the festival via Japan and Germany. Upon her return to South Korea in August 1989 she was sent to prison and was released after Kim Yŏng-sam took office in 1992. Chŏn Moon-hwan was a leader in Chŏndaehyŏp and played an active role in planning and organizing Im's journey to North Korea.

9. Em relates that "Marx, Lenin, along with intellectuals of the Frankfurt School and Third-World theorists like Samir Amin were required reading throughout the 1970s" (1993: 484). After the Kwangju massacre, however, the reading list was narrowed, and works about or relating to the *Chuch'e* Thought of Kim Il Sung gained in currency among student dissidents. Kim Il Sung's ideological emphasis on the centrality of the living subject as the active motivator of history, a view not shared by Marx or Lenin, allowed the movement to adopt an unabashedly nationalist stance. See Henry Em (1993).

10. This is an anonymous publication put forth by the Party History Institute of the Central Committee of the Workers' Party of Korea, eds. (Pyŏngyang: Pyŏngyang Languages Publisher's House, 1969).

11. *Korea Today* 3 (April 1982): 33.

12. In this sense, Kim Chŏng-il's political legitimacy as Kim Il Sung's successor stems solely from this Communist dynastic system of agnatic succession. Thus the enormous effort by the North Korean leadership to shape Kim Chŏng-il in the image of the "benevolent father," although I suspect he will never attain, for various obvious reasons, the prestige that his father enjoyed. Since Kim Il Sung's death on July 8, 1994, Kim Chŏng-il has been able to keep the mantle of the "revolution" alive, although I believe his role in the political process is largely symbolic.

13. Kwangju Commemoration, May 1989. These observations were made by students I interviewed in Kwangju city on the occasion of the 1980 Kwangju Uprising commemoration.

Chapter 7

1. Park Chung-hee (1970a: 167), from a speech given in 1962.

2. In July 1953, North Korea, China, and the United States signed an armistice agreement (South Korea refused to be a signatory). There was no peace treaty signed among the participants.

3. A good case in point is the inauguration of the Second Saemaul Undong (New Community Movement) and the Second Nation-Building Movement (Chae 2ŭi kŏn'guk) in 1998, both of which were modeled after successful national campaign movements initiated by former president Park Chung-hee in the 1970s. In addition, Kim's ebullient praise of Park Chung-hee, which came just two days before the thirty-seventh anniversary of Park's May 16, 1961, coup d'état, was viewed as a historical reevaluation of Park's place in Korean history. Further efforts to "make peace" with past military leaders was displayed in the dispatch of President Kim Dae-jung's junior coalition partner, Prime Minister Kim Jong-il, to Kwangju for a ceremony commemorating the nineteenth anniversary of the Kwanjgu Uprising on May 18, 1999.

4. The Righteous Army (*ŭibyŏng*) here refers to the guerrilla forces led by Hideyoshi that sprang up against the Japanese in 1592; the Independence Army (*tongnipkun*) refers to the guerrilla army (also referred to as *ŭibyŏng*) raised against the Japanese shortly after the assassination of Queen Min in 1895; and the Restoration Army (*kwangbokkun*) refers to the Korean Provincial Government (KPG)- and Kuomintang-allied army, whose officers later came to dominate the top levels of the Republic of Korea Army (ROKA).

5. *Chŏnjaeng Kinyŏmgwan chŏnsi yŏnch'u kyehoek* (Exhibition Display Plans for the War Memorial) (1990: 12). Hereafter *CCKNK.*

6. According to the actual record of Korean graduates from the Japanese Army Officer Military Academy, none went to North Korea. Instead, all of those who went on to pursue a military career went into the South Korean military, many of them occupying key positions in the ROK military in the 1940s through the 1960s.

Epilogue

1. The suggestive coincidence between nationalism and sexuality is the topic of concern in George Mosse's pioneering work, *Nationalism and Sexuality: Middle-Class Morality and Sexual Norms in Modern Europe* (1985). Analyzing the relationship between nationalism and the social norms associated with it, Mosse attempts to trace the proliferation of sexual ideas of middle-class respectability in Germany and, to a lesser extent, in Italy, England, and France. To a large extent, his work can be seen as a continuation of Foucault's *History of Sexuality*. While Foucault never addresses the problem of nationalism explicitly, both he and Mosse viewed sexuality essentially as a function of the power structure that seemed to repress it. Decency, respectability, and the social norms previously associated with religious doctrine of the seventeenth century reappeared in nationalism at the end of the eighteenth century as "the struggle to control sex—beyond those controls already attempted by the various churches" and as "part of a larger effort to cope with the ever more obvious results of industrialization and political upheavals" (Mosse 1985: 9). (For Foucault, this period marked the beginning of a "repressive discourse on sex"; for Mosse, it coincided with the emergence of a new form of communal imagining.) Thus, while Mosse locates the "repressive" constraints on sexuality in nationalism, Foucault sees the techniques of power and control exercised over sex implied everywhere in capitalist society as a whole: "This bio-power was without question an indispensable element in the development of capitalism; the latter would not have been possible without the controlled insertion of bodies into the machinery of production" (Foucault 1978: 140–41). The allegiance between the nation-state, capitalism, and bourgeois morality thus constituted a mechanism of social control by which nationalism—the natural by-product of all three—helped create modern middle-class mores of "respectability," which in turn enforced a whole code of social behavior and sexual practice considered to be "normal."

2. Kim Dae-jung's victory in the presidential election held on December 18, 1997, marked the first peaceful transfer of power from a ruling to an opposition party following national liberation in 1945.

3. The official Web site of the Chong Wa Dae (Blue House) writes of Kim's presidential victory: "This was not only a dramatic triumph for Kim, who had endured four decades of harsh suppression and tribulation, but a giant step toward the realization of full-fledged democracy in Korea" (see http://www.cwd.go.kr/english/president/profile). For representative news articles representing Kim Dae-jung's personal struggle as the nation's struggle, see *Nyusŭ p'ip'ul* (97.12.26–98.1.1): 10–14; *Hangyorae 21* (19981.1.): 16–18; *Chugan Chosŏn* (1998.1.1.): 20–21; *Tonga ilbo* 1997.12.22; *Wŏlgan Chosŏn* (1998.1): 110–22; *Hangyorae shinmun* (1997.12.20); *News* + (1998.1.1): 12–14. These are just a few of the many articles on this topic that appeared in the popular press shortly after the 1997 presidential elections.

4. For a description of this project and a detailed transcribed interview with President Kim about it and his views of Park Chung-hee, see *Wŏlgan Chosŏn* (1999.6): 186–97.

5. The official Web site of the Chong Wa Dae (Blue House) writes of Kim's "higher" endeavors: "Kim laid a firm foundation for peace and stability in Northeast Asia by reinforcing the nation's ability to deter war on the peninsula. Moreover, he threw his weight behind other pro-democracy movements in East Asia by dispatching Korean troops to the multinational force in East Timor. Indeed, he is endeavoring to bolster world peace and human rights under the banner of globalism." (See http://www.cwd.go.kr/english/president/profile.)

References

English Language

Allen, Horace. 1908. *Things Korean.* New York: Fleming H. Revell.

Anderson, Benedict. 1983. *Imagined Communities: Reflections on the Origin and Spread of Nationalism.* London: Verso.

Asad, Talal. 1973. "Two European Images of Non-European Rule." In *Anthropology and the Colonial Encounter,* ed. T. Asad. London: Athlone Press.

Baik Bong. 1969. *Kim Il Sung Biography: From Birth to Triumphant Return Homeland.* Tokyo: Miraisha.

Baker, Edward. 1976. "The Tale of Ong-nang." *Korea Journal.* Translated by E. Baker. Vol. 16, no. 5: 45–61.

Barlow, Tani. 1994. "Theorizing Women: *Funü, Guojia, Jiating* (Chinese Women, Chinese State, Chinese Family)." In *Scattered Hegemonies: Postmodernity and Transnational Feminist Practice,* ed. Interpal Grewal and Caren Kaplan. Minneapolis: University of Minnesota Press.

Baym, Nina. 1991. "Between Enlightenment and Victorian: Toward a Narrative of American Women Writers Writing History." *Critical Inquiry* 18, no.1 (Autumn 1991).

Beaver, Pierce. 1965. *All Loves Excelling: American Protestant Women in World Mission.* Ann Arbor: William Eerdmans.

Benjamin, Walter. 1968. *Illuminations: Essays and Reflections.* New York: Shocken Books.

———. 1999. *The Arcades Project.* Translated by Howard Eiland and Kevin McLaughlin. Cambridge, MA: Harvard University Press.

Bhabha, Homi. 1994. "The Location of Culture." New York: Routledge.

Braudel, Fernand. 1980. *On History.* Translated by S. Matthews. Chicago: University of Chicago Press.

Brooke, Timothy, and Andre Schmid. 2000. *Nation Work: Asian Elites and National Identities.* Ann Arbor: University of Michigan Press.

Brown, Arthur. 1919. *The Mastery of the Far East: The Story of Korea's Transformation and Japan's Rise to Supremacy in the Orient.* New York: Charles Scribner's Sons.

Brudnoy, David. 1970. "Japan's Experiment in Korea." *Monumenta Nipponica* 25: 172–216.

Butler, Judith. 1990. *Gender Trouble: Feminism and the Subversion of Identity.* New York: Routledge, Chapman & Hall.

Canary, Robert, and Henry Kozicki, eds. 1978. *The Writing of History: Literary Form and Historical Understanding.* Madison: University of Wisconsin Press.

Carr, David. 1986. *Time, Narrative and History.* Bloomington: University of Indiana Press.

Chan Wing-Tsit. 1963. *A Source Book in Chinese Philosophy.* Princeton: Princeton University Press.

Chandra, Vipan. 1986. "Sentiment and Ideology in the Nationalism of the Independence Club (1886–1898)." *Korean Studies* 10: 13–33.

Chang Duk-soon. 1970. *The Folk Treasury of Korea: Sources in Myth, Legend and Korean Oral Literature.* Seoul: Society of Korean Oral Literature.

Chatterjee, Partha. 1986. *Nationalist Thought and the Colonial World: A Derivative Discourse.* Dehli: Oxford University Press.

———. 1989. "Colonialism, Nationalism, and Colonialized Women: The Contest in India." *American Ethnologist* 16: 622–633.

Chen, Charles. 1969. *Neo-Confucianism, Etc.: Essays by Wing-tsit Chan.* Amherst: Oriental Society.

Cheong Ji-Woong. 1981. "Information, Education and Training in Saemaul Movement." In *Toward a New Community: Reports of International Research Seminar on the Saemaul Movement, 1980,* ed. Lee Man-gap. Seoul: Seoul National University.

Ching, Julia. 1985. "Yi Yulgok on the 'Four Beginnings and the Seven Emotions.'" In *The Rise of Neo-Confucianism in Korea,* ed. W. de Bary and John Haboush. New York: Columbia University Press.

Choe Dok-sin. 1987. *The Nation and I: For the Re-unification of the Motherland.* Pyŏngyang: Foreign Languages Publishing House.

Choi Jang-jip. 1993. "Political Cleavages in South Korea." In *State and Society in Contemporary Korea,* ed. Hagen Koo. Ithaca: Cornell University Press.

Clark, Allen. 1961. *History of the Korean Church.* Seoul: The Christian Literary Society of Korea.

Clifford, James. 1988. *The Predicament of Culture: Twentieth Century Ethnography, Literature and Art.* Cambridge, MA: Harvard University Press.

Cohn, Bernard S. 1980. "History and Anthropology: The State of Play." *Comparative Studies in Society and History* 22: 198–221.

———. 1981. "Anthropology and History in the 1980s: Towards a Rapprochement." *Journal of Interdisciplinary History* 12: 227–252.

———. 1987. *An Anthropologist Among the Historians and Other Essays.* New Delhi: Oxford University Press.

Comaroff, John, and Jean Comaroff. 1991. *Of Revelation and Revolution: Christianity, Colonialism and Consciousness in South Africa.* Chicago: University of Chicago Press.

———. 1992. *Ethnography and the Historical Imagination.* Boulder: Westview Press.

Conroy, Hillary. 1960. *The Japanese Seizure of Korea: 1868–1910: A Study of Realism and Idealism in International Relations.* Philadelphia: University of Philadelphia Press.

Cook, Harold. 1972. *Korea's 1884 Incident: Its Background and Kim Ok-kyun's Elusive Dream.* Seoul: Royal Asiatic Society.

Cott, Nancy. 1977. *The Bonds of Womanhood: "Women's Sphere" in New England, 1780–1835.* New Haven, CT: Yale University Press.

Craiger, John. 1968. "The Aims and Content of School Courses in Japanese History, 1872–1945." In *Japan's Modern Century,* ed. E. Skrzypczak. Tokyo: Voyagers Press.

Cumings, Bruce. 1981. *The Origins of the Korean War: Liberation and the Emergence of Separate Regimes, 1945–1947.* Princeton: Princeton University Press.

———. 1983. "Corporatism in North Korea." *Journal of Korean Studies* 4: 269–294.

———. 1997. *Korea's Place in the Sun: A Modern History.* New York: W.W. Norton.

de Bary, Theodore. 1958. *Sources of Japanese Tradition,* ed. T. de Bary. New York: Columbia University Press.

de Lauretis, Teresa. 1987. *Technologies of Gender.* Indiana: University of Indiana Press.

Deuchler, Martina. 1977. *Confucian Gentleman and Barbarian Envoys: The Opening of Korea, 1875–1885.* Seattle: University of Washington Press.

———. 1985. "Reject the False and Uphold the Straight: Attitudes Toward Heterodox Thought in Early Yi Korea." In *The Rise of Neo-Confucianism in Korea,* ed. W. de Bary and J. Kim Haboush. New York: Columbia University Press.

———. 1992. *The Confucian Transformation of Korea: A Study of Society and Ideology.* Cambridge, MA: Harvard University Press.

Douglas, Ann. 1977. *The Feminization of American Culture.* New York: Doubleday.

Douglas, Mary. 1966. *Purity and Danger: An Analysis of the Concepts of Pollution and Taboo.* London: Routledge and Kegan Paul.

Duara, Prasenjit. 1995. *Rescuing History from the Nation: Questioning Narratives of Modern China.* Chicago: University of Chicago Press.

———. 1997. "Why Is History Antitheorectical?" *Modern China* 24, no. 2: 105–120.

———. 1998. "Transnationalism and the Predicament of Sovereignty: China, 1900–1945." *American Historical Review* 102, no. 4: 1030–1051.

Duus, Peter. 1994. *The Abacus and the Sword.* Berkeley: University of California Press.

Eckert, Carter. 1991. *Offspring of Empire: The Koch'ang Kims and the Colonial Origins of Korean Capitalism, 1876–1945.* Seattle: University of Washington Press.

Elvin, Mark. 1984. "Female Virtue and the State in China." *Past and Present* (August 1984).

Em, Henry. 1999. "Minchok as a Modern and Democratic Construct: Sin Ch'aeho's Historiography." In *Colonial Modernity in Korea,* ed. Gi-Wook Chin and Michael Robinson. Cambridge, MA: Harvard University Press.

Fabian, Johannes. 1983. *Time and the Other: How Anthropology Makes Its Object.* New York: Columbia University Press.

Fairbank, John. 1989. *East Asia: Tradition and Transformation.* Boston: Houghton Mifflin.

Fenwick, Malcolm. 1911. *Church of Christ in Corea.* New York: Hodder and Stoughton.

Fiedler, Leslie. 1960. *Love and Death in the American Novel.* New York: Anchor Books.

Fogel, Joshua. 1995. *The Literature of Travel in the Japanese Rediscovery of China, 1862–1945.* Stanford: Stanford University Press, 1992.

Foucault, Michael. 1967. *Madness and Civilization: A History of Insanity in the Age of Reason.* Translated by R. Howard. London: Tavisock.

———. 1978. *History of Sexuality.* Translated by R. Hurley. New York: Pantheon Books.

Fukuzawa, Yukichi. 1985. *Fukuzawa Yukichi on Education: Selected Works.* Translated by Eiichi Kiyooka. Tokyo: University of Tokyo.

Gales, James. 1898. *Korean Sketches.* New York: Fleming H. Revell.

———. 1909. *Korea in Transition.* New York: Young People's Missionary Movement of the United States and Canada.

Gallagher, Catherine. 1985. *The Industrial Reformation of English Fiction: Social Discourse and Narrative Form, 1832–1867.* Chicago: University of Chicago Press.

Gann, Lewis. 1984. "Western and Japanese Colonialism: Some Preliminary Comparisons." In *The Japanese Colonial Empire, 1895–1945,* ed. R. Myers and M. Peattie. Princeton: Princeton University Press.

Gellner, Ernest. 1983. *Nations and Nationalism.* Ithaca, NY: Cornell University Press.

Geertz, Clifford. 1973. *The Interpretation of Cultures: Selected Essays.* New York: Basic Books.

Gilman, Sander L. 1985. "Black Bodies, White Bodies: Toward an Iconography of Female Sexuality in Late Nineteenth Century Art, Medicine, and Literature." *Critical Inquiry* 12: 204–242.

———. 1992. "Plague in Germany, 1939/1989: Cultural Images of Race, Space, and Disease." In *Nationalisms and Sexualities,* ed. A. Parker, M. Russo, D. Sommer and P. Yaeger. New York: Routledge, Chapman & Hall.

Gilmore, George. 1882. *Korea from Its Capital.* Philadelphia: The Presbyterian Board of Publication.

Ginzburg, Carlo. 1980. *The Cheese and the Worms: The Cosmos of the Sixteenth and Seventeenth Centuries.* Translated by J. Tedeschi and A. Tedeschi. London: Routledge and Kegan Paul.

Gossman, Lionel. 1990. *Between History and Literature.* Cambridge, MA: Harvard University Press.

Gluck, Carol. 1985. *Japan's Modern Myths: Ideology in Late Meiji Japan.* Princeton: Princeton University Press.

Grinker, Roy Richard. 1998. *Korea and Its Futures: Unification and the Unfinished War.* New York: St. Martin's Press.

Hall, Basil. 1818. *An Account of a Voyage of Discovery to the West Coast of Corea and the Great Loo-Choo Island.* Philadelphia: Abraham Small.

Hamilton, Agnus. 1904. *Korea.* New York: Charles Scribner's Sons.

Han Yong-un. 1970. *Meditations of a Lover.* Translated by Younghill Kang and Frances Keely. Seoul: Yonsei University Press.

Han Yŏng-wo. 1985. "Kija Worship in the Koryŏ and Early Yi Dynasties: A Cultural Symbol in the Relationship Between Korea and China." In *The Rise of Neo-Confucianism in Korea,* ed. W. de Bary and J. Kim Haboush. New York: Columbia University Press.

Hane, Mikiso. 1982. *Peasants, Rebels and Outcasts: The Underside of Modern Japan.* New York: Pantheon Books.

Hebdige, Dick. 1988. *Hiding in the Light: On Images and Things*. London and New York: Routledge.

Hill, Patricia. 1985. *The World Their Household: The American Woman's Foreign Mission Movement and Cultural Transformation, 1870–1920*. Ann Arbor: University of Michigan Press.

Ho, Samuel Pao-San. 1984. "Colonialism and Development: Korea, Taiwan, and Kwantung." In *The Japanese Colonial Empire, 1895–1945*, ed. R. Myers and M. Peattie. Princeton: Princeton University Press.

Hobsbawn, E.J. 1990. *Nations and Nationalism Since 1780: Program, Myth, Reality*. Cambridge: Cambridge University Press.

Hofstadter, Richard. 1992. *Social Darwinism in American Thought*. New York: Beacon Press.

Howard, Keith. 1987. "An Introduction to Korean Folk Bands and Folk Songs." *Korea Journal* 27, no. 8: 28–48.

Hulbert, Homer. 1906. *The Passing of Korea*. New York: Doubleday, Page and Company.

Hunter, Jane. 1984. *The Gospel of Gentility: American Women Missionaries in Turn-of-the-Century China*. New Haven, CT: Yale University Press.

Hutchison, William. 1987. *Errand Into the World: American Protestant Thought and Foreign Missions*. Chicago: University of Chicago Press.

Hwang Jong-yon. 1999. "The Emergence of Aesthetic Ideology in Modern Korean Literary Criticism: An Essay on Yi Kwang-su." *Korea Journal* 39, no. 4: 5–35.

Irokawa Daikichi. 1985. *The Culture of the Meiji Period*. Translated by Marius B. Jansen. Princeton: Princeton University Press.

Jackson, Leonard. 1991. *The Poverty of Structuralism: Literature and Structuralist Theory*. London: Longman.

Jager, Sheila Miyoshi. 1994. "Narrating the Nation: Students, Romance and the Politics of Resistance in South Korea." Ph.D. diss., Department of Anthropology, University of Chicago.

———. 1996a. "Women, Resistance and the Divided Nation: The Romantic Rhetoric of Korean Reunification." *Journal of Asian Studies* 55, no. 1: 3–21.

———. 1996b. "A Vision for the Future; or, Making Family History in Contemporary South Korea." *Positions: East Asia Cultures Critique* 4, no. 1 (Spring 1996): 31–58.

———. 1996c. "Woman and the Promise of Modernity: Signs of Love for the Nation in Korea." *New Literary History* 29, no.1 (February 1998): 121–134.

———. 2002. "Monumental Histories: Manliness, the Military, and the War Memorial, South Korea." *Public Culture* 14, no. 2 (Spring 2002): 387–409.

Jameson, Frederic. 1972. *The Prison-House of Language: A Critical Account of Structuralism and Russian Formalism*. Princeton: Princeton University Press.

———. 1981. *The Political Unconscious: Narrative as a Socially Symbolic Act*. Ithaca: Cornell University Press.

———. 1984. "The Politics of Theory: Ideological Positions in Postmodernism Debate." *New German Critique* 33: 53–65. Reprinted 1987 in *Interpretive Social Science: A Second Look*, ed. P. Rabinow and W.M. Sullivan. Berkeley and Los Angeles: University of California Press.

Karatani, Kojin. 1993. *Origins of Modern Japanese Literature*. Translated by T. de Bary. Durham, NC: Duke University Press.

Keene, Donald. 1971. *Landscapes and Portraits: Appreciation of Japanese Culture.* Tokyo: Kodansha International, Ltd.

Kendall, Laurel. 1985. *Shamans, Housewives and Other Restless Spirits.* Honolulu: University of Hawaii Press.

Kikuchi, Dairoku. 1985. "Japanese Education." In *Sources of Japanese Tradition,* ed. Theodore de Bary. New York: Columbia University Press.

Kim Byŏng-mo. 1986. "Archeological Fruits Since Liberation and the Reconstruction of Ancient History." *Korea Journal* 27: 50–57.

Kim Chi-ha. 1980. *The Middlehour: Selected Poems of Kim Chi-ha.* Translated by David McCann. Stanfordville, NY: Human Rights Publishing Group.

Kim, Eugene, and B.C. Koh. 1983. *Journey to North Korea: Personal Perceptions.* Berkeley: Institute of East Asian Studies.

Kim Il Sung. 1987. *Kim Il Sung Works.* Pyŏngyang: Foreign Publishing House.

Kim Jong-il. 1987. "On Establishing the Ch'uche Outlook on the Revolution." *Korea Today* 10: 9–14.

———. 1982. "The Inheritance of the Leader's Revolutionary Ideas." *Korea Today* 4: 2–10.

Kim Shi-ŏp. 1988. "Arirang, Modern Korean Folk Song." *Korea Journal* 28: 4–19.

Kim So-wŏl. 1977. "Chindalae kkot (Azaleas)." *A Lamp Burns Low.* Translated by Jaihiun Kim. Seoul: Seonji-sa.

Kim Sung-ok. 1993. *Seoul, 1964: Winter in the Land of Exile: Contemporary Korean Fiction.* Translated by M. Pihl. Armonk, NY: M.E. Sharpe.

Kim Tong-uk. 1980. *History of Korean Literature.* Translated by L. Hurvitz. Tokyo: Centre for East Asian Cultural Studies.

Kim Young-jik. 1986. *The Making of Korean Literature.* Seoul: The Korean Culture and Arts Foundation.

Kimball, Gayle. 1982. *The Religious Ideas of Harriet Beecher Stowe: Her Gospel of Womanhood.* New York: Edwin Mellon Press.

Koo, Hagen. 1993. "The State, Minjung and the Working Class in South Korea." In *State and Society in Contemporary Korea,* ed. Hagen Koo. Ithaca, NY: Cornell University Press.

Kwŏn Yi-gu. 1990. "Population of Ancient Korea in a Physical Anthropological Perspective." *Korea Journal* 30: 4–13.

Ledyard, Gari. 1975. "Galloping Along with the Horseriders: Looking for the Founders of Japan." *Journal of Japanese Studies* 1: 217–254.

Lee, Ann Sung-hi. 1991. "Yi Kwang-su and Early Modern Korean Literature." Ph.D. diss., Columbia University.

Lee, Chong-sik. 1963. *The Politics of Korean Nationalism.* Berkeley: University of California Press.

Lee, Jin-kyung. 2000. "Autonomous Aesthetics and Autonomous Subjectivity: Construction of Modern Literature as a Site of Social Reforms and Modern Nation-Building in Colonial Korea, 1915–1925." Ph.D. diss., University of California, Los Angeles.

Lee, Jung-young. 1981. *Korean Shamanistic Rituals.* New York: Mouton.

Lee Man-gap. 1981. *Toward a New Community: Reports of the International Research-Seminar Movement 1980.* Seoul: Institute of Saemaul Studies, Seoul National University.

Lee, Peter. 1965. *Korean Literature: Topics and Themes.* Phoenix: University of Arizona Press.

————. 1975. *Songs of the Flying Dragon: A Critical Reading.* Cambridge: Cambridge University Press.

————. 1980. *The Silence of Love: Twentieth Century Korean Poetry.* Honolulu: University of Hawaii Press.

————. 1981. *Anthology of Korean Literature: From Early Times to the Nineteenth Century.* Honolulu: University of Hawaii Press.

————. 1990. *Modern Korean Literature: An Anthology.* Honolulu: University of Hawaii Press.

————. 1993. *Sourcebook of Korean Civilization: From Early Times to the Sixteenth Century.* New York: Columbia University Press.

Lee, Sun-ja. 1981. "A *Saemaul Undong* Success Case Presented at the National Convention of *Saemaul* Leaders in 1975." In *Saemaul Undong: Determination and Capability of the Koreans.* Seoul: Institute of Saemaul Studies.

Lee Sung-kwan. 1997a. *Chŏnjaeng kinyŏmgwan* (Beyond the War Memorial). Unpublished manuscript.

————. 1997b/ Interview by the author. Seoul, 2 April.

LeRoy Ladurie, Emmanuel. 1979. *The Promised Land of Error.* Translated by B. Bray. New York: Vintage Books.

Liu, Lydia. 1994. "The Female Body and Nationalist Discourse: The Field of Dreams Revisited." In *Scattered Hegemonies: Postmodernity and Transnational Feminist Practice,* ed. Interpal Grewal and Caren Kaplan. Minneapolis: University of Minnesota Press.

————. 1995. *Translingual Practice: Literature, National Culture and Translated Modernity in China 1900–1937.* Stanford, CA: Stanford University Press.

Lowell, Percival. 1885. *Chosen: The Land of the Morning Calm.* Boston: Houghton, Mifflin and Co.

Lowenthal, David. 1985. *The Past Is a Foreign Country.* Cambridge: University of Cambridge Press.

Lukács, Georg. 1971. *The Theory of the Novel: A Historico-Philosophical Essay on the Form of Great Epic Literature.* Translated by A. Bostock. Cambridge: MIT Press.

McCann, David. 1986. "Formal and Informal Korean Society: A Reading of Kisaeng." In *Korean Women: View from the Inner Room,* ed. L. Kendall and M. Peterson. New York: East Rock Press.

McCarthy, Kathleen Louise. 1991. *Kisaeng in the Koryo Period.* Ph.D. diss., Harvard University.

McConnell, Michael. 1996. "Don't Neglect the Little Platoons." In *For Love of Country: Debating the Limits of Patriotism,* ed. Joshua Cohen. Boston: Beacon Press.

McDannell, Colleen. 1986. *The Christian Home in Victorian America, 1840–1900.* Bloomington: Indiana University Press.

McLennan, John. 1970. *Primitive Marriage: An Inquiry into the Origin of the Form of Capture in Marriage Ceremonies.* Chicago: University of Chicago Press.

McKeon, Michael. 1987. *The Origins of the English Novel, 1600–1740.* Baltimore, MD: Johns Hopkins University Press.

Marcus, George. 1986. "Contemporary Problems of Ethnography in the Modern World System." In *Writing Culture: The Poetics and Politics of Ethnography,* ed. J. Clifford and G. Marcus. Berkeley: University of California Press.

Mattielli, Sandra. 1977. *Virtues in Conflict: Tradition and the Korean Woman Today.* Seoul: Samhwa.

Megill, Allan. 1984. "Recounting the Past: 'Description' Explanation, and Narrative in Historiography." *American Historical Review* 94, no. 3: 627–653.

Miller, J. Hillis. 1979. "The Critic as Host." In *Deconstruction and Criticism*, ed. G. Hartman. London: Routledge and Kegan Paul.

Minh-ha, Trinh T. 1989. *Woman, Native, Other: Writing Postcoloniality and Feminism*. Bloomington: University of Indiana Press.

Mink, Louis. 1978. "Narrative Form as a Cognitive Instrument." In *The Writing of History*, ed. R.H. Canary and H. Kozicki. Madison: University of Wisconsin Press.

Miyoshi, Masa. 1969. *The Divided Self: A Perspective on the Literature of the Victorians*. New York: New York University Press.

———. 1974. *Accomplices of Silence: The Modern Japanese Novel*. Berkeley: University of California Press.

Moes, Robert. 1983. *Auspices Spirits: Korean Folk Paintings and Related Objects*. Washington, DC: International Exhibitions Foundation.

Mohanty, Chandra. 1991. *Third World Women and the Politics of Feminism*. Bloomington: University of Indiana Press.

Moore, Edward. 1902. *The Spread of Christianity in the Modern World*. Chicago: University of Chicago Press.

Morsel, F.H. 1884. "Events Leading to the Emeute of 1884." *Korean Repository* 4: 95–97.

Mosse, George L. 1985. *Nationalism and Sexuality: Middle-Class Morality and Sexual Norms in Modern Europe*. Madison: University of Wisconsin.

Myers, Ramon, and Mark Peattie. 1983. *The Japanese Colonial Empire, 1895–1945*. Princeton: Princeton University Press.

Nairn, Tom. 1977. *The Break-up of Britain: Crisis and Neo-Nationalism*. London: Lowe and Brydone Printers.

Nahm, Andrew. 1976. "Poetry and Songs from an Oppressed People, 1910–1945." *Korea Journal* 6, no. 10: 4–18.

———. 1983. "Korean Nationalism: Its Origins and Transformation." *Korea Journal* 23, no. 2: 19–37.

Noble, M.W. 1927. *Victorious Lives of Early Christians in Korea*. Seoul: Christian Literature Society of Korea.

Nussbaum, Martha C. 1996. "Patriotism and Cosmopolitanism." In *For Love of Country: Debating the Limits of Patriotism*, ed. Joshua Cohen. Boston: Beacon Press.

O Tak-sŏk. 1980. *The Benevolent Sun: Mt. Paektu Tells*. Pyŏngyang: Foreign Language Press.

Oberdorfer, Don. 1997. *The Two Koreas: A Contemporary History*. Boston: Addison-Wesley.

Okazaki, Yoshi, and V.H. Viglielmo. 1955. *Japanese Literature in the Meiji Era*. Tokyo: Ōbunsha.

Okuma, Shigenobu. 1985. "Fifty Years of New Japan." In *Sources of Japanese Tradition*, ed. Theodore de Bary. New York: Columbia University Press.

Poitras, Edward. 1983. "Gagach'isori" (The Cry of the Magpie). In *Korea Journal* 23: 38.

Park Chung-hee. 1962. *The Country, the Revolution and I*. Seoul: Hollym Corporation.

———. 1970a. *Major Speeches by President Park Chung-hee*. Seoul: Hollym Corporation.

———. 1970b. *Our Nation's Path*. Seoul: Hollym Corporation.

———. 1977. *The Road to National Survival.* Seoul: The Mail Kyunge Shinmun Co., Ltd.

———. 1979. *Saemaul: Korea's New Community Movement.* Seoul: Hollym Corporation.

Park Han-yong. 1981. "A Saemaul Success Case Study Presented at the National Convention of Saemaul Leaders in 1978." *Saemaul Undong: Determination and Capability of Koreans.* Seoul: Institute of Saemaul Studies.

Peattie, Mark. 1984. "Japanese Attitudes Toward Colonialism, 1895–1945." In *The Japanese Colonial Empire, 1895–1945,* ed. R.R. Myers and M. Peattie. Princeton: Princeton University Press.

Pecora, Vincent. 1989. "The Limits of Local Knowledge." In *The New Historicism,* ed. H. Aram Veeser. New York: Routledge, Chapman & Hall.

Pihl, Marshall. 1984. "Dramatic Structure and Narrative Technique in the Korean Oral Narrative Pansori." *Korea Journal* 24, no. 11: 27–32.

Pittau, Joseph. 1967. *Political Thought in Early Meiji Japan, 1868–1889.* Cambridge, MA: Harvard University Press.

Ponsonby-Fane, R. 1942. *Studies in Shintō and Shrines.* Kyoto: The Ponsonby Memorial Society.

Pratt, Mary Louise. 1987. "Linguistic Utopia." In *The Linguistics of Writing: Arguments Between Language and Literature,* ed. N. Fabb, D. Attridge, A. Durant, and C. MacCabe. New York: Methuen.

Pusey, James. 1983. *China and Charles Darwin.* Cambridge, MA: Harvard East Asian Monograph Series.

Rabinow, Paul, and W.M. Sullivan. 1987. *Interpretive Social Science: A Second Look.* Berkeley and Los Angeles: University of California Press.

Radhakrishnan, R. 1992. "Nationalism, Gender, and the Narrative of Identity." In *Nationalisms and Sexualities,* ed. A. Parker, M. Russo, D. Sommer, and P. Yaeger. New York: Routledge.

Reed, John Robert. 1975. *Victorian Conventions.* Athens: Ohio University Press.

Ricoeur, Paul. 1981. "Narrative and Time." In *The Writing of History: Literary Form and Historical Understanding,* ed. R. Canary and H. Kozicki. Madison: University of Wisconsin Press.

———. 1984. *Time and Narrative.* Translated by K. McLauglin and D. Pellauer. Chicago: University of Chicago Press.

Riley, Diana. 1988. *Am I That Name: Feminism and the Category of "Women."* Minneapolis: University of Minnesota Press.

Riley, Glenda. 1970. "The Subtle Subversion: Changes in the Traditionalist Image of the American Woman." *Historian* 32 (February).

Robinson. Michael. 1984. National Identity and the Thought of Shin Ch'ae-ho: *Sadaejuǔi* and *Ch'uche* in History and Politics." *Journal of Korean Studies* 5: 121–142.

———. 1986. "Nationalism and the Korean Tradition, 1896–1920: Iconoclasm, Reform, and National Identity." *Journal of Korean Studies* 10: 35–53.

Rutt, Richard. 1961. "The Flower Boys of Silla." *Transactions of the Korea Branch of the Royal Asiatic Society,* vol. 38.

Rutt, Richard, and Kim Chong-un. 1989. "The True History of Queen Inhyŏn." In *Virtuous Women: The Classical Korean Novels.* Translated by R. Rutt. Seoul: Kwang Myong.

Ryan, Mary. 1981. *The Cradle of the Middle Class: The Family in Oneida County, New York, 1790–1865.* Cambridge: Cambridge University Press.

Sahlins, Marshal. 1981. *Historical Metaphors and Mythic Realities: Structure in the Early History of the Sandwich Islands Kingdom.* Ann Arbor: University of Michigan Press.

_____. 1983. "Other Times, Other Customs: The Anthropology of History." *American Anthropologist* 85: 517–544.

_____. 1990. "The Return of the Event, Again; With Reflections on the Beginnings of the Great Fijiian War of 1843 to 1855 Between the Kingdom of Bau and Rewa." In *Clio in Oceania,* ed. A. Biersack. Washington, DC: Smithsonian.

_____. 1993. "Goodbye to Tristes Tropes: Ethnography in the Context of Modern World History." *Journal of Modern History* 65: 1–25.

_____. 1995. *How "Natives" Think, About Captain Cook, For Example.* Chicago: University of Chicago Press.

Said, Edward. 1978. *Orientalism.* New York: Pantheon.

Samson, G.B. 1929. "An Outline of Recent Japanese Archeological Research in Korea, in Its Bearing upon Early Japanese History." *Transactions of the Asiatic Society of Japan* 6: 6–19.

_____. 1961. *A History of Japan, 1334–1614.* Stanford, CA: Stanford University Press.

Scalapino, Robert A., and Chong-sik Lee. 1972. *Communism in Korea.* 2 vols. Berkeley: University of California Press.

Schama, Simon. 1988. *The Embarrassment of Riches: An Interpretation of Dutch Culture in the Golden Age.* Berkeley: University of California Press.

_____. 1989. *Citizens: A Chronicle of the French Revolution.* New York: Alfred A. Knopf.

Schmid, Andre. 1997. "Rediscovering Manchuria: Sin Ch'aeho and the Politics of Territorial History in Korea." *Journal of Asian History* 56, no. 1: 26–46.

———. 2000. "Decentering the 'Middle Kingdom': The Problem of China in Korean Nationalist Thought, 1895–1910." In *Nation Work: Asian Elites and National Identities,* ed. Timothy Brooke and Andre Schmid. Ann Arbor: University of Michigan Press.

———. 2002. *Korea Between Empires.* New York: Columbia University Press.

Schwartz, Vanessa . 2001. "Walter Benjamin for Historians." *American Historical Review* 106, no. 5: 1721–1743.

Shin, Michael. 1999. "Interior Landscape: Yi Kwangsu's 'The Heartless' and the Origins of Modern Literature." In *Colonial Modernity in Korea,* ed. Gi-Wook Shin and Michael Robinson. Cambridge, MA: Harvard University Press.

Sin Tŏng-yŏp. 1980. "Spring Comes." In *The Silence of Love: Twentieth Century Korean Poetry,* ed. P. Lee. Honolulu: University of Hawaii Press.

Sklar, Katherine. 1976. *Catherine Beecher: A Study in American Domesticity.* New Haven, CT: Yale University Press.

Smith-Rosenberg, Carroll. 1975. "The Female World of Love and Ritual: Relations Between Women in Nineteenth Century America." *Signs: Journal of Women in Culture and Society,* 1 (Autumn 1975).

———. 1988. "Domesticating 'Virtue': Coquettes and Revolutionaries in Young America." In *Literature and the Body: Essays on Populations and Persons,* ed. E. Scarry. Baltimore, MD: Johns Hopkins University Press.

Sommer, Dori. 1990. "Love and Country in Latin America: An Allegorical Speculation." *Cultural Critique* 16: 109–128.

———. 1991. *Foundational Fictions: The National Romances of Latin America.* Berkeley: University of California Press.

Spencer, Herbert. 1897. *The Principles of Sociology,* vol. 1–2. New York: D. Appleton.

Spivak, Gayatri. 1989. "The Political Economy of Women." In *Coming to Terms: Feminism, Theory, Politics,* ed. Elizabeth Weed. New York: Routledge.

Stocking, George. 1987. *Victorian Anthropology.* New York: Free Press.

Sym Myong-ho. 1982. *The Making of Modern Korean Poetry: Foreign Influences and Native Creativity.* Seoul: Seoul National University Press.

Szczesniak, Boleslaw. 1954. "The Sumu-Sanu Myth." *Monumenta Nipponica* 10, no. 12: 107–126.

Tae Hung-ha. 1988. *Poetry and Music in the Classical Age.* Seoul: Yonsei University Press.

Takekoshi, Yosaburō. 1912. Japan's Colonial Policy. *Oriental Review* 2: 101–120.

Tanaka, Stephen. 1993. *Japan's Orient: Rendering Pasts into History.* Berkeley: University of California Press.

Tang, Xiaobing. 1996. *Global Space and the Nationalist Discourse of Modernity.* Stanford, CA: Stanford University Press.

Taussig, Michael. 1984. "History as Sorcery." *Representations,* no. 7 (Summer 1984): 87–109.

Tokutomi Illchirŏ. 1985. "The Imperial Rescript Declaring War on the United States and the British Empire." In *Sources of Japanese Traditions,* ed. Theodore de Bary. New York: Columbia University Press.

Thompson, E.P. 1993. *Customs in Common: Studies in Traditional Popular Culture.* New York: New Press.

Troeltsch, Ernst. 1949. *The Social Teachings of the Christian Church.* 2 vols. Translated by O. Wyon. London: George Allen & Unwin.

Tu Wei-Ming. 1985. *Confucian Thought: Selfhood as Creative Transformation.* Albany: State University of New York Press.

Turkle, Sherry R. 1975. "Symbol and Festival in the French Student Uprising (May–June 1968)." In *Symbol and Politics in Communal Ideology: Cases and Questions,* ed. S. Moore and B. Myerhoff. Ithaca, NY: Cornell University Press.

Turner, Victor. 1981. "Social Dramas and Stories About Them." In *On Narrative,* ed. W.J.T. Mitchell. Chicago: University of Chicago Press.

Underwood, H.G. 1908. *The Call of Korea.* New York: Fleming H. Revell.

Underwood, H.H. 1926. *Modern Education in Korea.* New York: International Press.

Underwood, Lillias. 1904. *Fifteen Years Among the Top-knots.* New York: American Tract Society.

Van de Ven, Hans. J. 1996. "War in the Making of Modern China." *Modern Asian Studies* 30, no. 4: 737–756.

Van Den Abbeele, George. 1992. *Travel as Metaphor: From Montaigne to Rousseau.* Minneapolis: University of Minnesota Press.

Vaporis, Constantine Nomikos. 1994. *Breaking Barriers: Travel and the State in Early Modern Japan.* Cambridge, MA: Harvard University Press.

Varley, Paul. 1980. *A Chronicle of Gods and Sovereigns: Jinno Shotoki of Kitabatake, Chikafusa.* Translated by P. Varley. New York: Columbia University Press.

Waldron, Arthur. 1991. "The Warlord: Twentieth-Century Chinese Understandings of Violence, Militarism, and Imperialism." *American Historical Review* 96, no. 4: 1073–1100.

———. 1995. *From War to Nationalism: China's Turning Point, 1924–1925.* Cambridge: Cambridge University Press.

———. 1996. "China's New Remembering of World War II: The Case of Zhang ZiZhong." *Modern Asian Studies* 30, no. 4: 945–978.

Walraven, B.C.A. 1988. "Pollution Beliefs in Traditional Korean Thought." *Korea Journal* 28, no. 9: 16–23.

_____. 1989. "Symbolic Expressions of Family Cohesion in Tradition." *Korea Journal* 29, no. 3: 4–11.

Walzer, Michael. 1986. "The Politics of Michael Foucault." In *Foucault Reader,* ed. D.C. Hoy. London: Butler and Tanner.

_____. 1996. "Spheres of Affection." In *For Love of Country: Debating the Limits of Patriotism,* ed. Joshua Cohen. Boston, MA: Beacon Press.

Watt, Ian. 1957. *The Rise of the Novel: Studies in Defoe, Richardson and Fielding.* Berkeley: University of California Press.

Weber, Max. 1958. *The Protestant Ethic and the Spirit of Capitalism.* Translated by T. Parsons. New York: Charles Scribner.

Wells, Kenneth. 1990. *New God, New Nation: Protestants and Self-Reconstruction Nationalism in Korea, 1896–1937.* Honolulu: University of Hawaii Press.

Welter, Barbara. 1978. "She Hath Done What She Could: Protestant Women's Missionary Careers in Nineteenth Century America." *American Quarterly* 30 (Winter).

Wigen, Karen. 1999. "Culture, Power, and Place: The New Landscape of East Asian Regionalism." *American Historical Review* 104, no. 4 (October 1999): 1183–1201.

White, Hayden. 1973. *Metahistory: The Historical Imagination in Nineteenth-Century Europe.* Baltimore, MD: Johns Hopkins University Press.

_____. 1978. *Tropics of Discourse: Essays in Cultural Criticism.* Baltimore, MD: Johns Hopkins University Press.

_____. 1978. "The Historical Text as Literary Artifact." In *The Writing of History: Literary Form and Historical Understanding,* ed. R. Canary and H. Kozicki. Madison: University of Wisconsin Press.

———. 1981. "The Value of Narrativity in the Representation of Reality." In *On Narrative,* ed. W.J.T. Mitchell. Chicago: University of Chicago Press.

Williams, Raymond. 1973. *The Country and the City.* New York: Oxford University Press.

Wolf, Eric. 1982. *Europe and the People Without History.* Berkeley: University of California Press.

Woods, George. 1984. *Naval Surgeon in Korea.* Berkeley: University of California Press.

Yi In-jik. 1989. "Hyŏlŭinu." In *Korean Classical Literature: An Anthology,* ed. Chung Chong-hwa. New York: Kegan Paul International.

Yi Ki-baik. 1984. *A New History of Korea.* Translated by E. Wagner. Cambridge, MA: Harvard University Press.

Yi Ki-dong. 1987. "The Study of Ancient Korean History and Its Problems." *Korea Journal* 27: 41–50.

Yim, Louise. 1951. *My Forty-Year Fight for Korea.* Seoul: International Cultural Research Center, Chungang University.

Yoon Nae-hyun. 1987. "The True Understanding of Old Chosŏn." *Korea Journal* 27: 23–41.

Young Ick Lew. 1990. "The Conservative Character of the 1894 Tonghak Peasant Uprising: A Reappraisal with Emphasis on Chŏn Pong-jun's Background and Motivation." *Journal of Korean Studies* 7: 149–180.

Young, Louise. 1998. *Japan's Total Empire: Manchuria and the Culture of Wartime Imperialism.* Berkeley: University of California Press.

Yu Beong-cheon. 1992. *Two Pioneers: Han Yong-un and Yi Kwang-su of Modern Korean Literature.* Detroit: Wayne State University Press.

Yue, Meng. 1993. "Female Images and National Myth." In *Gender Politics on Modern China: Writing and Feminism,* ed. Tani Barlow. Durham, NC: Duke University Press 1994.

Žižek, Slavoj. 1993. *Tarrying with the Negative: Kant, Hegel, and the Critique of Ideology.* Durham, NC: Duke University Press.

Zŏng In-sob. 1959. *Folktales of Korea.* Seoul: Korean Cultural Series.

———. 1982. *Folktales from Korea.* Seoul: Hollym Corporation.

Korean Language

Chin Sŏng-ho. 1984. *Taehakŭi ŏlgul* (The Face of the University). Seoul: Ilwŏn sŏgak.

Cho Chŏng-nae. 1995. *T'aebaeksamaek* (Taebaek Mountain), vols. 1–10. Seoul: Haenaem.

Cho Sa-yŏn. 1989. "Taehakga saenghwalmunhwa undong ŭi kaenyŏm" (The University Life Cultural Movement: Its Conception). In *Taehak sori* (The Voice of the University). May: 130–135.

Cho Tong-il. 1978. *Han'guk munhak sasangsa siron* (Essays on the Ideology of Korean Literature). Seoul: Chisiksanŏpsa.

Cho Yong-man. 1969. "Iljehaŭi munhwa undong-sa" (History of the Cultural Movement under Japanese Rule). *Iljehaŭi han'guk yŏn'gu ch'ongso* (Collected Works of Studies on Korea under Japanese Rule). Seoul: Minjung sŏgwan.

Ch'oe Hung-kyu. 1983. *Sin Ch'aeho minchokjuŭisasang* (Research on Sin Ch'aeho's Ideology of Nationalism). Seoul: Tanje Sin Ch'aeho sŏnsaeng kinyŏmsaŏpsa.

Ch'oe Il Nam. 1975. *Seoul Saram* (Seoulites). Seoul: Sedaemun'go.

Ch'oe Yŏng-hŭi. 1969. Samil undonge irŭnŭn minchok tongnip undongŭi wŏnch'ŏn (The Origins of the National Independence Movement Leading to the March First Movement). *3.1 undong 50 chunyŏn kinyŏm nonmunjip* (Collection of Essays Commemorating the 50th Anniversary of the March First Movement). Seoul: Dong-a-ilbo.

Chŏn Moon-hwan. *Wŏlgan Chungang* 10 (October 1989): 186–195.

Ham Sŏk-hyŏn. 1965. *Ham Sŏkhyŏn Chŏnchip I* (The Collected Works of Ham Sŏk-hyŏn). Seoul: Hangil-sa.

Han Tong-min. 1988. *Aegugiran muŏsin'ga* (What Is Patriotism?). Seoul: Chamnam.

Han Yong-un. 1926. *Han Yongun sijip* (Collected Poems by Han Yong-un). Seoul: Han'guk minjungsayŏn'guhoe.

————. 1986. *Han'guk Minjuungsa* (The History of the Minjung). Seoul: P'ulpit.

Hwang P'ae-gan. 1982. *Han'guk munhak yŏn'gu inmun* (Introduction to the Study of Korean Literature). Seoul: Chisiksanŏp-sa.

Hwang Sok-yŏng. 1985. *Chukŭmŭl nŏmŏ, sidaeŭi ŏdumŏl nŏmŏ* (Over Death, Over the Darkness of the Age). Washington, DC: The Capital Union Presbyterian Church for Korea.

Im Su-gyŏng huwonsaophoe. 1990. *Ŏmŏni hanadoen choguke salgosip'ŏyo* (Mother I Want to Live in a Re-unified Fatherland). Seoul: Tolpaegae.

Kang Man-gil. 1973. *Chosŏn hugi sangŏp chabonjuŭi paltal* (Growth of Commercial Capitalism in the late Yi Dynasty). Seoul: Koryŏ Taehakkyo ch'ulp'anbu.

Kim Bong-sŏk. 1989. "Taehak chajumunhwaron" (An Essay on the Independent Cultural Movement of the University). In *Taehakŭi sori* (Voices from the University) 4: 126–129.

Kim Chi-ha. 1970. *Hwangt'o* (Yellow Earth). Seoul: Hanŏlmun'go.

Kim Chŏng-sin. 1970. *Nongminŭi adŭli taetŏngryŏngi toegiggachi Pak Chŏnghui taet'ongryŏng* (From Farmer's Son to President: Park Chung-hee). Seoul: Hallym Corporation.

Kim Chŏng-suk. 1987. *Ŭri ŏbŏi* (Our Parents). Pyŏngyang: Kŭmsŏng ch'ŏngnyŏnp'ansa.

Kim Dae-jung. 1997. *Naŭi sam, naŭi gil* (My Life, My Path). Seoul: Sinha.

————. 1998. *Tashi saeroŭn sichakŭl wehayŏ* (Again, in the Interest of a New Beginning). Seoul: Kim Yŏngsa.

Kim Dong-pae. 1986. "Sin Ch'aehoŭi much-ŏngbujuŭie kwanhan ilkoch'al" (An Examination of Sin Ch'aeho's Anarchism). In *Sin Ch'ae hoŭi sasanggwa minjok tongnip undong* (Sin Ch'ae-ho'sIdeology and the National Independence Movement), ed. Kim Chang-song. Seoul: Tanje Sin Ch'aehosŏnsaeng kinyŏmsaŏpsa.

Kim Nam-ju. 1988. *Nongbuŭi pam* (The Night of the Farmer). Seoul: Kidok saenghwal tongjihoe.

Kim Ran-ki. 1994. Kinyŏmkwanilga pakmulkwaninga? (Memorial? Museum?) *Plus* (July).

Kim Ta'e-jun. 1995. "Yi Kwangsuŭi munhakron" (Yi Kwang-su's Theory of Literature). In *Ch'uwŏn Yi Kwangsu munhakyŏngu*, ed. Han Bong-suk (Research on the Literature of Chuwon Yi Kwang-su). Seoul: Kukhak charyowŏn.

Kim Tong-in. 1959. *Ch'unwŏn yŏngu* (Research of Ch'unwon). Seoul: Koryŏ sibosa kongmubang.

Kim Yŏl-kyu. 1989. *Uri nara munhwaŭi ppuri* (The Roots of Our Culture). Seoul: Han'guk munhwa sŏnjip sirijŭ.

Kim Yŏng-ch'ŏl. 1986. "Han'guk taehaksaengŭi munhwa hwachŏng yŏngu" (A Study of the Korean University Students' Culturalization Process). Seoul National University Master's Thesis.

Kim Yŏng-sik. 1973. *Kŭndae han'guk munhak yŏngu* (Research on Modern Korean Literature). Seoul: Ilchisa.

Kim Yun-sik. 1982. *Han'guk kŭndaemunhak sasang* (Modern Korean Literary Theory). Seoul: Mundang.

————. 1986. *Han'guk kŭndae sosŏlsa yŏngu* (Research on the History of the Korean Modern Novel). Seoul: Ulyu munhwasa.

————. 1999. *Yi Kwangsuwa kŭŭi sidae* (Yi Kwang-su and His Times) Seoul: Solch'ulp'ansa.

REFERENCES 183

Ku In-hwan. 1983. *Yi Kwangsu sosŏlyŏngu* (Research on the Novels of Yi Kwangsu). Seoul: Samyŏngsa.

Lee Kwang-rin. 1969. *Han'guk kaehwasa yŏn'gu* (Studies on the History of Enlightenment in Korea). Seoul: Illchogak.

Lee Pyŏng-ju. 1988. *Chirisan* (The Chiri Mountains). Seoul: Hangilsa.

Mun Sun-tae. 1983. "Ch'ŏltchukche" (The Festival of Azaleas). In *Ŏich'imŭip'i* (Outcry of Blood). Seoul: Ilwŏlsŏgak.

Pak Chŏng-ch'ŏl yŏlsa kinyŏmsaŏphoe. 1989. *Kŭdae onmom kitpaltoeŏ* (Your Whole Body Became a Banner). Seoul: Sonamu.

Pak Chŏnghui [Park Chung-hee]. 1965–1979. *Pak Chŏnghui taet'ongnyŏng yŏnsŏlmunjip* (President Park Chung-hee's Collected Speeches). Vols. 1–3, 5–16. Seoul: Taet'ongnyŏng pisŏsil. Vol. 4. Seoul: Tonga ch'ulp'ansa, 1967.

Pak Kyŏng-ri. 1969–1994. *T'oji* (Land). Seoul: Chishik sanŏpsa.

Pak Se-gil. 1988. *Tashi ssŭnŭn han'guk hyŏndaesa* (Re-writing Modern Korean History). Seoul: Tolbaegae.

Pak Ŭn-sik. 1906. "Koguryŏ yŏngak taewang myobidŭngbon" (I Read a Rubbed Copy of the Stele of Koguryŏ King Yon'gak). *Sŏbukhakhae wŏlbo* 1, 9: 99.

———. 1910. *Han'guk T'ongsa* (The Painful History of Korea). Seoul.

Sin Ch'ae-ho. 1995. "Toksa Sillon" (A New Reading of History) (1908). In *Sin Ch'ae ho yŏksanonsŏljip* (Collected Essays of Sin Ch'ae-ho) (hereafter SYNC), ed. Chong Hae-Ryŏm. Seoul: Hyŏndaesilhaksa.

———. 1990. "Ŭlchi mundŏk" (1908). In *Kŭm Hanul: Sin Ch'aeho ch'akp'um jip* (Dream Sky: Collected Works of Sin Ch'ae-ho): 173–208 (hereafter *KHSCC*), ed. Song Chae-so and Kang Myŏng-kwan. Seoul: Tongkwang ch'ulp'ansa.

———. 1962. "Sŏho mundap" (West Lake Dialogue) In *Tanjae Sin Ch'aeho chŏnchip* (Complete Works of Tanjae Sin Ch'ae-ho) (hereafter *TSCC*). Separate Collection: 131–145, ed. Tanjae Sin Ch'aeho sŏnsaeng kinyŏmsaŏphoe. Seoul: Hyŏngsŏlch'ulpal sa.

———. "Chaegukchuŭiwa minjokchuŭi" (Imperialism and Nationalism) (1909). In *TSCC*, vol. 3: 108.

———. 1962. "Munhwawa muryŏk" (Culture and Military Power) (1910). In *TSCC*, Separate Collection: 200–201.

———. 1962. "Yisusang ege tosŏllangŭl yoch'ŏnghanŭn p'yŏnji" (A Letter of Request to Prime Minister Yi Regarding an Inspection of Books). (Undated). In *TSCC*, Separate Collection: 367–368.

———. 1995. "Ŏnmusumun" (偃 武 修 文) (End War, Bring Peace) (1910). In SYNC: 396.

———. 1990. "Kkum hanŭl" (Dream Sky) (1916). In *KHSCC*: 9–47.

———. 1976. "Chosŏn hyŏngmyŏngsŏnŏn" (Declaration of Korean Revolution) (1923). In *Han'guk kundae sasangga sŏnjip: Sin Ch'aeho* (An Anthology of Korea's Modern Thinkers: Sin Ch'ae-ho): 187–196. (Hereafter *HKSSC*), ed. An Pyŏng-sik. Seoul: Hangilsa.

———. 1976. "Yanggaekŭi sinnyŏnmanp'il" (New Year's Ramblings of a Vagabond) (1925). In *HKSSC*: 175–184.

———. 1976. "Munyegye ch'ŏngnyŏn ege ch'amgorŭl kuham" (Soliciting a Consultation with the Youths of the Literary World). (Undated). In *HKSSC*: 169–173.

———. 1990. "Yongkwa yongŭi taegyŏkchŏn" (The Great War of the Dragons) (1925). In *KHSCC*: 100–118.

————. 1976. "Chosŏn sanggosa" (History of Ancient Korea) (1931). In *HKSSC:* 13–57.

Sin Il-ch'ŏl. 1981. *Sin Ch'aehoŭi yŏksasang yŏngu* (Research on the Historical Ideology of Sin Ch'ae-ho). Seoul: Koryŏ taehakkyŏ ch'ulp'anbu.

————. 1986. "Sin Ch'aehoŭi kŭndae kukkagwan: chagang chuŭi (kukka) esŏ muchŏngbu (sahoe) ero" (Sin Cha'e-ho's View of the Modern Nation: From [National] Self-Strengthening to [Social] Anarchism). In *Sin Ch'aehoŭi sasanggwa minjok tongnip undong* (Sin Ch'ae-ho's Ideology and the National Independence Movement), edited by Kim Chang-song. Seoul: Tanje Sin Ch'aeho sŏnsaeng kinyŏmsaŏpsa.

Sin Tong-yŏp. 1967. *Sin Tongŏp chŏnjip* (Collected Works of Sin Tong-yŏp). Seoul: Ŭryu munhwa-sa.

Sin Yong-ha. 1984. *Sin Ch'aehoŭi sahoesasang yŏngu* (Research on the Social Ideology of Sin Ch'ae-ho). Seoul: Hangilsa.

————. 1985. *Han'guk minjok tongnipundŏngsa yŏngu* (Research on the Korean National Independence Movement). Seoul: Ŭlyumunwhasa.

————. 1986. "Sin Ch'ae hoŭi minjok tongnipundŏngnonŭi t'ŭkchin" (Sin Ch'ae-ho's Theory of the Korean National Independence: Its Distinctive Features). In *Sin Ch'aehoŭi sasanggwa minjok tongnip undong* (Sin Ch'ae-ho's Ideology and the National Independence Movement), ed. Kim Chang-song. Seoul: Tanje Sin Ch'ae ho sŏngsaeng kinyŏmsaŏpsa.

————. 1996. "Tanjae Sin Ch'aehoŭi minjokchuŭi sasangŭi sŏnggyŏk" (The Distinctive Traits of Tanjae Sin Ch'ae-ho's Nationalist Ideology). This paper was presented at the conference entitled *Sin Ch'aehowa han'guk minjokchuŭi* (Sin Ch'ae-ho and Korean Nationalism), which was sponsored by the Tanjae Sin Ch'ae ho sŏnsaeng kinyŏmsaŏphoe to commemorate the sixtieth anniversary of Sin Ch'ae-ho's death. It was held on December 4, 1996, at the Seoul Press Center, South Korea.

Wŏn Ŭi-tang. 1964. "Sinŭng mugwanhakkyŏ" (The Sinŭng Military Officer School) *Sin Dong-a* (9/20): 236–244.

Yi Chae-sŏn. 1979. *Han'guk hyŏndae sosŏlsa* (A History of the Modern Korean Novel). Seoul: Honsŏng-sa.

Yi Kwang-rin. 1979. *Han'guk kaehwasasangyŏn'gu* (Research on Korea's Enlightenment Movement). Seoul: Ilchogak.

Yi Kwang-su. 1972. "Saranginga." *Muhaksasang* 2, 2: 442–446.

————. 1979a. "Munhakŭi kach'i" (The Value of Literature). In *Yi Kwang-su chŏnjip* (Collected Works by Yi Kwang-su). Seoul: Yusinsa.

————. 1979b. "Munhakiran hao?" (What Is Literature?). In *Yi Kwang-su chŏnjip* (Collected Works by Yi Kwang-su). Seoul: Yusinsa.

————. 1993a. "Sonyŏnŭi pi" (The Sorrows of Youth). In *Mumyŏng* (Nameless). Seoul: Yusinsa.

————. 1993b. "Ŏrinbŏt ege" (To My Young Friend). In *Mumyŏng* (Nameless). Seoul: Yusinsa.

————. 1996. *Mujŏng* (Heartless). Seoul: Ilsinsŏchŏkch'ulp'ansa.

Yi Man-yŏl. 1980. *Hanmal kidokkyŏwa minjok undong* (Christianty and National Movements at the End of the Chosŏn Dynasty). Seoul: P'yŏngminsa.

————. 1981. *Han'guk kidokkyŏ wa minjok ŭisik* (Korean Christianity and Historical Consciousness). Seoul: Chisik sanŏpsa.

Yoon Nae-hyun. 1986. *Han'gukkodaesa sinron* (Ancient Korean History: A Reinterpretation). Seoul: Ilchi-sa.

Yun Hu-chŏng. 1994. *Ehwa 100 nyŏnsa p'yŏnch'anwiwonhoe* (Committee for the Compilation of 100 years of Ehwa's History). Seoul: Ehwa yŏchahakkyŏ ch'ulp'anbu.

Newspapers, Magazines, Journals, and Government Publications

Chugan Chosŏn
Chosŏn Ilbo
Hangyorae shinmun
Kajong chapchi
Korea Herald
Korea Report
Korean News Review
Korea Today
Korea Times
Kwangsŏng sinmun
Mal
MOGAMA (Ministry of Government Administration and Home Affairs) [Haechŏng cha ch'ibu], records, 1970–1980
News +
News People
Nyusŭ p'ip'ul
Sahoewa sasang
Seoul sinmun
Sin donga
Stars and Stripes
Taehan maeil sinbo
Tonga ilbo
Wŏlgan Chosŏn
Wŏlgan Chungang
Wŏlgan Ssiŭlui sori

Interviews

Chang Chŏng-dok 1997. Interview by author. Seoul, 21 April.
Choi Young-jeep. 1997. Interview by author. Seoul, 25 March.

Index

Sheila Miyoshi Jager is the Henry Luce Assistant Professor of East Asian Studies at Oberlin College. She received her Ph.D. in anthropology from the University of Chicago. She has published articles in the *Journal of Asian Studies, positions: east asia cultures critique, New Literary History*, and *Public Culture*.